Innovation and Entrepreneurial Networks in Europe

Routledge International Studies in Business History

EDITED BY RAY STOKES AND MATTHIAS KIPPING

Innovation and Entrepreneurial Networks in Europe

Edited by Paloma Fernández Pérez
and Mary B. Rose

Routledge
Taylor & Francis Group
New York   London

Fundación **BBVA**

First published 2010
by Routledge
711 Third Avenue, New York, NY 10017

Simultaneously published in the UK
by Routledge
2 Park Square, Milton Park, Abingdon, Oxfordshire OX14 4RN

First issued in paperback 2015

Routledge is an imprint of the Taylor & Francis Group, an informa business

Library of Congress Cataloging-in-Publication Data
Innovation and entrepreneurial networks in Europe / edited by Paloma Fernández Pérez and Mary B. Rose.
    p. cm. — (Routledge international studies in business history ; v. 18)
    Includes bibliographical references and index.
    1. Entrepreneurship—Europe.   2. Technological innovations—Europe.   3. Business networks—Europe.   4. Innovation relay centers—Europe.   I. Fernández Pérez, Paloma, 1964–   II. Rose, Mary B.
    HB615.I5632 2009
    338.8'7—dc22
    2009005118

ISBN 13: 978-0-415-63572-1 (pbk)
ISBN 13: 978-0-4154-5451-3 (hbk)

Contents

Figures

Tables

Acknowledgements

The raw material for this book originated from a rather innovative cooperation between European scholars gathered to develop research on innovation and networks during the years 2004–2006. They were supported by a grant from the Spanish Banco Bilbao Vizcaya Argentaria (BBVA) Foundation. This cooperation, which included discussions between academics and an entrepreneur, led to research, debates and knowledge exchange, all achieved without too much travelling thanks to the Internet. The scholars involved were Mary Rose and Mike Parsons from the Institute of Entrepreneurship and Entrepreneurial Development at the University of Lancaster, Matthias Kipping from Schulich Business School in Canada, Andrea Colli from Bocconi Università in Italy, Nuria Puig from Universidad Complutense de Madrid, and Paloma Fernández Pérez from Universitat de Barcelona in Spain. The aim of broadening the network and getting more European scholars involved in the discussions led Mary B. Rose and Paloma Fernández Pérez to organize a session on innovation and networks in Europe during the International Economic History Association Conference in Helsinki in 2006. In that session perceptive comments were received from all the participants and the audience, among them a good number of North American scholars. The editors organized a book proposal, which received comments, suggestions and finally generous acceptance from Routledge. We must particularly thank Terry Clague for his initial enthusiasm and support and Laura Stearns for her help in the last stages of the process. We greatly acknowledge editorial and language editing assistance from Tony Breakell in Lancaster. For research, writing, debates and editorial and language assistance we must acknowledge financial support from Fundación BBVA, from the Spanish public research project SEJ 2005–02788 and from the Institute for Entrepreneurship and Enterprise Development, Lancaster University Management School. We would like to thank Tony Breakell for language and copy editing the manuscript.

1 Introduction
Innovation and Entrepreneurial Networks in Europe

Paloma Fernández Pérez and Mary B. Rose

The chapters in this volume draw on business history, alongside the literatures of entrepreneurship, innovation and networks, to reflect the experience of innovation in Europe in the twentieth century. America is often used as a bench mark for studies of innovation in large-scale, technologically intensive firms. We know considerably less about models of innovation that consider comparative empirical evidence from heterogeneous European countries and regions. Insights are drawn from small- and medium-sized firms, from managerial and organizational innovation, from innovation in 'traditional' sectors such as consumer-goods industries and from service innovation.

Chapters in this book, to a greater or lesser extent, all touch upon the idea of systems of innovation. With a national, sectoral or regional character, European systems of innovation involve collaborative links, usually between universities, industry and government. For this reason it provides a useful framework to explore the links between chapters. Varying international experience, however, demonstrates the importance of analyzing the way in which distinctive histories, business and national cultures, as well as institutions, shape innovation practice and processes.

The book is interdisciplinary, but academic boundaries are surprisingly acute, even where interrelatedness is anticipated:

> Given the inherent interrelatedness of entrepreneurship, innovation and creativity, one would expect there to have been a natural conscious blending of research interests, results, methodologies and diverse applications; yet each field is neatly compartmentalized with little cross pollination. For example, creativity is rooted firmly in psychology and innovation has primarily been examined in fields of technology and engineering. (Brazeal and Herbert 1999)

This view was echoed in a recent Harvard Business School interview with Geoffrey Jones, co-editor of *The Oxford Handbook of Business History* (2008). He observed that despite having much to offer the study of entrepreneurship and management, business history has developed in a separate silo, which has 'resulted in the spread of influential theories based on ill-informed understandings of the past' (Jones 2008). This makes combining historical perspectives with theories of entrepreneurship, innovation and networks especially rewarding. This introduction explores how this can be achieved and the implications for analyzing European innovation experience. The book is organized in four sections covering respectively theories of entrepreneurship, innovation and networks, innovation and international competitive advantage and collaboration and knowledge transfer.

The cases analyzed in the book come from firms whose business activity has taken place in a wide variety of European territories, including Scandinavian and Mediterranean countries, the United Kingdom, the Netherlands and Germany. Diversity is the rule, but despite the differences, the empirical evidence contained in the chapters offers manifold insights into the significance of personal networks linking entrepreneurs, governments and regional or national associations in the creation or transfer of innovative knowledge in Europe. Within multinationals such as the case of Philips analyzed by Davids et al., the big banks touched upon by Kipping, or among small and medium firms, as Colli's chapter indicates for Italian chemical firms and Puig's and Fernández Pérez's chapters for Spanish pharmaceutical and metal manufacturing firms, respectively innovation was above all a social process of communication among persons belonging to different intellectual and cultural groups. The creation of 'communities of practice' where entrepreneurial people crossed borders and could regularly meet has been in fact a common thread in the vast majority of innovative experiences analyzed in this book. The chapter by Parsons and Rose in this book presents a good overview of the theoretical literature about this concept, so useful to understanding the creation of European systems of innovation in a long-term historical perspective.

The book contains first of all two strong theoretical chapters by Casson and by Parsons and Rose that overview common concepts and ideas about innovation and its relationship with entrepreneurial networks as described by the authors of the book. Then follow nine chapters with case studies that present very different empirical results about how and why innovation has taken place in firms of different size and economic specialization. These chapters include small firms through to big multinationals, from industries with diverse technological content and added value (food production, forestry industry, chemical and pharmaceutical manufacturing, metal production and bath tube equipment industries, IT sector etc.) through to services provided within clusters and services distributed worldwide (as in the case of consultancy). The chapters are methodologically diverse, though they all coincide in emphasizing that innovation in Europe has definitely not been an isolated technological process. Also, that it has rarely been the outcome of isolated public policies of innovation. Rather, the diverse firms and experiences analyzed strongly confirm that it has been a social and institutional process, where interest groups and associations have played a role as important as the one played by outward-looking entrepreneurs well connected with such interest groups and associations. Of course Schumpeterian creative and imaginative individuals have played a role, but this has been the case because they have been able to connect with teams prepared to develop and commercialize individual innovative ideas. This introduction does not therefore repeat what is already summarized at the end of each chapter, but concentrates on surveying the common themes addressed in the volume and their relationship to wider debates surrounding the idea of innovation as a social and learning process.

ENTREPRENEURSHIP AND NETWORKS

Entrepreneurial decision making is a dynamic process, where what is needed and what is possible are constantly changing. What is needed reflects what the consumer wants, whereas what is possible is shaped by the knowledge and skill embedded in the firm, combined with technology and shaped by engagement with networks of suppliers within the organization, with other organizations, with government and with customers. Innovation involves the commercialization of a product, a service or a process, or a combination of all three. This only occurs when there is an appreciation of the changing relationship between consumer demand, technological capabilities and the wider business and economic environment. Creativity and imagination are vital to innovation, but alone they do not lead to commercialization or diffusion, and it is here that the link with entrepreneurship becomes crucial. Entrepreneurship involves the recognition and assessment of opportunities and is often the bridge between creativity and innovation. This is because the entrepreneur is involved in what can be described as the dance of two questions—what is needed and what is possible—and the interplay of these two questions is an ongoing and dynamic process (Stefik and Stefik 2004, 27–46). Responses are shaped by the changing knowledge of the external environment, by social and business networks, by changes in the legal system, by changes in the competitive environment and by market changes. The idea of innovation as an entrepreneurial dance of two questions is introduced by Parsons and Rose in this volume.

'Networks are everywhere', as Casson points out in his chapter on networks in economic and business history. But they are not all benign or beneficial, and some malfunction. Several chapters in this book explore the diverse ways communication occurs or fails to occur through social networks in different time periods, sectors and regions to identify and develop new combinations of old and new knowledge, or to build awareness of ideas which respond to changing needs.

INNOVATION SYSTEMS

Innovation systems provide an important platform for making sense of knowledge exchange within and between firms and sectors, as well as between individuals, across communities, regions and nations. Innovation systems are about how innovation takes place, who is involved and how and where they interact. They provide a good starting point for analyzing how and why entrepreneurial networks are crucial to the innovation process and the way in which they function.

Innovation, or the commercialization of a new product, service or process, is rarely carried out in isolation, but is socially embedded. Taking Schumpeter's definition as a starting point, innovation involves 'combining productive services . . . combining factors in a new way or that it consists of "new combinations"' (Schumpeter 1939, 87–88).

This observation points to innovation taking place at the boundaries of areas of knowledge and expertise and being underpinned by interactive learning processes, involving exchange of both codified and tacit knowledge. But the iterations that occur have the potential for developing new knowledge, which may stimulate innovation. The role is crucial here for entrepreneurship because

> [s]ometimes, an innovation might be almost inevitable—the new combination might be easy to find and to realize. In other cases, it might take an enormous intellectual effort or an extremely creative mind, to identify a potential new combination. (Lundvall 1992, 8)

These ideas lie at the heart of wide-ranging research on national, regional and sectoral systems of innovation (Ludvall 1992; Edquist 1997). As Edquist observed,

> In the pursuit of innovation they interact with other organizations to gain, develop and exchange various kinds of knowledge, information and resources. These organizations might be other firms (suppliers, customers, competitors) but also universities, research institutes, investment banks, schools, government ministries. Through their innovative activities firms often establish relations with each other and other kinds of organizations; therefore it does not make sense to regard innovating firms as isolated, individual decision making units. (1997, 1)

Small and medium firms that succeed in commercializing products or services in distant markets—such as the ones described in the chapters by Parsons and Rose; Fernández Pérez; Colli; Davids et al.; Ojala, Lamberg and Melander; and Puig—are particularly good case studies that show how, in different sectors and regions, European innovation in the twentieth century was essentially about establishing links with other firms and organizations. And chapters dealing with banks (Kipping) and diversified multinationals (Davids et al., Saarinen) indicate the importance of developing efficient internal processes of organization to make innovation possible in larger firms. In all cases, and particularly after the 1950s, the chapters of this book show that contacts with outward-looking universities and institutions made the flow of information and people and the crossing of knowledge boundaries possible. In a recent conference about large family firms in the world, John Davis, from Harvard University, indicated that U.S. business schools are noticing nowadays that, in contrast with the previous century, big U.S. multinationals seem to be relying less and less on business-school expertise and training. Instead they are creating their own knowledge-exchange centres for creative and innovative employees working in their businesses around the world. This is reminiscent of practices in some Asian countries a few decades ago and is developing as a key new strategy for innovation training among Dutch multinationals (Sluyterman and Westerhuis 2008). In contrast with big corporations, large European family firms have been increasing their links with one another and with outward-looking institutions and organizations (Tàpies and Ward 2008; Fernández Pérez and Puig 2007, 2008). Innovation then is complex and based on social interaction.

The inspiration for what we now call 'national systems of innovation' had its origins in the second half of the nineteenth century, when the needs of emerging industries became increasingly reliant on science and academic research. Businesses in Germany and the United States, where the R&D departments of large firms in chemicals and electronics developed close ties with universities, enjoyed considerable international competitive advantage. Fears of foreign competition in established industrializers such as Britain, along with the quest for catch up by later industrializers, led in the twentieth century to the spread of three-pronged initiatives where governments promoted closer ties between industry and universities. From the 1970s there was an acceleration in the number of government plans to link university and industrial research to stimulate economic development and regeneration (Mowery and Sampat 2005, 209). This stimulated a growing body of academic literature around national, regional and sectoral innovation systems (Lundvall 1992; Edquist 1997; Cooke 1996, 2001). Alongside this literature, and often overlapping with it, has been a growing interest in industrial districts, sometimes described as regional production systems. Interest has been prompted by the dramatic and well-known economic success of 'Third Italy' with the innovative flexibility of such labour-intensive sectors as clothing and shoes in Northern Italy, or in the innovative, dynamic hi-tech clusters of universities, companies and venture capital in Silicon Valley or Route 128 in the United States (Zeitlin 2008, 220).

The development of close synergistic relationships between universities and businesses, however, is just one dimension of innovation systems. Innovation systems reflect the interactions involved in achieving innovation. They may involve government initiative, but this is by no means inevitable, as much depends on timing, on the type of knowledge involved and on economic, social and political factors. Systems are sometimes supranational, while national systems are frequently underpinned by and intertwined with regional and sectoral systems (Edquist 1997, 11).

THE IMPACT OF HISTORY ON INNOVATION SYSTEMS

History is central to much theorizing about the development of national systems of innovation. This is because

> [t]o have a historical perspective is not only an advantage when studying processes of innovation, but also necessary if we are to understand them. This is because innovations develop over time . . . History matters very much in processes of innovation as they are often path dependent: small events are reinforced and become crucially important through positive feedback. (Edquist 1997, 18)

In addition, looking at innovation systems historically gives profound insight into the way in which varying types of expertise, along with economic, technological, political and social conditions, create differing arrangements for exchanging knowledge to achieve innovation. Historical analysis helps explain why a simple linear 'stages' approach to innovation systems through time can be misleading. It helps identify the reasons why, within any historical period, a range of systems may exist—varying regionally and internationally. History therefore shapes behaviour, attitudes and social processes and is intimately related to the 'rules of the game' or 'institutions' which underpin all forms of human activity. These

> humanly devised constraints . . . shape human interaction. In consequence they structure incentives in human exchange whether political, social or economic. Institutional change shapes the way societies evolve through time and is the key to understanding historical change. (North 1991, 3)

Formal 'rules of the game' include regulations, laws, property rights and so forth, while norms of behaviour, taboos, customs, attitudes and values can be described as informal institutions (North 1991, 97). Since they regulate interaction between individuals or groups, they lie at the heart of the interactive learning processes that are so crucial to systems of innovation (Edquist and Johnson 1997, 51). The following overview of the development of national and regional innovation systems demonstrates how differing histories shape innovation processes.

INNOVATION SYSTEMS THROUGH TIME

The form which a system of innovation takes depends very much on the type of knowledge being exchanged, whether predominantly tacit or formalized. This in turn depends on the industrial base, its needs and the society in which it is embedded. There is evidence therefore of shifts in the nature of innovation systems through time and of national and sometimes regional differences in experience. These in turn mould future choices and patterns. During the Industrial Revolution in Britain, for example, knowledge exchange typically occurred at an informal community level, rather than at a national level. Innovation depended heavily on deeply embedded practical skill and reflected,

> primarily, learning inside firms which developed and tested new production equipment, either developed in house, or in co-operation with artisans from small workshops. (Lundvall 1992, 13)

Tacit community-based practical knowledge, therefore, formed the basis of innovation in early British industrialization. Improvements to machines were typically made by their users (Macleod 1992, 290). Yet science played a significant role in many sectors including, for example, pottery, textile finishing and metallurgy. The transfer of scientific knowledge occurred as a 'bottom up' process, based on informal social contacts between scientists and industrialists through scientific societies, which sprang up in newly industrializing areas in the late eighteenth century (Schofield 1972). By 1815 every British industrial town had its scientific society, leading Benjamin Disraeli (1844) to comment,

> what Art was to the ancient world, Science is to the modern . . . Rightly understood, Manchester is as great a human exploit as Athens. (Thackery 1974, 675)

Such informal arrangements existed to a greater or lesser extent throughout Europe in the early stages of industrialization. The co-evolution of new science, new technology and new forms of business organization in the late nineteenth century led to the emergence of distinctive systems of innovation and the involvement of different actors in the innovation process. This was linked to greater government involvement in stimulating ties between universities and industry to promote the diffusion of innovation. The extraordinary combination of scientific, organizational and technological advance, in what has been described as the 'Age of Synergy' (Smil 2005), is touched on by Parsons and Rose in this book.

New science contributed to the development of technologies, materials and ways of communicating. It contributed to the emergence of industries such as electricity, organic chemistry, synthetics and automobiles. This had implications for the type of knowledge involved in innovation, for the way it was developed and for the configuration of innovation systems. These developments 'changed the innovation nexus and brought it closer to the R&D departments of large firms' (Lundvall 1992, 10). It also increased the role of science in the innovation process, and this in turn stimulated and was partly encouraged by an emerging role for research-oriented universities. The form this took, the extent to which governments became involved and the impact on innovation varied internationally.

The origin of innovation systems based on the company R&D laboratory, with strong university links, was seen in Germany in the 1870s, especially through the industrial role of the Technische Hochschulen. By the First World War this had evolved into a powerful national system which became a model for other industrial nations. This system consisted of

> university laboratories . . . in house R&D laboratories . . . national research institutes and libraries, a network of national scientific and technical societies and publications, all supported by a growing supply of qualified people from the education system and thorough industrial training system for a variety of craft and technical skills. (Freeman 1992, 173)

Germany's research-based, industry-facing universities lay at the heart of this system and were its foundation. The close relationship between university and industrial research, and the flows of personnel between the two, created an ideal environment for innovation in science-based industries. It helped to create common languages and norms of behaviour and to develop communities of shared practice, so important to knowledge exchange. A similar network emerged in the United States before the end of the nineteenth century and was reinforced by institutes of technology, such as the Massachusetts Institute of Technology (MIT). Founded in 1861, MIT was to be 'a school of industrial science [aiding] the advancement, development and practical application of science in connection with arts, agriculture, manufactures, and commerce' (Etzkowitz and Leydesdorff 2000, 116).

In Britain the development of the civic universities and Mechanics' Institutes in the large industrial cities occurred. This reflected continued community-based development of innovation, linked primarily to the staple industries (Sanderson, 1972). Beginning in the 1830s and gathering pace in the 1880s, concern over foreign competition for British industry—especially from Germany—led to a series of government inquiries into technical and scientific education. For a range of reasons, including early industrialization, tardiness in the rise of the large firms and social and political attitudes, there were few signs of the emergence of a German-style national innovation system before the First World War. The nearest to it was Prince Albert's vision for South Kensington in London—home of the 1851 Great Exhibition. As he envisaged it,

> gathered [in] South Kensington would be the learned societies funded by the national government, along with the national museums, and a variety of schools, in a grouping that would function as a University. (Robertson 2004, 1)

Funded by the surpluses of the Great Exhibition, this complex ultimately spawned the Victoria and Albert Museum, the Science Museum, the

Natural History Museum and eventually the Imperial College of Science and Technology in 1907 (Gay 2007, 58).

By contrast in twentieth-century continental Europe, later industrializers developed national and local innovation systems around university-industry ties and company research laboratories in science-based sectors (Freeman 1992, 174); they also developed them around regional institutions, such as the Mancomunitat de Catalunya in the early twentieth century, and entrepreneurial associations dominated by some industrialized sectors, such as the textiles, metal-mechanic or shipping industries studied by Jordi Nadal and Jordi Maluquer for Catalonia and Jesús M. Valdaliso for the Basque Country in Spain. But success or failure very much depended on personal relationships and networks within these systems and on perceptions of the role of universities and of academic research. The nature of the relationships and the innovation processes involved was shaped by national, regional, industrial and sometimes company and social conditions.

Chapters in this book offer a warning against assuming that the development of national systems of innovation was a simple linear process, especially among later industrializers. In his study of Finland from 1945 to 1984 Saarinen shows how the importance of business collaboration with universities and research centres grew during the late 1960s and 1970s. But in several other cases the relationship was far more complicated. The case of the Dutch electronics firm Philips, discussed in this volume by Davids et al., is especially instructive here. Philips' industrial-research laboratory, established in 1914, was vital to the company's ability to innovate. Interestingly gaps in Dutch university science made access to American technological knowledge crucial. The laboratory had a lively intellectual climate, and regular visits by its scientists to American research centres forged powerful, international, interpersonal links. These proved crucial to maintaining the company's competitive strength in the second half of the twentieth century. It is also misleading to assume that competitive success among late industrializers always depends on the national innovation system. The success of innovation systems based on university-industry links depends on there being overlapping cultures. Puig, in her study of twentieth-century Spanish pharmaceutical companies, shows that industry and academia occupied different cultures. In this industry successful innovation in twentieth-century Spain depended more on the development of international strategic alliances than the national innovation system. Puig also demonstrates the importance of personal contacts and relationships in successful knowledge exchange.

The centrality of the R&D laboratory in national systems of innovation since the nineteenth century has been linked to economic prosperity (Freeman 1992, 174–175). Among business historians there is, however, considerable debate about the role of the R&D laboratories and the impact of their scientists on the competitive advantage, even of American firms. Much depended on the extent to which the scientists related to the business world they moved into:

Histories of laboratories staffed by university researchers, especially phys-
icists with no business experience, chronicle decisions that undermined
the companies' previous capacity to innovate. (Graham 2007, 356)

By the late twentieth and early twenty-first centuries, several factors have
altered the significance of the R&D laboratory still further. For many large
industrial companies globalization has meant a shift in the basis of their
competitive advantage from product to service development. This is especially illustrated in the case of small- and medium-sized Italian chemical
companies, discussed by Colli in this book. He shows that the repositioning of these producers of intermediate products and co-design of services
with their users has enhanced the competitive advantage of these niche
companies. This has some resonance with Ojala, Lamberg and Melander's study of Finnish family firms, which demonstrates the development of
intensive customer relationships to facilitate product development in wood
pulp. Such trends reflect a growing emphasis on user-driven innovation
(von Hippel 2005).

The systems of innovation literature focuses strongly on technological
innovation and for the most part neglects the diffusion of organizational
and managerial innovations. In part, of course, this has also been associated
with the development of university-management education and research,
from the nineteenth century onwards. Again there have been striking international differences in its shape and relationship to business (Locke 1989).
But there were a range of actors involved in the diffusion of management
innovation. Scientific management and work study was intimately related
to the spread of mass production techniques in the twentieth century. Diffusion of the process in Europe, with its different industrial, social and
political history, was neither automatic nor uniform. Kipping's analysis of
the role of management consultants shows how distinctive national conditions affected the actors involved in terms of their behaviour and their
impact on the diffusion process. By analyzing the twentieth-century experience of Britain, Germany and Spain, he identifies sharply differing roles for
management consultants and their relations with both entrepreneurs and
government.

CONCLUSION: INNOVATION AS INTERACTIVE LEARNING

Throughout the book personal relationships are shown to lie at the heart of
successful knowledge exchange and innovation. Since innovation systems
reflect socially embedded interactive learning, this is to be expected. As
Casson implies in his chapter, the key to understanding the role of networks lies in analyzing the ways in which shared values ease communication and reduce uncertainty. Successful collaboration leading to innovation
within and between firms, between firms and universities, between sectors

or across national boundaries depends on individuals developing an under-standing of another world. As Wenger observed,

> Being alive as human beings means that we are constantly engaged in the pursuit of enterprises of all kinds, from ensuring our physical sur-vival to seeking the most lofty pleasures. As we define these enterprises and engage in their pursuit together, we interact with each other and with the world accordingly. In other words, we learn. Over time this collective learning results in practices that reflect both the pursuit of our enterprises and the attendant social relations. These practices are thus the property of a kind of community created over time by the sustained pursuit of a shared enterprise. It makes sense therefore to call these kinds of communities, communities of practice. (Wenger 1998, 45)

Mutual experience and practice therefore builds understanding and espe-cially the tacit knowledge and trust needed for successful communication and collaboration. Sharing a history means that routines, expectations and patterns of behaviour are taken for granted. Deeply embedded values can of course become a barrier to innovation in inward-looking commu-nities or organizations. Fernández Pérez's study of Spanish family firms demonstrates the way in which successful collaborations and the develop-ment of outward-looking innovative environments have helped transform several Spanish family firms that started in the iron and steel industry and are now increasingly diversifying like Roca and CELSA. Her study also shows interesting cases of failure due to lack of team work at the top and inward-looking managerial attitudes in technologically mature firms such as Rivière. Where past experience involves differing languages, ways of doing, as well as the quest for differing goals, this can inhibit innova-tion. The same applies within institutions and involves boundary crossing one of the biggest innovation challenges and social skills. Change can be achieved by what has been described as 'mindful deviation' from existing pathways. As such it means building understanding of those engaged in the process and empathizing with their concerns and perceptions suffi-ciently to carry them forward (Garud and Karnøe 2001). By emphasizing the importance of social processes in escaping from the past's wheel ruts takes a combination of imagination, determination to achieve change and social understanding.

REFERENCES

Brazeal, D. V., and T. T. Herbert. 1999. The genesis of entrepreneurship. *Entrepre-neurship: Theory and Practice* 23 (3): 29–45.
Cooke, P. N. 1998. Introduction: Origins of concept. In *Regional innovation sys-tems: The Role of governances in a globalised world*, Hans Joachim Braczyk, Philip N. Cooke and Martin Heidenreich, 2–27. London: Routledge.

————. 2001. Regional innovation systems, clusters and the knowledge economy. *Industrial and Corporate Change* 10 (4): 945–974.

Edquist, C., ed. 1997. *Systems of innovation: Technologies, institutions, and organizations.* London: Pinter.

Edquist, C., and B. Johnson. 1997. Institutions and organizations in systems of innovation. In *Systems of innovation: Technologies, institutions, and organizations,* ed. C. Edquist, 36–61. London: Pinter.

Etzkowitz, H., and L. Leydesdorff. 2000. The dynamics of innovation: From national systems and mode 2 to a triple helix university-industry-government relations. *Research Policy* 29:109–123.

Fernández Pérez, P., and N. Puig. 2007. Bonsais in a wild forest. A historical interpretation of the longevity of large Spanish family firms. *Revista de Historia Económica: Journal of Iberian and Latin American Economic History* 25 (3): 459–497.

————. 2008. Global businesses, global lobbies: The birth of the Spanish lobby of family firms in an international perspective. Paper presented at the European Business History Association in Bergen, Norway, 21–23 August 2008.

Freeman, C. 1992. Formal scientific and technical institutions in the national system of innovation. In *National systems of innovation: Towards a theory of innovation and interactive learning,* ed. B.-A. Lundvall, 169–187. London: Pinter.

Garud, R., and P. Karnøe. 2001. Path creation and the process of mindful deviation. In *Path Dependence and Creation,* ed. R. Garud and P. Karnøe, 1–40. London: Laurence Erlbaum Associates.

Gay, H. 2007. *The history of Imperial College London, 1907–2007: Higher education and research in science, technology, and medicine.* London: Imperial College Press.

Graham, M. B. W. 2008. Technology and innovation. In *The Oxford handbook of business history,* ed. G. G. Jones and J. Zeitlin, 347–376. Oxford: Oxford University Press.

Jones, G. G. 2008. The lessons of business history: A handbook. Interview with S. Silverthorne. *Harvard Business School Working Knowledge,* 17 March. http://hbswk.hbs.edu/item/5849.html.

Locke, R. 1989. *Management and higher education since 1940: The influence of America and Japan on West Germany, Great Britain, and France.* Cambridge: Cambridge University Press.

Lundvall, B.-A., ed. 1992. *National systems of innovation: Towards a theory of innovation and interactive learning.* London: Pinter.

Macleod, C. 1992. Strategies for innovation: The diffusion of new technology in nineteenth-century British industry. *Economic History Review,* n.s., 45 (2): 285–307.

Mowery, D. C., and B. N. Sampat. 2005. Universities in national innovation systems. In *The Oxford handbook of innovation,* ed. J. Fagerberg and D. C. Mowery, 209–239. Oxford: Oxford University Press.

North, D. C. 1990. *Institutions, institutional change, and economic performance.* Cambridge: Cambridge University Press.

————. 1991. Institutions. In *Journal of Economic Perspectives,* 5(1): 97–112.

Robertson, B. 2004. The South Kensington Museum in context: An alternative history. *Museum and Society* 2 (1): 1–14.

Sanderson M. 1972. *The universities and British industry, 1850–1970.* London: Routledge and Keegan Paul.

Schofield, R. E. 1972. The industrial orientation of science in the Lunar Society of Birmingham. In *Science, technology, and economic growth in the eighteenth century,* ed. A. E. Musson, 136–147. London: Methuen.

Schumpeter, J. A. 1939. *Business cycles: A theoretical, historical, and statistical analysis of the capitalist process.* 2 vols. New York: McGraw-Hill.

Sluyterman, K., and G. Westerhuis. 2008. The flow of people: Globalization and the organization of the international workforce in multinationals companies. Paper presented at the European Business History Association conference in Bergen, Norway, 21–23 August 2008.

Smil, V. 2005. *Creating the twentieth century: Technical innovations of 1867–1914 and their lasting impact.* Oxford: Oxford University Press.

Stefik, M., and B. Stefik. 2004. *Breakthrough: Stories and strategies of radical innovation.* Cambridge, MA: MIT Press.

Tàpies, J., and J. Ward. 2008. *Family values and value creation: The fostering of enduring values within family-owned businesses.* Barcelona: IESE Business School.

Thackray, A. 1974. 'Natural knowledge in cultural context: The Manchester model'. *American Historical Review* 79 (3): 672–709.

von Hippel, E. 2005. *Democratising innovation.* Cambridge, MA: MIT Press.

Wenger, E. 1998. *Communities of practice.* Cambridge: Cambridge University Press.

Zeitlin, J. 2008. Industrial districts and regional clusters. In *The Oxford handbook of business history*, ed. G. G. Jones and J. Zeitlin, 219–243. Oxford: Oxford University Press.

2 Networks in Economic and Business History
A Theoretical Perspective

Mark Casson

INTRODUCTION

Networks as an Inter-disciplinary Subject

Networks are everywhere. In physics there are electrical circuits; in civil engineering there are structures such as bridge trusses; in information technology there are telephones and the Internet; while in geography there are transport systems, such as motorways and railway systems. Agriculture and industry depend upon distribution systems (pipelines, electricity grids) and disposal systems (drainage ditches, sewage systems). In biology the brain is analyzed as a network of neurons, and in anthropology family networks are created and sustained through reproduction. Economists refer to networks of trade, investment and technology transfer when discussing international and inter-regional resource flows. Sociologists analyze social groups in terms of interpersonal networks and use network effects to explain 'chain migration' flows, while business strategists analyze networks of strategic alliances between firms.

Networks are a powerful way of understanding the historical evolution of economic and social institutions. Institutions are often analyzed in terms of firms, markets and the state (North 1981). Networks are then introduced as a fourth type of institution. However, this approach is not sufficiently radical. Networks are an emerging paradigm for economic and social history. But to exploit the potential of this paradigm fully, there needs to be more agreement and greater clarity over the definition of terms. There are many different types of networks, involving different types of elements connected up in different ways using different kinds of relationships. Confusion is created when researchers fail to define their terms and to specify which type of network they are writing about.

Ambiguities of the Subject

When analyzing networks, different disciplines refer to the same concepts by different names. The members of a network are variously referred to as elements, nodes, vertices and points, while the connections between them are referred to as linkages, edges, paths and so on.

Ambiguities exist even within a single discipline. For example, economic and business historians have used the term 'network' in several ways (see Thompson 2003). All four of the concepts described next have been applied to industrial districts based on flexible specialization, but it is not always clear, in any given instance, which type of network a writer has in mind.

- A *'network' as a distinctive organizational form, intermediate between firm and market.* In this context, a network comprises a web of long-term cooperative relationships between firms.
- A *'network firm' as a set of quasi-autonomous subsidiaries.* Japanese *keiretsu* and Italian business groups are often described in these terms.
- A *'local business network' which involves key actors, such as bankers, entrepreneurs and government officials, who informally coordinate activities within an economic region or urban centre.* This network involves a mixture of organizations of different types. The relationships are used to finance strategic investments in local public goods, such as training colleges or dock improvements, whose benefits accrue to businesses in general rather than to any single business in particular.
- A *'network industry', such as transport, water, energy and other utilities.* Network industries typically sink large amounts of capital into specialized infrastructure, which links different locations and facilitates the movement of resources between them (Foreman-Peck and Millward 1994).

There is a tension between these specific connotations of a network and the generality of the underlying concept. It can be argued, for example, that firms and markets are not alternatives to networks, but simply special types of networks—the firm being a relatively rigid and hierarchical network, and a market a flat and flexible one. On this view, almost everything is a network, and so it is fruitless to argue about what is a true network and what is not. The research question is not so much 'Is it a network?' as 'What type of network is it?' The key to understanding networks is to have a scheme by which to classify them.

Role of Networks in the Coordination of Economic Activity

The key economic role of networks is to coordinate activities. Whatever the activities, networks are crucial in communicating crucial information, controlling conflict and fostering cooperation. Without the benefits of coordination, it would often not be worthwhile to invest in networks.

A common objection to this approach is that networks are created because people like to belong to them. In other words, the benefits generated by networks are intrinsic, rather than instrumental. Intrinsic benefits are certainly an important benefit of belonging to small and cosy groups like a happy family. But not all networks are a pleasure to belong to; some professional networks can be very competitive, for example, and, far from welcoming new members, act more like a clique or a cartel. People still seek entry, however, because of the economic advantage that can be obtained. If emotional benefits were the only benefits that people derived from networks, it seems likely that networks would be much less common than they are.

Taking an instrumental view of networks helps to explain why there are so many different varieties of network in practice. Different network structures are best adapted to coordinating different types of economic activities. If emotional benefits were the only reward then it is likely that networks would be much more homogeneous: in particular, they would be much smaller and friendlier than many of them really are. To explain why network structures vary, it is necessary to recognize that different types of networks coordinate different types of activities.

A SIMPLE TYPOLOGY OF NETWORKS

Social Networks versus Physical Networks

If 'everything is a network' then clearly there must be different types of networks. A river and its tributaries, for example, exemplify a *physical* network that distributes water, while an extended family exemplifies a *social* network that connects descendants of common ancestors (Haggett and Chorley 1969). More precisely, a physical network connects material elements such as natural features, buildings and plants, while a social network connects people.

Physical networks have *spatial* characteristics. These are usually represented in two dimensions—for example, by a map of a road or river system—although some networks are inherently three-dimensional—for example, crystalline structures and aircraft flight paths.

The spatial dimension is also relevant to social networks, but not to the same extent. An individual's social network may be summarized by the names in his address book, but it would be a mistake to suppose that those who live further away are contacted less frequently. In social networks, *social distance* is more relevant than *Euclidean distance*—thus two people who live on either side of a national border may be 'farther apart' than two people who live at opposite ends of the same country. Social distance may be expressed using a metric of communication costs, provided that these costs include not merely the cost of a letter or telephone call, but the costs of overcoming linguistic and cultural barriers too.

Networks can be analyzed at different levels of aggregation. An element of a physical network may comprise a single unit, such as an individual factory, or a collection of units, such as a town or region; this leads to a difference between the inter-plant network studied in industrial complex analysis (Isard, Schooler and Vietorisz 1959) and the inter-regional network studied by regional policy analysts (Armstrong and Taylor 2000). In the social sphere, single individuals constitute an interpersonal network while groups of people make up an inter-organizational network. Inter-organizational networks are often best analyzed in interpersonal terms, however, since relations between organizations are usually mediated by representatives, and relationships may alter radically when the representation changes.

Investment in Networks

Another important distinction is between *natural* networks and networks *engineered* by human agency. Both physical and social networks can be engineered: thus a canal is an analogue of a natural river, while a club is an analogue of a family.

Engineering a network can involve a major investment and requires entrepreneurship of a high order. Canals were financed using an early form of joint stock company, while the establishment of early professional societies required major commitments of time by their founders and trustees.

Any given network is almost invariably part of a wider system. Thus engineered networks are typically embedded in natural networks—for example, canals developed from cuts made in navigable rivers, and railways followed river valleys because the gradients were easy. The only network that is not part of a wider system is the global network that encompasses the totality of all the networks: it is the network that links every person, every resource and every location, directly or indirectly, to every other, through different types of physical and social connections. Every other network is a sub-set of this encompassing network. It is necessary to base analyses on subsidiary networks because this encompassing network is so complex that, while it can be analyzed at a high level of aggregation, it is too large to analyze fully at a disaggregated level. It must be recognized that every subsidiary network selected for study is therefore an 'open system' which connects with the rest of the global network at various points. For analytical purposes it is often useful to ignore these external connections in order to focus on the internal structure of a subsidiary network, but it is important not to forget that the analysis is then based on the assumption that the structure of the wider network remains constant.

Coordination: The Interdependence of Physical and Social Networks

Physical networks are often analyzed as though they were independent of social networks, and vice versa, but in reality the two types of networks are closely linked. Social networks are used to coordinate flows through physical networks and to coordinate strategic investments in them. Conversely, social networks require supporting services supplied by physical networks—for example, transport to and from the meetings organized by a club. Geographers often study physical networks in isolation from social networks, while sociologists often study social networks in isolation from physical ones. Such partial perspectives provide a distorted picture of networks and can lead to misleading conclusions.

Physical networks involving flows of goods and services emerge because the *division of labour* leads individuals to specialize in particular tasks. A single complex task is broken down into a set of simpler tasks, each performed by a different person. The different elements of the physical network are created by this differentiation of tasks. A social network is created to coordinate the actions of the people who have been assigned to these different tasks, using special channels of communication.

Different stages of production are usually carried out at different locations, due to local availability of natural resources or special labour skills. This requires a physical network to transport intermediate products and ensure that scales of activity at different locations are compatible with each other.

Different products may also be produced at different locations. When consumers like variety, a high proportion of the output at each location must be exported. This requires a distribution network to transport the product and a social network to ensure that each consumer obtains the particular mixture of goods that he desires.

Engineering Trust in Social Networks

Where resources are scarce and people are selfish, everyone has an incentive to claim the ownership of a resource for himself. Criminals steal, transactors cheat, workers shirk and citizens 'free ride'. A social network can resolve such problems by developing a stock of mutual obligations (Granovetter 1985). Engineering trust through mutuality addresses a number of simple everyday problems.

- *Maintaining social order.* Perhaps the most fundamental coordination problem of all is to avoid accidents and collisions. It is a basic law of nature that two people cannot occupy the same space at the same time. Families and communities develop informal customs and rituals which avoid conflict between members. Conformity with local custom reinforces the sense of 'belonging to' the network and encourages loyalty to fellow members of the group.
- *Organizing enjoyable group activities.* Work can be interesting and playful if it is not too repetitive or demanding, and shared participation in such activity can also strengthen group identity (Veblen 1922; Knight 1935). Organizing and participating in a local festival is an example; so too are team sports. People earn respect as much for

making the effort as for getting a result. It becomes a form of coop-erative self-improvement in which each person is 'competing against himself' in order to improve upon his 'personal best'.

- *Counselling and care.* In a volatile environment where coordination is costly, coordination failures, leading to setbacks and disappointments, are always liable to occur. Providing care and counselling to victims of misfortune is a task in which everyone can share, even though some may have more professional skill than others. The person who is the victim one day may be counsellor the next, and may even turn his own setback to an advantage by drawing on his own misfortunes to counsel others. Alternating roles in this way can therefore develop empathy and encourage reciprocity and thereby engineer trust.

Engineering trust is particularly easy when membership is small and every-one is close together.

- Proximity facilitates face-to-face communication, and so, unlike with remote communication, information does not have to be written down and codified. Furthermore, verbal emphasis, gesture and posture give added clarity and conviction to face-to-face communication.
- Small membership means that everyone is personally known to oth-ers, and so deviants are easier to detect. Relationships are more per-sonal, and less anonymous, than in larger groups.
- The combination of proximity and small size means that chance encounters are common. Gossip is intense, and so reputation effects are strong. A person with a bad reputation can be punished by being shamed or shunned in subsequent encounters. Finally, it is easy to arrange consultative meetings at which everyone can express his views on matters of common concern. This encourages a relatively democratic approach to collective decision making.

A Market in Trust

While small local networks are particularly important in building trust, large dispersed networks create a major demand for trust. The value of resources coordinated by a large dispersed network can be very high—for example, a network of international trade in high-value products, or an international banking network transmitting large amounts of cash and loans. If we call the small local network a bonding network and the large dispersed network a commercial network, then the problem is applying the trust generated by the bonding network to facilitate coordination within the commercial network. The difficulty is that the commercial network is very different from the bonding network. Interpersonal relationships within a bonding network are relatively intense, in emotional terms, while interpersonal relationships in a commercial network are more detached.

The distances covered by a commercial network mean that to support a commercial network the members of a bonding network must disperse in some way. There are three main ways in which this can be achieved.

- *The movement of people.* People brought up in the same community can emigrate, creating a diaspora of people with common roots. Once introduced to each other they remain bonded for life. In the case of families and communities, they may pass on this sense of bonding to their children, creating a distinctive ethnic group. The effect may also apply to alumni, former work colleagues, fellow professionals and so on.
- *Regular visits to a central meeting place.* People can meet up at regular intervals for intensive bonding experiences. Within families, baptisms, weddings and funerals play a useful role in forming new bonds and replacing obsolete ones. Similarly, the annual meetings of professional associations provide opportunities for bonding at dinner and the bar. The fact that people travel enormous distances to such events underlines their importance in engineering trust.
- *The federation of local networks.* Different local networks may embrace the same culture. This may be a religion, a political outlook, a common interest or a hobby. The leader may travel around to 'spread the word' or send out teams of missionaries or representatives to form local satellite networks. These networks then federate within the parent organization. In this model it is the leader and the representatives who do the travelling, rather than the individual members; it is particularly appropriate for situations in which travel costs for ordinary members are very high.

These three mechanisms complement each other. For example, a family may disperse to create a diaspora, and then the different local communities established by the emigrants may affiliate into an organization that promotes their traditional values. From time to time the whole family may reassemble for an important 'rite of passage' of one of its leading members, or for some ceremony to honour the common ancestors.

Volatility and Innovation

If a physical network operated in a totally stable environment then there would be little day-to-day need for coordination. Each day the same routine would be followed. A rigid system of command and control working on a regular cycle would be perfectly adequate to coordinate physical flows—much like a railway-signalling system driven by the dictates of a daily timetable.

In fact the economic environment is constantly changing, creating a continual need to modify levels of production and patterns of trade throughout the global economy. As new trade routes open up, new demands for infrastructure arise. Networks of transport and communication evolve, breaking some connections, but also bringing distant places into closer contact with each other.

In addition, intellectual curiosity and the quest for greater economy stimulates scientific discovery. In a private enterprise economy individuals can profit from discoveries through innovation. To produce and distribute new products, innovators create new networks of customers and suppliers and possibly destroy the networks built up by their established competitors in the process. Thus while established networks influence the type of information discovered, the discovery of new information feeds back to alter the structure of networks too.

Social networks also spread news, including information about new investment opportunities. The diffusion of news speeds up adjustment to change. News can be spread in two main ways: by local contact, through conversation with neighbours in a small group, or through broadcasting to members of a larger group. A leader may emerge who controls broadcast information. The leader may promote particular beliefs about the environment and censor or discredit competing views. He may also favour certain types of institutions over others—for example, preferring large firms to markets, or government to private enterprise. He may decide to promote certain moral values as conducive to trust, such as honesty, loyalty and hard work.

Intermediation

The division of labour applies not only to production activities, but to the design and operation of a network too. In a physical network, specialized hubs may emerge where different traffic flows converge. These hubs provide flexibility by allowing traffic to be switched from one route to another.

In social networks, entrepreneurs and leaders act as information hubs. Individual consumers go to entrepreneurs to buy their goods, relying on the entrepreneurs to procure the goods on their behalf from the producer, who is the ultimate source of supply. Individuals who need to make contact with other individuals may go to a leader and ask him to arrange an introduction. The leader may expect the individual to join his group, and possibly pay a membership fee, in return for receiving this service.

In a private enterprise economy, entrepreneurs compete with each other for custom. Similarly, leaders of rival groups compete for members and also to gain influence for their views. As a result, both physical networks and social networks develop a multiplicity of competing hubs. Ordinary members use these hubs as gateways to the rest of the network. In effect, relationships between ordinary members of the network are mediated by the entrepreneurs from whom they buy, the leaders of the groups to which they belong and the hubs through which they travel and through which the goods they buy are consigned to their homes. While individuals also have direct connections to other individuals, the number of such direct connections is very small compared to the number of people to whom they are indirectly connected through the hubs. This would make the hubs extremely powerful if it were not for the competition between them. This competition reflects the fact that an individual usually has more than one hub through which he can reach another individual who is able to fulfil his needs.

BASIC CONCEPTS OF NETWORK THEORY

Connectivity and Configuration

The basic principles of network representation are set out in the mathematical theory of graphs (Biggs, Lloyd and Wilson 1986; Diestel 1997). The defining feature of a network is *connection*. A set of *elements* which are connected to each other form a *network*. Every pair of elements belonging to a network is connected up, either *directly* or *indirectly*. Indirect connections are effected through other elements of the network.

From an economic and social perspective, there are four key aspects of networks:

- *size*, as measured by the number of elements that belong to the network;
- *diversity*, as measured by the number of different *types* of elements that belong to the network;
- the types of *relationships* that connect the members; and
- the *configuration* of the network, which describes the pattern in which the different elements are connected up.

Economic historians have discussed relationships in considerable detail but have said surprisingly little about size and diversity, that is, about the characteristics of the elements that are connected up. Configuration has been studied even less by historians, and it is therefore useful to begin by addressing this issue.

Considerable research has been carried out into the configurations of physical networks, but remarkably little into the configuration of social networks (though see Doreian and Stokman 1997; Wasserman and Faust 1994; Wellman and Berkowitz 1988). Conversely, far more research has been carried out into the nature of relationships in social networks than in physical networks. Only a small number of writers, such as Leibenstein (1978), Pattison (1993) and Burt (1992), have integrated the analysis of relationships with the analysis of configurations.

There are many different ways of connecting up a given set of elements. The configuration of a network is defined by the set of direct pair-wise linkages between its elements. As the number of elements increases, the number of different ways in which elements can be connected up increases dramatically. Network analysis is bedevilled by the complexity created by this 'combinatorial explosion'.

Hubs

Hubs are points at which three or more linkages converge: they act as consolidation centres and distribution centres for the traffic over the network. Hubs are often connected to other hubs by trunk connections which carry high-volume traffic (Watts 2003).

The power of a hub can be measured by the proportion of through traffic that it handles in proportion to the amount of traffic originating or terminating at the hub itself. When every linkage in a network carries the same amount of traffic, the power of a hub is proportional to the number of linkages it possesses. With n elements, including a solitary hub, and two-way flow of traffic x between each pair of elements, the total traffic through the hub will be $(n-1)(n-2)x/2$. The traffic originating from, or destined for, the hub will be $(n-1)x$, and so the power of the hub will be the ratio of the first term to the second, namely, $(n-2)/2$.

Webs

A weakness of the hub configuration is that there is no 'redundancy', that is, there are no alternative routes between any pair of elements. A failure in any link will completely disconnect one of the elements from the network, and a failure of the hub itself is fatal. A natural solution is to use more than one hub. In the limiting case, every element becomes a hub. This creates a web configuration, in which every element is directly connected to every other.

It is often said that networks afford significant economies of scale, but these economies are in fact attributable to hubs. In a web, where every element is directly connected to every other, the number of linkages, $n(n-1)/2$, is equal to the number of connections achieved, and so there is no saving in linkages as the number of elements in the network increases. On the other hand, the number of linkages in a corresponding hub is only $n-1$, and so network economies increase without limit when a hub configuration is adopted. The difference between the hub and the web becomes more pronounced as the number of elements increases, as moving from a hub to a web increases the number of linkages by a factor $n/2$.

THE SCHEMATIC REPRESENTATION OF NETWORKS: AN APPLICATION TO TRADE

Entrepreneurial intermediation and the coordination of trade

To illustrate the application of network analysis in economic and social history it is useful to set out an example which has widespread relevance and which exemplifies many of the general points already made. The evolution of trade is a suitable example: trade is a generic feature of economic development and demonstrates very clearly the importance of studying all the aspects of network structure—size, diversity, relationships and configurations—rather than just a single one of them.

As indicated earlier, social networks are used to coordinate physical networks. Trade in manufactures, raw materials or agricultural products involves networks of physical flows which are coordinated by information flows mediated by social networks. Long-distance trade is generated by a physical division of labour in which producers at one location serve consumers at another location (Putterman 1990).

An accurate representation of a trade network calls for a clear distinction between the flow of resources that needs to be coordinated and the flow of information that effects the coordination. Figure 2.1 introduces the convention, used in subsequent figures, that physical flows are indicated by thick lines and flows of information by thin lines. The thick black line in the figure illustrates the flow of product which results when one person— the producer S—decides to specialize in the production of a good, which customer D consumes.

The physical activities that generate the physical flows are denoted by square boxes while the people who control the activities, and coordinate the flows, are denoted by circles. Thus the embedding of a circle within a

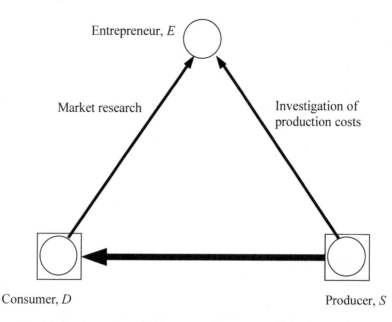

Figure 2.1 Intermediation as information synthesis: Role of the entrepreneur in promoting coordination.

square denotes that the individual concerned not only communicates with other individuals, but controls physical activities too (for a more complete discussion of these conventions, see Casson 1997, 2000).

Connections in networks can be either one-way or two-way. The direction of the arrow from right to left illustrates the one-way flow of the product from S to D. In economic and social networks most flows are two-way, but the flows in each direction are different. For example, when product flows from S to D, there is a reverse flow of payment from D to S, but this is not shown in the interests of simplicity.

It is assumed that trade is intermediated by an entrepreneur, E. The entrepreneur is the first to recognize the opportunity for S to specialize in production, because S himself is not aware of D's latent demand. Information flow is illustrated by a thin line. The left-hand line DE illustrates the entrepreneur's market research, which identifies D's demand, while the right-hand line SE indicates the entrepreneur's investigation of production possibilities, which identifies S as a source of supply. The arrows indicate the direction of information flow.

To understand relationships properly, however, it is necessary to examine how the entrepreneur extracts profit from the opportunity. The answer is that he will block direct communication between D and S by interposing a retailer, N, in the product flow. The entrepreneur may set up as a retailer himself: he buys from the producer and then marks up the price for resale to the consumer. Alternatively, he may use an independent retailer, in which case he acts as a wholesaler instead, buying from the producer and reselling to the retailer.

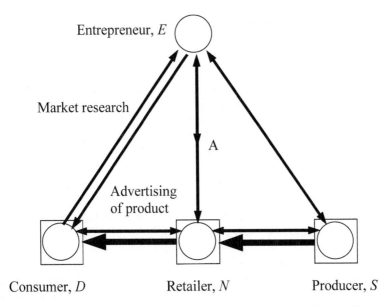

Figure 2.2 The market-making entrepreneur: Establishing a distribution channel.

The simple case where the entrepreneur acts as retailer is illustrated in Figure 2.2. The entrepreneur negotiates with the producer over the price of the good, as indicated by the two-way flow of information *ES*. As a retailer, he negotiates with the customer, as indicated by the two-way flow of information *ND*. As a retailer, he also places orders with the producer in order to maintain sufficient stock to service demand, and the producer invoices him in return; this two-way information flow is represented by the line *NS*. The entrepreneur continues to observe the customer, as indicated by the one-way flow of information *DE*, and in addition he uses the media to advertise the product to the customer. These are two distinct information flows that go in opposite directions—not a form of dialogue, unlike the other information flows—and therefore they are represented by two separate lines.

The relationship between the entrepreneur and the manager of the retail facility involves authority. It is fundamentally different from the other relations connecting *E* and *N* to *S* and *D*, which involve negotiation instead. While communication between entrepreneur and manager is two-way, it is asymmetric because the entrepreneur gives orders and the manager reports back when they have been carried out. In Figure 2.2 the authority relation is indicated by a letter, *A*, placed next to an arrow in the middle of the connecting line, where the arrow indicates the direction in which orders are given.

Entrepreneurship is normally viable only when market size is sufficient to cover the fixed costs of creating the market—that is, making contact with customers and suppliers and establishing a retail facility. It follows that *D* indicates a representative consumer rather than a solitary consumer. Representing each consumer individually would make the figure impossibly complicated. There may be several producers too, particularly if the demand is large and production plants are small scale.

Trust as a Basis for Trade

In a market economy, 'buyer' and 'seller' are important roles. They carry certain expectations about conduct. Such expectations relate to the two-way flows of information *ES* and *ND* in Figure 2.2, which involve the negotiation of contracts for the supply of the product and its resale to the consumer. These information flows occur before the delivery of the product has commenced; after the date for delivery has passed, there may be further communication arising from delays or quality problems. Trust reduces the costs of these contracts by encouraging compromise in negotiation, compliance with delivery requirements and a speedy resolution of any disputes (Williamson 1985).

Trust can be generated in two main ways. If one of the parties has a reputation for being trustworthy, then the other parties can place themselves in his hands. If the intermediator has a strong reputation, for example, then the producer will accept payment after delivery, allowing the entrepreneur to check the quality before he pays. Similarly, the consumer will be willing to pre-pay for the product, provided that he has sufficient funds.

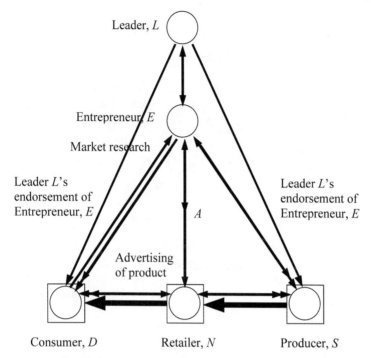

Figure 2.3 Leader of elite social group endorses integrity of entrepreneur.

The entrepreneur's reputation may derive from the fact that he belongs to an outward-looking social network that enjoys a good reputation. The situation is illustrated in Figure 2.3, where *E* belongs to a network whose membership is known to consumer *D* and producer *S*. This network has a leader, *L*, who makes it known to everyone that *E* is a member. Provided that everyone is also aware that *E* controls *N*, they will be happy for *N* to hedge his credit risk at their expense.

E's reputation means that *D* and *S* trust *E* and *N*, even though *E* and *N* do not trust *D* and *S*. The resultant pattern of trust is indicated in the figure using a 'double arrow' notation. The links *ES*, *NS* and *ND* all carry a double arrow facing away from either *E* or *N*, so that the arrow represents the additional weight to be attached to information flowing from the reputable party.

Engineering Mutual Trust

The role of a social network in supporting a trading relationship is illustrated in Figure 2.4, and its application to the market model is shown in Figure 2.5. Just as the entrepreneur intermediates market relationships, so the leader of a social network, *L*, intermediates voluntary non-profit

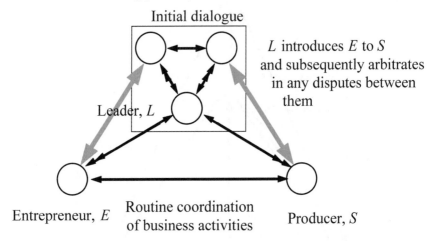

Meeting facility at central location

Initial dialogue

L introduces *E* to *S*
and subsequently arbitrates
in any disputes between
them

Leader, *L*

Entrepreneur, *E*   Routine coordination
of business activities   Producer, *S*

Figure 2.4 Role of social network in building trust to support economic activity.

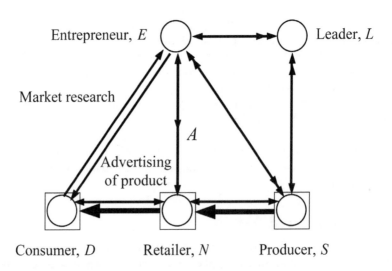

Entrepreneur, *E*   Leader, *L*

Market research

A

Advertising
of product

Consumer, *D*   Retailer, *N*   Producer, *S*

Figure 2.5 Role of social network in building mutual trust between a producer and
a market-making entrepreneur.

activity. Participants in this activity form a bonding network. According to Figure 2.4, L introduces E to S within the context of the bonding network, and as a result they both incur additional obligations which then underpin their business relationship. In the absence of intermediation by the bonding network the business relationship would be impersonal and sustained by remote communication. Relations within the bonding network are, by contrast, personal and face-to-face. To effect face-to-face communication, E and S travel to meetings of the bonding network; at the first meeting they are introduced by L, while at subsequent meetings L is on hand to supply further support if necessary—for example, mediating in any disputes between them. The return travel to the meeting is represented by the thick grey line, which carries two arrows to indicate a round trip.

The consequences of embedding the business relationship within a bonding network are shown in Figure 2.5. E trusts S and S trusts E, so there are double arrows pointing in each direction along this link. This represents the mutual trust that exists between E and S and indicates that a lower level of transaction cost is incurred by this connection now that it does not depend on E's reputation alone.

It can be seen, therefore, that social networks reduce transaction costs in two distinct ways. Outward-looking networks confer reputations on entrepreneurs (and others) which facilitate the intermediation of trade (and the advancement of the division of labour as a whole). These reputations create one-sided trust, which allows the entrepreneur to deal with other people who place themselves in his hands. Ordinary networks that promote shared interests also confer reputations on their members through emotional bonding, but these reputations are more localized, and in inward-looking networks the obligations that members accept are limited to fellow members of the group. The advantage of the emotional bonding effected by the ordinary network, however, is that it develops mutual trust between people who might not qualify to join an elite group.

Thus while elite outward-looking networks develop unilateral trust in people who take on intermediating roles, ordinary inward-looking networks develop mutual trust between less influential people. These two roles complement each other in improving the performance of the market system.

Competition between Entrepreneurs

The essence of a market is that a customer can choose between alternative sources of supply. While an entrepreneur may have a temporary monopoly when he sets up a new market, as assumed previously, competitors will soon appear, who either imitate his product or market a variant of it instead. A mature market therefore features competition between rival entrepreneurs. This is illustrated in Figure 2.6, which portrays two rival entrepreneurs, $E1$ and $E2$, drawing on distinct sources of supply $S1$ and $S2$. Each entrepreneur acts as a retailer. Two representative consumers are shown, $D1$

and *D*2, to emphasize the possibility that that the two entrepreneurs can divide the market between them. Prior to contract, each consumer solicits price quotations from each entrepreneur. Having compared the prices, *D*1 decides to buy from *E*1 and *D*2 from *E*2; this is illustrated by the pattern of thick lines representing the product flows. It should be noted that under competition the network of information flows is far more dense than the network of product flows. This is because product only flows when a contract has been agreed, while information flows every time a potential contact is investigated.

Confidentiality

Most writers on networks assume that, if considerations of cost are ignored, more linkages are always better, because this will shorten the paths between some pairs of elements and thereby reduce overall communication costs. But in practice, many people devote a lot of effort to avoiding communication with other people. One reason is simply that communication is time consuming and therefore costly. There is no point in wasting time talking to someone who has no contribution to offer.

There are numerous people whom we walk past everyday and with whom we do not stop and talk because we are hurrying to meetings with people to whom we do wish to talk. Although a link has already been created by chance, which has placed us at the same location at the same time, we do not wish to take advantage of the opportunity; on the contrary, we

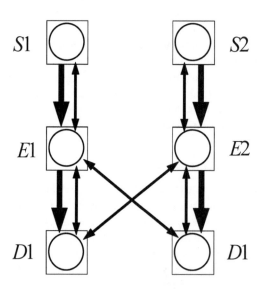

Figure 2.6 Stylized view of a competitive market intermediated by entrepreneurs.

actively decline it. Even people we already know may be avoided if we do not trust them, for there is no point in talking to someone whom you do not trust, since you would not wish to trade with him, and in any case you cannot believe what he says.

Other people are positively dangerous. This is not just a question of physical danger, but of economic danger. An entrepreneur will not wish to communicate with a competitor because he does not wish the competitor to know his price, because if the latter did then he could steal the former's customers away by quoting a marginally lower price.

It is possible, though, that some entrepreneurs can trust each other not to steal customers. In this case they can profit from collusion by raising price. By raising price above the competitive level, the suppliers can redistribute income from customers. Because higher prices will also restrict demand, the customers will lose more than the suppliers gain, which is one reason why collusion is regarded as anti-social. To avoid complaints from the consumers, the entrepreneurs may disguise their collusion. They therefore communicate in secret rather than in public, in the hope that customers will not realize what is going on. Thus if there is a link between $E1$ and $E2$, it will normally be secret. This is illustrated in Figure 2.7, where a link between $E1$ and $E2$ is shown in a box to indicate that it is hidden from other parties.

Consumers can also communicate with each other, as illustrated by the link between $D1$ and $D2$ in Figure 2.7. In most product markets, however, consumers lack market power because there are far more consumers

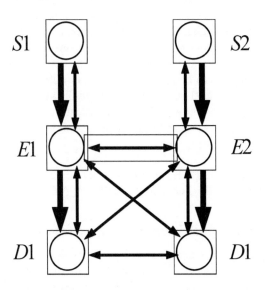

Figure 2.7 Vertical and horizontal communication in a market with secret collusion between suppliers and learning between consumers.

than producers and therefore it is too costly for them to coordinate their purchasing strategies. Consumers can, however, compare the prices they have paid through normal social channels such as gossip. This tends to strengthen consumer market power in a different way. Each consumer can 'free ride' on the shopping experiences of other consumers and therefore economize on the amount of shopping that they do themselves. Furthermore, any entrepreneur that reduces his price can expect to gain a larger share of the market when consumers pool their information since his reputation will spread more quickly. Thus even when consumers are unable to coordinate their purchasing decisions formally, they can still improve their position by harnessing social networks to distribute price information within the group.

It should be noted that issues relating to confidentiality vary according to the type of product traded in the market. Thus in labour markets, trade unions organize collusion among the workers conspicuously in order to maximize their strike-threat power, while employers similarly organize their labour purchasing to maximize their lock-out power, creating a system of collective bargaining underpinned by 'countervailing power'.

A set of linkages between consumers and producers exemplifies a 'vertical' network in which the flow of communication follows the same path as the flow of the product, while a network of producers and a network of consumers both exemplify a 'horizontal' network between people operating at the same stage of product flow. It is often claimed that vertical linkages strengthen competition and improve trade, while horizontal linkages are anti-competitive and damage trade, but this is not always the case, as the example of consumer learning makes clear. More generally, within any network composed of different types of elements, it is useful to distinguish linkages between elements of the same type from linkages between elements of a different type. Once again, links between elements of different types may be presumed to be pro-competitive, and links between elements of the same type to be anti-competitive, although these presumptions will not always be correct as the competitive implications depend not only on the configuration but also on the type of relationship involved.

THE SPATIAL DIVISION OF LABOUR AND THE DEMAND FOR TRANSPORT AND COMMUNICATION NETWORKS

The Demand for Personal Transport Derived from Social Networking

The preceding analysis has emphasized the close links between social networks and physical networks, with the flow of information through the former being used to coordinate the flow of resources through the latter. The links between social and physical networks become even closer when the spatial dimension of economic activity is examined in more detail.

There is a crucial difference between remote communication and face-to-face communication: while the former creates a demand for communications infrastructure, the latter creates a demand for transport infrastructure. Everyone cannot live 'next door' to everyone else, and so face-to-face communication creates a demand for travel to meetings. When just two or three people plan to meet, people may take it in turn to act as host, but when a significant number of people need to meet, a central location will normally be used. A specialized central location reduces overall travelling distance, while large meetings economize on the use of time as it is possible to meet lots of people by making just one trip.

Attending large meetings is also an efficient way of obtaining introductions: each person can not only be introduced, but can also introduce others. The structure of the meeting is important in this respect. People need to be able to circulate so that they can be paired up with appropriate people. Breakout areas in which people can hold confidential one-to-one discussions are also useful when the function of a meeting is to help broker business deals.

Efficiency of communication is increased if different meetings take place at the same central location, so that people can attend several meetings on the same trip. Different meetings of interest to the same groups of people can be scheduled to run in sequence, as with the annual conferences of related professional associations.

Other meetings are in continuous operation. A shopping centre, for example, may be construed as a continuous open meeting where people can come and go as they please. People who are attending scheduled meetings can 'pop out to the shops' at their convenience. Retailing is a prominent activity at many of the hubs where people meet. Historically, abbeys and castles attracted retailers, especially on saints' days, while many of today's major retail centres originally developed around ports or centres of government.

Emergence of Personal Transport Hubs Through Economies of Agglomeration

Retailing affords economies of agglomeration to consumers. Where different retailers stock different types of products, the consumer can collect an entire 'basket' of different goods on a single trip. Where different retailers stock different varieties of the same product, the customer can assess the design and quality of different varieties on the spot. Where different retailers stock the same product, customers can compare prices. In each case the agglomeration of retailers reduces the marginal cost of a customer's search.

Retailers supplying complementary goods have a direct incentive to locate close together. If one shop is already selling outerwear, for example, then a shop that sets up next door selling underwear can anticipate a substantial 'passing trade'.

It is not so clear, though, why competing retailers would locate together. One reason is that customers refuse to buy from a local monopolist because they believe that they will be cheated. This reflects a lack of trust in society. Thus retailers who locate together gain credibility: they acquire a small share of a large market instead of the entire share of the very small market that they would otherwise enjoy.

Another explanation relates to innovation. An effective way to advertise a new product is to display it adjacent to its closest competitor. Customers can be 'intercepted' on their way to their usual source of supply. The 'market test' may well put one of the suppliers out of business: if the new product is successful then the established retailer may quit, while if it fails then the innovator will quit. An established retailer defeated by an innovation may retire to a more remote location where it can monopolize a small market with its traditional product.

The link between innovation and agglomeration explains why a market may be regarded as a 'self-organizing' system. Volatility in the environment continually creates new consumer problems and a consequent demand for new products to solve them. At the same time, the social accumulation of technological knowledge allows new types of products to be developed. But an innovation is only viable if it can find a market, and its market is to be found where its closest competitor is sold. To make as much profit as early as possible, a confident innovator will head for the largest market (possibly after 'proving' the product in a smaller market first), which is where the contest between the new product and the old product will be played out.

The continuous influx of new products increases both the novelty and the diversity of the products available at a major hub. The greater intensity of competition means that older, obsolete products will be expelled from large markets before they are expelled from smaller ones. The larger the market, therefore, the greater the diversity and the lower the average age of the product.

On the other hand, the risks faced by the consumer are greater in a large market because a higher proportion of the products will be unproven. A large market will therefore attract buyers who are confident of their ability to judge design and quality and who value novelty for its own sake, while smaller markets will retain the custom of less confident people and those who prefer proven traditional designs. Optimal innovation strategy therefore explains both the capacity of the market system to renew itself continually by updating its product range and also the concentration of novelty in the largest markets.

Varieties of Transport Hubs

Meeting points and major markets constitute information hubs. People visit these centres specifically to meet other people. Travel to the hub both sustains the existing division of labour and also helps to effect changes in it. Shopping sustains profitable production, while meetings support the innovation process: researchers 'network' at conferences, entrepreneurs meet venture capitalists at elite gala events and inter-firm alliances are planned at trade fairs.

With so many visitors to the hub, accommodation, catering and entertainment facilities are required. Infrastructure may be built to facilitate mass transit to the hub. The ease of access and the variety of services available at the destination attracts tourists. A *visitor hub* of this type is, in principle, quite distinct from the *transit hub*, such as a railway junction or airport hub, at which people change from one trunk route, or transport mode, to another. People travel *through* a transit hub in a particular direction, whereas they travel *to and from* a visitor hub as part of a return journey.

The essence of a transit hub is that a number of connecting trunk lines all converge on the same point. Through traffic is switched from the incoming link to the outgoing link. Some traffic can be switched from one route to another without stopping—for example, express trains at country railway junctions and car traffic at motorway intersections—but in other cases a stop is required so that a connection can be made with another route. It is when traffic has to stop that it may 'stop over' rather than proceed on its way at the first available opportunity.

There is little point in stopping over at a pure transit hub, as there are no major services to attract the visitor. A visitor hub, on the other hand, can attract stop-overs if it can also be used as a transit hub. In order to act as a transit hub, however, it needs to occupy an appropriate location on the transport network, at the intersection of important routes. A transport hub without visitor potential is exemplified by the railway town of Crewe, which is an important junction that provides few visitor services. By contrast nineteenth-century London became a great metropolis by combining the roles of transit hub and visitor hub. Many railway trunk routes converged on London from different points of the compass, but each had its own terminal, so through travellers were obliged to change terminals as well as trains. However, the railway companies provided massive station hotels which not only allowed travellers to break their journey with an overnight stop, but also encouraged them to spend several days in the capital, consulting with doctors, bankers and solicitors and attending theatres and museums.

Combining the role of transit hub and visitor hub, however, can lead to congestion. In the late twentieth century, visitor attractions have tended to concentrate in the centres of the cities while transit hubs have moved to airports and motorway junctions on the periphery. London has strengthened its visitor appeal by excluding through traffic from the centre using a congestion charge, while Birmingham has acquired visitor appeal by building shopping centres and exhibition halls close to its motorway transit hubs. In the global economy of the twenty-first century, competition between 'world cities' is based on finding an efficient way of combining the roles of transit hub and visitor hub.

CONCLUSION

Networks have stimulated a lot of interest among economic and business historians over the past decade. Part of this is due to their ideological significance. They have been hailed as an alternative to large impersonal organizations such as the multinational firm or the state. Indeed, it has been suggested that the modern capitalist system took a 'wrong turning' about a century ago when the large managerial corporation superseded the networks of flexible specialization that prevailed in the industrial districts of the time (Piore and Sabel 1978).

Networks are inherently complex, but this does not mean that they cannot be properly understood. The structure of a network is governed by four main factors.

- *The size of the network, as measured by the number of elements.* Size is an important determinant of both the type of relationship and the configuration of flows. Large size encourages network members to opt for a multiplicity of impersonal relationships rather than a small number of personal ones. It also calls for the consolidation of network flows along trunk connections and the emergence of specialized trunk hubs where trunk traffic is sorted and sent on.
- *The membership of the network, as reflected in the types of elements that belong to it and the extent to which different types are mixed.* A typical trade network, for example, will contain at least three types of elements: a consumer, a producer and an intermediator such as an entrepreneur.
- *The types of relationships between members, which reflect the roles that they play.* Social relationships, for example, vary from highly impersonal relationships sustained by remote communication, which are characteristic of commercial networks, to highly personal relationships sustained face-to-face, which are characteristic of smaller and more localized bonding networks.
- *The configuration of the network, which describes the pattern in which the different elements are connected up.* Intermediators often act as hubs in networks. Multiple hubs stimulate competition within the network and provide redundancy, which makes the network resilient to shocks.

Recent analysis of social networks has been dominated by the study of relationships, and in particular by the issue of trust. This has distracted attention from the issue of configuration. Configuration is an important influence on the cost of operating a network. Configuration is the major focus of graph theory and has received much attention in research on physical networks, but most writers on economic and social history have ignored it.

This chapter has outlined the structure of a positive theory of networks which explains why certain types of networks are particularly common in certain situations. A simple approach is to identify the function that a network exists to perform. The division of labour provides the rationale for many physical networks. It creates a wide variety of industries whose products are distributed to millions of individual consumers. The division of labour needs to be coordinated, and a social network is well adapted to this task. Some networks coordinate long-distance trade, while others coordinate production processes; others regulate access to public goods, such as heritage sites, or facilitate mutual support between individuals.

Specialized intermediators emerge within networks, acting as communications hubs. If these intermediators work for profit then they normally re-sell products to the members, and if this is not possible then they charge a brokerage fee. Intermediation for profit is a classic example of entrepreneurial activity. Entrepreneurship is often presented as a highly individualistic activity, but in fact it depends heavily on the use of networks. A successful entrepreneur will identify the key networks that he needs to join, and for this purpose he requires a good understanding of the relationships that exist within the various networks and their implications for the ways in which the members of those networks behave.

Many intermediators, however, do not work for profit. They may be charismatic idealists seeking to improve society; operating for profit would be incompatible with their moral principles. Alternatively they may be high-status individuals who are rewarded by deference and respect. In some cases non-profit intermediators can cover their costs from voluntary donations to their organization or by charging membership fees.

Different coordination requirements are best satisfied by different network structures. Hence the nature of the division of labour determines the pattern of coordination required, which in turn determines the most appropriate network structure. If coordination is efficiently organized then the most efficient network structure will be the one that is used.

Long-distance trade, for example, is usually coordinated by for-profit entrepreneurs through inter-firm contracts, while the delivery of local social services is usually coordinated by non-profit leaders who establish schools, hospitals, churches, sports clubs and community associations for this purpose.

The leader of a non-profit group has a significant advantage over an entrepreneur who runs a for-profit firm in establishing a reputation for integrity. His selection of non-profit activity suggests altruistic motives, while the absence of charges for services eliminates the incentive to offer services that he does not intend to supply. This in turn is a significant advantage in establishing the external reputation of the network to which the leader belongs.

Any given person will belong to a substantial number of networks: family, church, sports club, work group, political party, professional association and so on. The fact that many non-profit networks recruit part-time volunteers and rotate tasks gives people ample opportunity to join many networks and to get acquainted with a high proportion of the membership of each. It is therefore probable that, quite by chance, they encounter someone with whom they are able to trade—for example, a distant family member may become a business partner, or a fellow member of a sports club may become a customer or employee.

Membership of one network can influence a person's behaviour in another network. For example, a supplier will be more reluctant to cheat on quality if his customer is a friend. There is scope for significant positive externalities from the membership of different social networks. It has been argued, however, that a person's behaviour in one network may be quite unrelated to his behaviour in another, and in particular that a person's private life is no indicator of his behaviour in public life, and vice versa. This could be the case, for example, if a person adapted his behaviour fully to the strategic requirements for success in each particular sphere. However, if an individual belongs to a network that imposes universal moral obligations on him then these obligations, if honoured, are bound to spill over into conduct in other networks. The individual will gain a reputation based upon his commitment to universal standards of behaviour, and this will in turn influence the range of economic activities that he is able to undertake. The reputation of eighteenth-century Quaker businessmen for probity is a case in point.

The greatest impact on economic performance will, in theory, be made by outward-looking social networks that promote functionally useful moral values. These are values that reduce transaction costs and promote productivity, namely, values such as honesty, willingness to compromise, hard work and thrift. These values are embodied in the obligations to which the members commit themselves. The universal nature of these values gives the members a reputation outside the network. As a result, members of such networks are well equipped to intermediate in trade.

By actively recruiting new members, the leaders of such networks can add to the total stock of reputation in the economy. The stock of reputation can be multiplied further by encouraging experienced members to found new networks or start up satellite networks based on similar principles.

Because each person in the economy belongs to so many different networks, all the networks to which people belong are intertwined. Every network is connected, directly or indirectly, to every other network by multiple links. Thus every network is a sub-set of a single giant network that encompasses the entire global economy.

To cut through this complexity, it is necessary to analyze any given network phenomenon by concentrating on just one part of the global system. Research must proceed by abstracting the network under scrutiny from the system as a whole, in order to examine its internal structure in full detail. It must not be overlooked, however, that the network under scrutiny is connected to the rest of the system at numerous points—it is an 'open system', in other words. Disturbances originating elsewhere in the economy can impinge on the network at any point, and sometimes at several points at once.

This methodology of examining the part in relation to the whole is common to all social science, however, and so in this respect the study of networks merely conforms to general research practice. What has been missing from the study of networks so far is not so much an awareness of this interdependence as a reluctance to examine the structure of individual networks in adequate detail. It is hoped that the survey of network structure presented in this chapter, and the analysis of its economic significance, will encourage business and economic historians to pay more attention to network structure in the future.

ACKNOWLEDGEMENTS

I am grateful to Paloma Fernández Pérez, Mary B. Rose, Marina Della Giusta, Zella King and Bob Fessop for comments on earlier drafts of this chapter.

REFERENCES

Armstrong, H., and J. Taylor. 2000. *Regional economics and policy*. 3rd ed. Oxford: Blackwell.

Biggs, N. L., E. K. Lloyd, and R. Wilson. 1986. *Graph theory, 1736–1936*. Oxford: Oxford University Press.

Burt, R. S. 1992. *Structural holes: The social structure of competition*. Cambridge, MA: Harvard University Press.

Casson, M. 1997. *Information and organization: A new perspective on the theory of the firm*. Oxford: Clarendon Press.

———. 2000. *Entrepreneurship and leadership*. Cheltenham, U.K.: Edward Elgar.

Diestel, R. 1997. *Graph theory*. New York: Springer.

Doreian, P., and F. N. Stokman. 1997. *Evolution of social networks*. Amsterdam: Gordon and Breach.

Foreman-Peck, J. S., and R. Millward. 1994. *Public and private ownership of industry in Britain, 1820–1980*. Oxford: Clarendon Press.

Granovetter, M. 1985. Economic action and social structure: The problem of embeddedness. *American Journal of Sociology* 91 (3): 481–510.

Haggett, P., and R. J. Chorley. 1969. *Network analysis in geography*. London: Arnold.

Isard, W., E. W. Schooler, and T. Vietorisz. 1959. *Industrial complex analysis and regional development*. London: Chapman & Hall.

Knight, F. H. 1935. *The ethics of competition and other essays*. London: Allen & Unwin.

Leibenstein, H. 1978. *General X-efficiency theory and economic development*. New York: Oxford University Press.

North, D. C. 1981. *Structure and change in economic history.* New York: W. W. Norton.

Pattison, S. 1993. *Algebraic models for social networks.* Cambridge: Cambridge University Press.

Piore, M. J., and C. F. Sabel. 1978. *The second industrial divide: Possibilities for prosperity.* New York: Basic Books.

Putterman, L. 1990. *The division of labour and economic welfare.* Oxford: Oxford University Press.

Thompson, G. F. 2003. *Between hierarchies and markets: The logic and limits of network firms.* Oxford: Oxford University Press.

Veblen, T. 1922. *Instinct of workmanship: And the state of the industrial Arts.* New York: B. W. Huebsch.

Wasserman, S., and K. Faust. 1994. *Social network analysis: Methods and applications.* Cambridge: Cambridge University Press.

Watts, D. J. 2003. *Six degrees: The science of a connected age.* London: William Heineman.

Wellman, B., and S. D. Berkowitz, eds. 1988. *Social structures: A network approach.* Cambridge: Cambridge University Press.

Williamson, O. E. 1985. *Economic institutions of capitalism: Firms, markets, relational contracting.* New York: Free Press.

3 Innovation, Entrepreneurship and Networks

A Dance of Two Questions

Mike Parsons and Mary B. Rose

INTRODUCTION: WHAT IS INNOVATION?

Innovation is as old as mankind and lies at the heart of human survival, progress and, of course, destruction. Controlling fire to keep warm, making basic tools, growing food—all had their origins thousands of years ago and were as innovative as the development of automobiles, computing and telecommunications today. Definitions of innovation vary enormously and the concept is treated differently across disciplines and through time and space.

From a business perspective, innovation is about turning opportunity or need into new products and services, which are commercially exploited. Only around 3 percent of patented inventions are commercialized, many remaining just clever ideas. Creativity alone does not lead to commercialized innovations, and it is here that the link with entrepreneurship becomes crucial. Entrepreneurship involves the recognition and assessment of opportunities and is often the bridge between creativity and innovation. This is because the entrepreneur is involved in what can be described as the dance of two questions—what is needed and what is possible—and the interplay of these two questions is an ongoing process.

Innovation is the often precarious balancing of these two priorities to create, anticipate and respond to change and to solve problems. Understanding the shifting relationships between competitors, consumer demand, technological capabilities and the wider social, legal and economic environment for business is therefore crucial to successful innovation (Stefik and Stefik 2004, 27–46; Fagerberg 2005, 4–8).

Radical new technologies, such as electricity, the internal combustion engine or telecommunications, have altered the innovation environment for new products and services. Such change has stretched far beyond power generation, transport and communication. This is especially so when a number of changes converge, creating novel and previously unimagined horizons leading to paradigm shifts in both what is possible, in terms of process, and what is expected, in terms of product.

Innovation is not just about technology or even new products or machines. It is linked to and shaped by the knowledge, skills, practices and experience of entrepreneurs, employees and customers and is embedded within organizations, industries, regions and nations.

This means that innovation is moulded by past experience and accumulated expertise. It is an evolutionary process which can in turn be shaken by discontinuities, which fundamentally alter the 'rules of the game'. Discontinuities in the macro-environment may be stimulated by new technologies or materials, by variations in laws or attitudes or by fundamental economic shocks and can have profound effects, especially on established businesses, which can become trapped by their past (Tushman and Anderson 1986, 444–460).

Most innovation occurs on the boundaries between areas of expertise, since bodies of knowledge (old and new, familiar and unfamiliar) can be combined to achieve innovation, and often involves collaboration. Whether individuals, firms or regions become imprisoned by history depends on attitudes to change, to boundary crossing and to awareness of shifts outside an immediate area of expertise. The essence of entrepreneurship is interpreting information that is available to others in original ways. In addition, the ability to evaluate, combine and utilize 'outside knowledge' lies at the heart of the innovation process (Shane 2003, 41; Cohen and Levinthal 1990, 128).

Inevitably this makes successful innovation a social rather than a solitary process, and the majority of the most successful entrepreneurs have been embedded in extensive networks which facilitate knowledge and technology exchange and financial support (Hargadon 2003, 5–7). This chapter analyzes the complex and shifting relationships between innovation, entrepreneurship and networks to demonstrate the changing ways, through time, in which innovative entrepreneurs have balanced what is needed with what is possible. It also explores types and sources of innovation and the way in which they have been shaped by the past. The chapter shows that, far from being a linear process, innovation is often a chaotic and complex process.

TYPES OF INNOVATION

Innovation has conventionally been categorized as product (or service), process, radical or incremental (De Propsis 2002, 337–353). But the boundaries are often blurred, and this categorization does not entirely capture the nuances and subtleties of innovation. As a result these types of innovation are just a starting point for its understanding, and there are significant interrelationships, overlaps and shifts through time.

Product and process innovation are, for example, intimately intertwined, and discernible phases of innovation can be identified for both products and services. Very often radical innovation has been linked to and has contributed to the development of new products and new processes and may be associated with paradigm shifts—shifts in mental maps of the way we think about products, processes and human behaviour. The conventional categories ignore the impact of an innovation on the mental map—whether at the level of society or that of the firm.

Changing the way we think about a product or service, or indeed an organization, is a critical dimension of any innovation which can have far-reaching implications. A good example is the lean production methods developed initially by the Japanese in the 1950s and 1960s. By the 1970s these achieved variety, small batches, high quality and productivity through self-managing teams (Kenney and Florida 1993, 16). This fundamentally challenged deeply held beliefs of how efficiency was achieved. Although the actual diffusion of lean production, in the United States and Europe in the 1980s and 1990s, did not lead to the disappearance of mass and large-batch production in manufacturing, lean thinking has impacted attitudes to work practice far beyond the factory shop floor, to embrace services, including retailing and office practice (Bowen and Youngdahl 1998, 207–225). Taken to its logical conclusion, lean thinking, with its emphasis on waste reduction and value enhancement for the customer, has formed a basis for product and service innovations. But because transformation in the mental map involves changes in human behaviour, it is rarely fast and requires the 'undoing' of learning by doing, often through 'learning by trying' (Fleck 1999, 244–257).

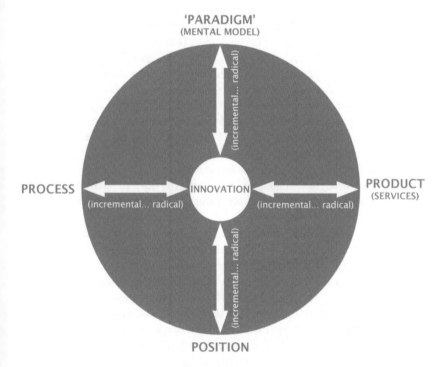

Figure 3.1 Innovation space. (Source : Tidd, Bessant and Pavitt 2005: 13)

Figure 3.1 categorizes innovation as product (or service), process, paradigm or positioning. These categories range from the radical to the incremental, and for each individual innovation the precise placing depends not just on the individual innovation, but also on the context for the specific sector and company within the sector (Tidd, Bessant and Pavitt 2005, 13).

There are many innovations where commercial success has been dependent upon developing a new process or means of distribution. Two good examples of process innovation are electricity and the telephone, both of which involved developing a system of long-distance distribution. In other words we witness the interplay between product and process innovation and its relationship with the wider technological environment. We associate Thomas Edison with the light bulb, but this was not his main contribution as an innovator. He recognized the need to combine a (service) system with a product. The light bulb could not function without electricity and therefore could not diffuse on its own; it diffused when it was combined with a range of supporting systems (Stefik and Stefik 2004, 69–70).

Similarly George Eastman did not invent the camera, but he did develop a new photographic process or system: '*You press the button and we do the rest*'. This was a 'new combination' of the known inorganic chemical process of light-reactive materials with one of the very first plastics—celluloid—the very beginning of exploitation of organic materials and the supporting science. The manufacturer of the camera took advantage of the mass-manufacturing technologies of the day to produce something at very low cost. This transformed both photography and photographers (Utterback 1996, 173–176).

In a very different sector and with a very different product, the same principles apply if we consider McDonald's and fast food. McDonald's did not invent the hamburger, but they standardized both the process and product and developed a process for delivering it which created a new business model, and hence a market was developed with the new product/service. The McDonald's burger was not itself innovative, but the whole McDonald's process was, transforming both business and consumer expectations of fast food (Drucker 1985, 15). All these innovations also involved a paradigm shift because they helped to transform the way particular products or services were perceived by both producers and consumers (Tidd, Bessant and Pavitt 2005, 10).

The intertwining of product, process, radical and incremental innovations is also apparent from the evolution of path-breaking products. In the early life of a radical new product there is likely to be a 'fluid' period of intensive incremental innovation, as a dominant design emerges from the plethora of possibilities. There is no guarantee that the most technologically sophisticated product will become the industry standard, and the combined forces of competitive strategy, usability and consumer perceptions are all influences on what we have come to take for granted in a product category. Once the dominant design has settled, a transition phase follows, when there is likely to be growing emphasis on process innovation to improve efficiency. There is therefore interplay between innovation and the competitive process. While product innovation can initially be completely separate from process innovation, competitive pressures often stimulate changes in system, organization and work practice.

In the mature phase, innovation is likely to be increasingly incremental. These patterns are not confined to complex assemblies such as the motor car, refrigerator or the personal computer, but can be identified in non-assembled products such as textiles, glass or steel. In this category of products, emphasis on process innovation and the development of processing equipment, often initially by lead users, is especially noticeable (Utterback 1996, 103–144). Indeed, in practice, it is the act of combining an existing product with a wider innovative process, rather than the product on its own, which brings competitive advantage. This in turn may have implications for service innovation because, when a product innovation diffuses through the establishment of a system, that system invariably involves the provision of services.

In services, however, while innovation types are similarly intertwined they follow differing patterns. In the first phase innovation will be about improving efficiency of existing services; in the second phase, the effectiveness and quality of services; and only in the third phase, radical innovations and transformation (Utterback 1996, 124; Damanpour and Gopalakrishan 2001, 45–65).

CONTINUITIES AND DISCONTINUITIES IN INNOVATION

Innovation and its diffusion are associated with continuity and discontinuity and are shaped by a combination of evolutionary forces and networks with knowledge, skill and expertise at their core (Malerba 2006, 12). This means they are not simple linear procedures at the level of nation, industry, region or firm. They are instead complex and uncertain and play out differently according to variations in history, knowledge, economic conditions, legal frameworks, attitudes and social processes.

History is not just about the past, but can be used to understand the present and the future. The links between past and future and the cumulative nature of innovation are the result of the social-learning processes associated with innovation (Lazonick 2003, 33–39). Innovation is by implication evolutionary, with the discontinuities typically coming from boundary crossing, which leads to new combinations (Ziman 2000; Hargadon 2003).

Discontinuity as well as continuity lies at the heart of innovation at both the macro and micro level. For Schumpeter, for whom innovation was about much more than simply new products,

> Change, particularly that resulting from new technology, offers a continuous supply of new information about different ways to use resources.

It is this information that allows enterprising individuals to engage in the dis-equilibrating process of recombining resources in ways that are made valuable by the technological changes that have occurred. (Schumpeter 1934, 121)

At the macro level, major radical innovations created economic change through what has been described as a ripple effect associated with a period of creative destruction. The implication of Schumpeter's ideas is to suggest that the impact of such radical innovations (e.g., changes in motive power, communications, materials, design) was to encourage firms to introduce refinement in existing practice or to lead to the disruption of current practice, products and processes.

This was of course reflected in the competitive behaviour of firms and in the 'swarming' of innovations before the emergence of a dominant design. This applied to established sectors—where entrepreneurs might be looking for refinements in their existing products and processes to improve cost competitiveness. It also applied in non-traditional sectors and firms through recognition of potential new combinations (Abernathy and Clark 1985, 3–22). The resultant upsurge of investment, business formation and associated product and process development, according to Schumpeter, created periodic upswings in the economic cycle. These upswings have been identified as 'long waves' in economic growth, normally lasting around fifty years (Schumpeter 1965, 45–64).

Few periods in history have witnessed such a convergence of new scientific and technological knowledge as occurred between 1867 and 1914. It has been argued that the

period ranks as history's most remarkable discontinuity not only because of the extensive sweep of its innovations but also because of the rapidity of the fundamental advances that were achieved during the time. (Smil 2005, 5)

According to Smil, a combination of rapid patenting of science-based innovation, the coincidence of major path-breaking scientific and technical advances which were rapidly improved after introduction and the sheer boldness of the innovations provided Western society with an entirely 'different programme to guide its future'.

What distinguished this period from many others was a remarkable synergy of change which included electricity, the internal combustion engine, new and synthetic materials and advances in communication and information. The synergy and high level of knowledge exchange between pure science and industry was reinforced by the R&D laboratories of large companies. These appeared first in the late nineteenth-century German chemical industry and soon after in the American electricity industry. These fundamental changes provided the knowledge foundation for the major technological and organizational changes of the twentieth and twenty-first centuries. Their initial association with cheap oil set the world on an energy-intensive journey of productivity gain which global warming has rendered unsustainable (Smil 2005, 9–27; Pavitt 2005, 90).

Although these changes fundamentally and permanently changed the canvas of business, consumption and indeed society, the speed and pattern of their diffusion varied internationally. These variations have nothing much to do with science and technology and a lot to do with history, demographics, social attitudes and the institutional environment.

For example, these technological changes were associated with the rise of mass production in the United States, which itself was stimulated and reinforced by the size and wealth of the domestic market. Between 1820 and 1914 the population of the United States grew from 10 million to 100 million, making it the world's largest domestic market (Atack and Passell 1992, 213). Such demographic buoyancy, combined with relatively high levels of real income and supported by high-wage strategies and ease of credit, fuelled innovation, especially in consumer-goods industries, machinery and of course automobiles. Schmookler, in his study of the economics of invention, concluded,

It seems almost obvious . . . that the automobile came when it did more because of economic and social changes than because of technological change as such. In the first place, in the automobile, prestige, flexibility, privacy, recreation and utility are combined in ways which only an individualistic, high-per capita income society could afford to develop. (1962, 226–227)

These characteristics, so noticeable in the United States, were simply not shared in Europe in the same period. As a country of recent settlement, American attitudes differed significantly from those in Europe, and there were sharp contrasts in the formal and informal rules of the games of business, technology and innovation (Davis and North 1971, 270). These affected the ways in which business was organized, the opportunities for innovation and its shape. Certainly there were product and factor-market contrasts which shaped technological change. Yet, whereas in Europe social status was derived from land and birth, in America it came from wealth, business success and resulting community endowment (Cochran 1981, 12). Nevertheless, there was growing international awareness that a shift in international efficiency was occurring. In the first half of the twentieth century, European industrialists and engineers began monitoring the American system of manufacturing, adapting mass-production techniques to their domestic circumstances. Before and after the First World War, owners, managers and engineers from Europe's car manufacturers including André Gustav Citroën and Louis Renault from France, Giovanni Agnelli (Fiat) from Italy, and Herbert Austin and William Morris of

England all visited Ford works at both Highland Park and River Rouge. The process of hybridization of mass-production methods, to suit conditions outside the United States, accelerated after the Second World War and contributed to rising productivity levels in Europe during the post-war period (Zeitlin 2000, 19). European productivity growth outstripped the United States for much of the second half of the twentieth century. Recent research has shown, however, that this trend has reversed, and the United States has again moved ahead of Europe by several percentage points. This phase began in 1995 when for the first time high levels of investment in information technology (IT) began to be matched by significant productivity gains.

This has not been equalled in Europe, where investment came later and where the so-called productivity paradox continues. The reasons for the widening productivity gap between the United States and Europe include American use of lean manufacturing for IT equipment, the spread of IT equipment and related work practices, especially in the service sector, including retailing. The crucial issue for Europe is linked to differing path-dependent patterns since the United States—with its early start in computing—has developed deeper expertise than is to be found in Europe (van Ark et al. 2003, 295–318; Brown and Duguid 2001, 198–213).

The differences in experience between the United States and Europe in particular demonstrate the hazards of assuming that patterns of innovation appropriate in one environment will be easily replicated elsewhere. In addition, as discussed in the introduction to this book, international differences in innovation systems and the relationships between governments, universities and businesses reinforce these variations (Edquist 2005, 182–208). This is especially true for later industrializers such as Spain and other Mediterranean economies, as is shown in the chapters by Puig and Fernández Pérez in this volume.

THE 'DANCE OF TWO QUESTIONS' AS A MULTIPLAYER GAME: INNOVATION AND ENTREPRENEURIAL NETWORKS

Major, radical technological changes affect the environment faced by individual firms, large and small. Other sources of discontinuity include the emergence of new markets, new technologies in apparently unrelated sectors, changes in the political or legislative environment, shifts in social attitudes, or major wars (Philips et al. 2006, 178–180). It can be especially difficult for established firms to respond to and engage in what has been described as 'discontinuous innovation' because this type of innovation requires 'new skills, new ways of organizing and often new ways of managing' (Tushman and Nadler 1986, 77). Much depends upon sensitivity to new knowledge (whether that generated within a firm or externally) or to 'absorptive capacity' (Cohen and Levanthal 1990, 128). Where established firms have limited 'absorptive capacity' there is the opportunity for 'disruptive technologies' to creep in, upturning existing 'rules of the game' from the outside. Examples include reel film and digital photography, land-line and mobile telephony, electric lighting and light-emitting diodes (LEDs), London and New York stock exchanges and electronic communications networks, standard textbooks and custom-assembled modular digital textbooks (Christensen 1997, xxv).

Path dependency, or the influence of past events and knowledge on the future, has been likened to the 'deepening of wheel ruts by each successive vehicle' (David 1997, 123). Knowledge and skill, built on past experience through 'learning by doing', can of course become a constraint, where organizations and the individuals within them become trapped by their past. An inward-looking culture, unchanging embedded routines and suspicion of outside influences all potentially lead to path-dependent lock in. However, the decisions of entrepreneurs (whether in large or small firms) engaged in their dance of two questions—what is needed and what is possible—can still be shaped by past knowledge and experience without being trapped by it. The entrepreneur's imagination has the potential to change the shadow of the past into an inspiration for the future. Many innovations have combined existing bodies of knowledge in novel ways but have involved no new technology or ideas. Where linked with new or external knowledge, old knowledge becomes an asset rather than a liability.

As shown in Colli's case study in this book, such new combinations may bring together established techniques with services to achieve innovative delivery and design systems and a repositioning of the company. An alternative approach is to link products to innovative distribution systems which bring a company closer to customers. A classic example of this is Dell, the computer company which, in 1996, linked its product distribution to the Web in a highly imaginative way. It allowed the company to understand and respond to customer needs.

> In its first 4 years, Dell's on-line initiative proved very successful, helping the company better understand user priorities and further customize service and product support offerings to them. The Website quickly became a dynamic market place; by the early twenty-first century, company sales through its Web site averaged more than $40m a day. (Koehn 2001, 304)

That said, it is important to understand that Dell began selling by mail order and telephone. The success of Dell is again a new combination: grasping the Internet as a new business platform and combining it with lean manufacturing/pull systems which emerged strongly in the United States as a response to the Japanese threat.

Rather than staying trapped by their past, entrepreneurs may, therefore, engage in 'mindful deviation' and in so doing create new innovative pathways. This can be achieved by a combination of external and internal awareness or receptivity to the unfamiliar, combined with an understanding of the need to convince hearts and minds of the benefits of change (Garud and Karnøe 2001, 6; Bessant, Birkinshaw and Delbridge 2004, 32–33). All this implies that the dynamic dance of two questions will not be conducted in isolation, but will be embedded in and underpinned by social networks within and outside firms.

Awareness of and receptivity to people, ideas and technologies from outside the familiar arenas of activity lie at the heart of successful innovation. The observation that 'the ability to exploit external knowledge is a critical component of innovative capabilities' (Cohen and Levinthal 1990, 128) implies that successful innovation is a multiplayer game, involving networks rather than lone individuals. Collaborative networks of people from differing backgrounds are often crucial in innovation. This is because innovation frequently occurs at the boundaries of knowledge and where boundaries between areas of knowledge cross. However, it takes imagination to see beyond those boundaries and to see the wide range of possibilities they bring and judgment to choose between them (Shane 2003, 41; Casson 1982). It also requires knowledge of what has gone before and an ability to learn from it, as well as appreciation of the present, to understand the available choices.

Innovation is therefore a social process, with knowledge built through engagement within communities of practice where learning is based on participation and engagement with others (Lave and Wenger 1991; Wenger 1998, 45). Applied to the innovation process this theory forms a crucial bridge between theories and history since the building of communities of practice are based upon the evolution of shared experience among those with common histories. This helps us understand the entrepreneurial process and how, through operating within overlapping communities of practice, entrepreneurs may develop innovative ideas through new combinations. In addition they could be used to explain the diffusion of innovation and, especially, differing patterns of diffusion within different societies.

New combinations of knowledge will be facilitated by collaboration between people from different backgrounds but who share understanding and have built successful bridges. The most successful entrepreneurs and companies tend to be those with the widest and most interactive networks, as the case studies by Puig and Fernández Pérez show.

Collaborations between individuals and companies allow the sharing of knowledge. This sharing helps create informal communities of people like the ones created in the university chairs financed by the Rubiralta family, which provide useful contacts and information for firms, scholars and students, as shown in Fernández Pérez's case study. They mean that firms do not always need to invest directly in an area of competence, but can derive it from others. Interestingly this can also be illustrated by Kodak in the 1990s. The development of digital imaging technology saw Kodak making alliances to develop capabilities which would allow them to play in this arena. They hired George Fisher from Motorola to be their new CEO and in 1998 set up a joint venture with Intel to develop the picture CD. These developments meant that by 2004 Kodak had 20 percent global market share of the digital-camera market (Tidd, Bessant and Pavitt 2005, 334).

But collaborations—often new collaborations—can also go horribly wrong where there is a lack of shared vision or trust and mutual understanding, or where governance systems or arrangements for intellectual property rights (IPR) lead to conflict or inhibit innovation. An example of the negative effects of the lack of a shared vision or trust was the end of the ownership of the Rivière family of their one hundred—year-old steel-wire firm. On the other hand, conflicts that inhibit innovation have become increasingly prominent with the emergence of e-businesses—often operating within a global supply chain where the challenges of creating virtual communities should not be underestimated.

Social processes also play a crucial role in determining whether or not innovations will diffuse—within a company, within economies or into the market place. Some companies may develop major breakthroughs which are not commercialized simply because there are profound cultural gaps between those developing the ideas in the R&D departments and those involved in marketing or engineering. Or because the past experience and capabilities of the company prevented appreciation of the significance of the innovation, as happened when the Xerox Palo Alto Research Center developed the mouse and graphic-user interface—the significance of which passed the Xerox strategy team by (Brown and Duguid, 2000, 150–151).

It is equally clear, as is shown in the chapters by Kipping and Puig, that sometimes distrust and misunderstanding between groups engaged in facilitating innovation and those potentially adopting it can restrict diffusion. In part this can be a result of a lack of mutual understanding and a high level of distrust, stemming from lack of overlapping communities of practice. In this context, Puig has shown that, in the case of Spanish pharmaceuticals, we are looking more at a network of opportunity, rather than necessarily a network of innovation.

The diffusion of innovations into the market place is also a social process, which is heavily dependent on word of mouth and the attitudes of consumers, which are in turn linked to economic and cultural forces. Innovation is certainly about identifying new uses for existing innovations and technologies—but these must be recognizable to users, otherwise they will not diffuse as Hargadon observed of Edison:

> Edison paid great attention to the publicizing, packaging and delivering of new systems to the non technical user in user friendly form—

for example making his lighting systems as identical as possible to the more familiar and established gas systems. (Hargadon 2003, 67)

An entrepreneur's networks are likely to be based on experience, which not only determines the range of contacts, but may also influence perceptions of opportunities and courses of action. Such linkages are often based upon personal ties and operate through informal social contact, but individual contacts alone, while reducing uncertainty, may become constraints on both the entrepreneur and the business unless reinforced by a wider external network. External networks frequently involve more formal contractual arrangements, including strategic alliances with other companies, which may themselves initially derive from personal contacts. It is relatively easy to understand why networks are so crucial to innovation in small firms—they drastically extend the knowledge and expertise of the firm beyond those of the Small and Medium Sized Enterprise (SME) owner (Freel 2000, 245–266).

There is considerable research on the role of business-to-business networking in the supply chain and the potential benefits derived from collaborating with suppliers in bringing innovative products to market. Not only does close collaboration with suppliers reduce uncertainty, in terms of delivery, but, at the same time, it also allows for exploitation of synergies in the design process—vital, given the ways in which the behaviour of materials can influence the design and performance of products. With the arrival of lean manufacturing, networking within the supply chain changed considerably. The previous mentality had been to keep suppliers at a distance, ensuring there were many different suppliers for the same thing, negotiating at arms length and certainly not sharing information now considered vital to the smooth running of supply chains. The new methodology has involved sharing information much more closely between manufacturer and supplier (Wilms et al. 1994). But supply-chain networks are not just restricted to business to business, as business-to-customer networks are also vital to innovation.

By engaging in a networked dance of two questions entrepreneurs increase their awareness and reduce the obstacles to 'what is possible'. Seventy-five percent of successful innovations arise in response to a recognized need—the challenge is identifying and responding to that need (Rothwell and Gardiner 1985, 168). Lead-user innovation is not new and can be traced back to the Industrial Revolution, when cotton textile machinery and machine tools were developed respectively by the textile manufacturers and the machine makers themselves (Macleod 1992, 295–296). Increasingly contemporary research has shown that lead users, rather than market research, provide more reliable insight into future needs (von Hippel 2005, 14).

Lead-user innovation is where the users themselves, as those with the best understanding of their demands, innovate to produce what they need. They benefit from using rather than selling the product, in the first instance, and 'learn by using' a product or process. This brings them far nearer to understanding need than the provider of the good or service (von Hippel 2005).

These users operate at the cutting edge of activity and have needs in advance of the majority of users. This gives them the incentive to innovate, while 'usage' gives them the capability to develop and improve (Lüthje and Herstatt 2004, 556). Use of a product is knowledge enhancing and builds experience which informs understanding of the capabilities and shortcomings of existing products. By facing more extreme or more specialized problems, lead users are also able to build the knowledge needed to provide innovative solutions, rather than relying on established suppliers. Where lead users are themselves industrial or indeed service customers, their user innovation is likely to be a process innovation, which enhances efficiency or perhaps allows them to develop the sophistication of their product (Pavitt 1984, 259). Occasionally a few lead users themselves set up businesses, but this is comparatively rare. However, where entrepreneurs collaborate with lead users there can emerge

> a learning process consisting of learning by doing, learning by using, learning by interaction and learning by diffusion, which results in the speed and flexibility of new product development being dependent on an overlapping approach and information sharing. (Shaw 1994, 275)

Since innovative networks are based on learning by doing they are embedded in the history of industries and of regions, as can be shown in the U.K. outdoor trade. During the 1960s the northwest region of the United Kingdom became the home of several innovative design-based companies, producing clothing and equipment for mountaineering and outdoor sports. This region borders on the Pennines. It includes North Cheshire, Manchester, Lancashire, Derbyshire, Sheffield and parts of what is now Yorkshire. From the early eighteenth century, these adjoining regions played a central role in the newly emerging Industrial Revolution. Design activity in Manchester and Sheffield led to hundreds of new technologies and products, many of them world changing. At the time, Manchester was a world leader in design activity that resulted in radical technical, social, commercial, organizational, educational and political changes.

In contrast, the cutting-edge design activity in Sheffield was focused more tightly on steel production. From as early as the fourteenth century, the Sheffield area specialized in cutlery production. In early eighteenth-century Sheffield, the design of the crucible process, a new way of making better steel, facilitated new engineering and product design in the emerging Industrial Revolution. From that time to the middle of the twentieth century, Manchester and Sheffield were the home of design and manufacture in cotton, textile engineering and specialist steel manufacturing, together with related industries such as printing, linoleum making and machine production.

The twentieth-century industrial decline of Manchester and Sheffield, with the accompanying decay and unemployment, came with rising foreign competition. They left a legacy of experience and skill and a deeply embedded culture of design and innovation, which, combined with new knowledge and applied to new activities, contributed, among other things, to the design of new outdoor clothing and equipment and sporting innovation. New outdoor clothing and equipment businesses included Karrimor, Troll and Mountain Equipment. During the 1970s, these and other outdoor clothing and equipment firms emerged as international brands (Parsons and Rose 2005; Rose, Love and Parsons 2007).

CHANGING NETWORKS AND MASS COLLABORATION

Beginning in the 'Age of Synergy', in the late nineteenth century, the R&D laboratory has lain at the heart of innovation in large corporations in both the United States and Europe for over a century. By the early twenty-first century, the combination of lead-user innovation and rapid and interrelated shifts in technology are altering the innovation process, which is in turn being shaped by emerging social processes. The development of open-source software by communities of programmers and hackers has emerged as a major cultural and economic phenomenon in recent years (von Hippel 2005). Such communities include Linux, Moodle and Sakai, where software development is almost exclusively undertaken by users, rather than by commercial software companies. The emergence of LAMP (Linux, Apache, MySQL, Perl/PHP) or the bundles of open-source software have transformed Web sites from static sources of information to dynamic collaborative spaces. This 'new collaboration' is closely linked to the phenomenon of Web 2.0, where users are becoming 'disruptors', creeping up on established manufacturers influencing their approach to R&D, innovation and indeed productivity (O'Reilly 2005; Tapscot and Williams 2006, 10–11).

New technologies, including broadband, collaborative software platforms, Web applications and collaborative tools such as wikis and blogs, are affecting the way we communicate and collaborate. Indeed these are making many consumer products (e.g., games and mobile phones) the focus of consumer improvement for their own use. Because the resulting new ideas can be so readily distributed on the Internet, manufacturers are seriously afraid of 'losing control of their platform'. On the other hand, strong legal reactions are avoided since they would be against the very loyal users of their product (Tapscot and Williams 2006, 270–272).

Other factors, including global shifts in economic activity, are speeding up the innovation cycle and leading to the repositioning of Western companies away from core competences in manufacturing, towards those in service and design. This combination of forces is contributing to a paradigm shift in attitudes to innovation and in company and consumer behaviour.

The attitudes of large companies towards innovation are beginning to shift from a closed system, where the R&D laboratory is the prime basis of competitive advantage. Intellectual property remains a company's major strategic asset; it is being exploited more successfully by a number of new strategies which can be described as 'nurturing the collaborative capabilities of the organization'. This can include the shifting of some resources to open-source collaboration. Alternatively innovations may be put into 'protective commons', while some companies have made intellectual property available for licensing via online techniques and communities, rather than simply being reliant on personal networks. This is more than a technical change—it is a cultural one of some magnitude (Tapscot and Williams 2006, 270). Engagement in open innovation requires the development of 'porous boundaries' to firms, allowing a growing proportion of innovation to be undertaken outside the company (Chesbrough and Crowther 2006, 229–336).

The situating of large and small companies within 'communities of innovation' can be identified within industrial clusters, dating back to the eighteenth and nineteenth centuries. The unusual twentieth-century success of Silicon Valley, as a dynamic hi-tech industrial cluster, has encouraged governments across the developed world to launch initiatives designed to build and strengthen links between research universities and industry. By no means have all these 'top downwards' initiatives been successful, not least because industrial clusters need to be embedded rather than imposed (Mowery and Sampat 2005, 207, 225–226). Since 2000 a trend towards 'communities of networks', based around open-innovation processes and lead users, has been gathering pace, initially in the United States but also in Europe. Mass collaboration across borders, facilitated by proactive Internet use, is therefore gathering pace. Large companies increasingly rely on massive international networks of users, scientists and inventors, linked through collaborative software platforms. By so doing they are able to diversify their innovation portfolio and meet those needs lying outside their core competences (Tapscot and Williams 2006).

Established in 2001, InnoCentive describes itself as the world's first innovation marketplace. The InnoCentive Web site (http://www.innocentive.com/) brings together corporations, government agencies and non-profit organizations with scientists, universities and lead users, offering cash rewards of up to $1 million for those that meet their specification. For its part InnoCentive raises revenue by offering the IPR support when the solver transfers the copyright to solution-seeking companies. In autumn 2007, 110,000 'solver' scientists had signed up from 175 countries engaging with many companies, including Boeing, Dow, DuPont Novartis and Procter and Gamble (Tapscot and Williams 2006, 98). Open innovation of this kind allows the companies to tap diversity at lower risk and lower cost than under closed-innovation models or the outsourcing of R&D (Bingham 2008). InnoCentive is one of several Internet-based 'communities of communities' to emerge. Most are U.S.-based initiatives, but TechEx is a European initiative, and Innovation Xchange Australian, and all have a global reach. By engaging in this way, these companies are synergizing their intellectual property resources by licensing outwards and at same time pulling solutions inwards, instead of automatically briefing their own R&D team.

eBay-style innovation markets are not the only way companies build diversity beyond the scope of their R&D laboratories. By engaging with and learning from consumers, especially from lead-user consumers, a number of companies are demonstrating a more open approach to innovation. European corporations, including BMW, Audi, Nokia, the BBC, Peugeot, Philips and Lego, are all building open-innovation networks into their culture through engaging with their lead users (Trend watching 2005). For example, within the BMW Customer Innovation Labs,

> participants are handed online tools helping them develop ideas and showing how the firm could take advantage of advances in telematics, online services and driver assistance. (http://www.hyve-special.de/bmw/index1.php)

Similarly Philips, the Dutch electronics company, set up http://www.LeadUsers.nl in 2005. They are also engaging with *Second Life*—the virtual world set up by Linden Labs but entirely designed by its users. Many companies use *Second Life* as a market place, but by engaging with its users, Philips aims to understand why people want to inhabit a virtual world and introduce these insights into the design process (http://www.philips.co.uk/mt_theme_2007_06_secondlife.page?). As Tapscot and Williams have written,

> This [type of activity] . . . has reached a tipping points where new forms of mass collaboration are changing how goods and services are invented, produced and distributed on a global basis. (2006, 10)

Active Web-based participation is contributing, then, to a paradigm shift in the process of innovation and the role of collaboration within it.

CONCLUSIONS

This chapter has demonstrated that innovation is both uncertain and complex and is based as much on human relationships as on technology. The knowledge-based evolutionary processes underpinning innovation mean that it is shaped by history, though it need not be constrained by it. It has demonstrated the interplay between types of innovation, demonstrating the way that competence enhancing creates continuity. The analysis of the sources and impact of major macro-discontinuities highlights the difficulties faced, especially by established players when the familiar landscape shifts. Mediated deviation can allow new pathways to be created and requires an understanding of the people affected—whether employees or customers. Engaged in a dynamic dance of two questions, the innovative entrepreneur relies on networks to move the boundaries of what is possible and to build better understanding of what is needed. As Schumpeter identified in his later work, much of the focus of innovative activity shifted to the R&D laboratories of large corporations from the late nineteenth century. Yet over the next one hundred years there is considerable evidence of networked-based innovation within the supply chain. More recently there has been the beginning of a change in both business and consumer behaviour which is contributing to open-innovation processes. This combined shift in technology and economic and social processes is not without its hazards, not least the aligning of attitudes and arrangements for IPR with expectations. Yet taken together there is the potential for a paradigm shift in the relationship between entrepreneurship, innovation and networks through this new collaboration.

REFERENCES

Abernathy, W., and K. B. Clark. 1985. Innovation: Mapping the winds of creative destruction. *Research Policy* 14 (1): 3–22.

Atack, J., and P. Passell. 1992. *A new economic view of American history: From colonial times to 1940*. New York: Norton.

Bessant, J., J. Birkinshaw and R. Delbridge. 2004. Innovation as unusual. *Business Strategy Review* 15:32–35.

Bingham, A. 2008. Risk sharing. 13 January 2008 InnoBlogger (Alph Bingham is one of the founders of InnoCentive, the open innovation community established in 2001 for companies to find innovation solutions and inventors to find companies).

Bowen, D. E., and W. E. Youngdahl. 1998. Lean service: In defense of a production-line approach. *International Journal of Service Industry Management* 9 (3): 207–225.

Brown, J. S., and P. Duguid. 1991. Organizational learning and communities of practice: Toward a unified view of working, learning and innovation. *Organizational Science* 2 (1): 40–57.

———. 2000. *The social life of information*. Boston: Harvard Business School Press.

———. 2001. Knowledge and organization: A social practice. *Organizational Science* 12 (2): 198–213.

Broadberry, S. N. 1997. *The productivity race: British manufacturing in international perspective, 1850–1990*. Cambridge: Cambridge University Press.

Casson, M. 1982. *The entrepreneur: An economic theory*. Cheltenham: Edward Elgar.

Chesbrough, H., and A. K. Crowther. 2006. Beyond high tech: Early adopters of open innovation in other industries. *R and D Management* 36 (3): 229–236.

Christensen, C. M. 1997. *The innovator's dilemma: When new technologies cause new firms to fail*. Boston: Harvard Business School Press.

Cochran, T. C. 1981. *Frontiers of change: Early industrialism in America.* New York: Oxford University Press.

Cohen, W. M., and D. A. Levinthal. 1990. Absorptive capacity: A new perspective on learning and innovation. *Administrative Science Quarterly* 35: 128–152.

Damanpour, F., and S. Gopalakrishan. 2001. The dynamics of the adoption of product and process innovations in organizations. *Journal of Management Studies* 38 (1): 45–65.

David, P. 1997. Path dependence: Putting the past into the future of economics. In *Evolutionary economics and path dependence* ed. L. Magnusson and J. Ottosson Cheltenham, UK: Edward Elgar, 115–135.

Davis, L. E., and D. C. North. 1971. *Institutional change and American economic growth.* Cambridge: Cambridge University Press.

De Propsis, L. 2002. Types of innovation and inter firm co-operation. *Entrepreneurship and Regional Development* 14 (4): 337–353.

Drucker, P. F. 1985. *Innovation and entrepreneurship: Practices and principles.* London: Elsevier.

Edquist, C. 2005. Systems of innovation: Perspectives and challenges. In *The Oxford handbook of innovation*, ed. J. Fagerberg, D. C. Mowery and R. R. Nelson, 181–208. Oxford: Oxford University Press.

Fagerberg, J. 2005. Introduction: A guide to the literature. In *The Oxford handbook of innovation*, ed. J. Fagerberg, D. C. Mowery and R. R. Nelson, 1–27. Oxford: Oxford University Press.

Fleck, J. 1999. Learning by trying: The implementation of configurational technology. In *The social shaping of technology*, ed. D. Mackenzie and J. Wajcman, 244–256. 2nd ed. Maidenhead, U.K.: Open University Press.

Freel, M. 2000. External linkages and product innovation in small manufacturing firms. *Entrepreneurship and Regional Development* 12:245–266.

Garud, R., and P. Karnøe. 2001. Path creation and the process of mindful deviation. In *Path dependence and creation*, ed. R. Garud and P. Karnøe, 1–40. London: Laurence Erlbaum Associates.

Hargadon, A. 2003. *How breakthroughs happen: The surprising truth about how companies innovate.* Boston: Harvard Business School Press.

Kenney, M., and R. Florida. 1993. *Beyond mass production: The Japanese system and its transfer to the United States* New York: Oxford University Press.

Koehn, N. 2001. *Brand new: How entrepreneurs earned consumers' trust from Wedgwood to Dell.* Boston: Harvard Business School Press.

Lave, J., and E. Wenger. 1991. *Situated learning: Legitimate peripheral participation.* Cambridge: Cambridge University Press.

Lazonick, W. 2003. Understanding innovative enterprise: Towards the integration of economic theory and business history. In *Business history around the world*, ed. F. Amatori and G. Jones, 31–61. Cambridge: Cambridge University Press.

Lüthje, C., and C. Herstatt. 2004. The lead user method: An outline of empirical findings and issues for future research. *R&D Management* 34 (5): 553–568.

Macleod, C. 1992. Strategies for innovation: The diffusion of new technology in nineteenth-century British industry. *Economic History Review*, n.s., 45 (2): 285–307.

Magnusson, L., and J. Ottosson, eds. 1997. *Evolutionary economics and path dependence.* Cheltenham, U.K.: Edward Elgar.

Malerba, F. 2006. Innovation and the evolution of industries. *Journal of Evolutionary Economics* 16:3–26.

Mowery, D. C., and B. N. Sampat. 2005. Universities in national innovation systems. In *The Oxford handbook of innovation*, ed. J. Fagerberg and D. C. Mowery, 209–239. Oxford: Oxford University Press.

O'Reilly, T. 2005. What is Web 2.0: Design patterns and business models for the next generation of software. 30 September. http://www.oreillynet.com/pub/a/oreilly/tim/news/2005/09/30/what-is-web-20.html

Parsons, M., and M. B. Rose. 2005. The neglected legacy of Lancashire Cotton: Industrial clusters and the UK outdoor trade, 1960–1990. *Enterprise and Society* 6 (4): 682–709.

Pavitt, K. 2005. Innovation processes. In *The Oxford handbook of innovation*, ed. J. Fagerberg and D. C. Mowery, 86–114. Oxford: Oxford University Press.

Philips, W., R. Lamming, H. Noke and J. Bessant. 2006. Beyond the steady state: Managing discontinuous product and process innovation. *International Journal of Innovation Management* 10 (2): 175–196.

Rose, M. B., T. Love and M. Parsons. 2007. Path dependent foundation of global design-driven outdoor trade in NW of England. *International Journal of Design* 1 (3): 57–68.

Rothwell, R., and P. Gardiner. 1985. Invention, innovation re-innovation and the role of the user. *Technovation* 3 (3): 167–186.

Schmookler, J. 1962. Changes in industry and in the state of knowledge as determinants in industrial invention. In *The rate and direction of inventive activity*, ed. R. R. Nelson, 195–232. Princeton, NJ: Princeton University Press.

Schumpeter, J. A. 1934. *Theory of economic development*. Cambridge, MA: Harvard University Press.

———. 1965. Economic theory and entrepreneurial history. In *Explorations in enterprise*, ed. Hugh G. J Aitken, 45–64. Cambridge, MA: Harvard University Press.

Shane, S. 2003. *A general theory of entrepreneurship*. Cheltenham, U.K.: Edward Elgar.

Shaw, B. 1994. User/supplier links and innovation. In *The handbook of industrial innovation*, ed. M. Dodgson and R. Rothwell, 260–278. Cheltenham, U.K.: Edward Elgar.

Smil, V. 2005. *Creating the twentieth century: Technical innovations and their consequences*. Oxford: Oxford University Press.

Stefik, M., and B. Stefik. 2004. *Breakthrough stories and strategies of radical innovation*. Cambridge, MA: MIT Press.

Tapscott, D., and A. D. Williams. 2006. *Wikinomics: How mass collaboration changes everything*. London: Atlantic Books.

Tidd, J., J. Bessant and K. Pavitt. 2005. *Managing innovation: Integrating technological, market and organizational change*. New York: Wiley.

Trend watching. 2005. http://www.trendwatching.com/trends/CUSTOMER-MADE.htm

Tushman, M. L., and P. Anderson. 1986. Technological discontinuities and organizational environments. *Administrative Science Quarterly* 31:439–465.

Tushman, M., and D. Nadler. 1986. Organizing for innovation. *California Management Review* 28 (3): 74–92.

Utterback, J. M. 1996. *Mastering the dynamics of innovation*. Boston: Harvard Business School Press.

van Ark, B., R. Inklaas, and R. H. McGuckin. 2003. ICT and productivity in Europe and the United States: Where do the differences come from? *Casio Economic Studies* 49 (3): 295–318.

von Hippel, E. 2005. *Democratizing innovation*. Cambridge, MA: MIT Press.

———. 2006. Ideas on the edge: Interview with Eric Von Hippel. *Innovations*, Winter, 14–18.

Vise, D. A. 2005. *The Google story*. New York: Bantham.

Wilms, W. W., A. J. Hardcastle, and D. M. Zell. 1994. Cultural transformation at NUMMI. *Sloan Management Review* 36 (1): 99–113.

Wenger, E. 1998. *Communities of practice*. Cambridge: Cambridge University Press.

Zeitlin, J. 2000. Introduction: Americanization and its limits: Reworking US technology and management in post-war Europe and Japan. In *Americanization and it limits: reworking US technology and management in post-war Europe and Japan*, ed. J. Zeitlin and G. Herrigel, 3–25. Oxford: Oxford University Press.

Ziman, J. M. 2000. *Technological innovation as an evolutionary process*. Cambridge: Cambridge University Press.

URLs

http://www.trendwatching.com/newsletter/previous_26.html. Trendwatching allows tracking of customer contributions to innovation.

http://www.innocentive.com/ The open innovation community established in 2001 for companies to find innovation solutions and inventors to find companies.

video clip : http://freethinkr.wordpress.com/2007/09/05/must-watch-tv-innocentives-business-model-explored/

Philips and Second Life:

http://www.philips.co.uk/mt_theme_2007_06_secondlife.page? This shows the use Philips makes of second life.

4 Management Consultancies and Organizational Innovation in Europe

Matthias Kipping

INTRODUCTION

The purpose of this chapter is to examine the role of consultants in the dissemination of management innovations in different institutional contexts. The chapter looks in particular at how consultants competed or cooperated with other diffusion channels. It also pays attention to the ways in which they managed (or not) to connect to existing entrepreneurial networks in different countries. As the detailed empirical analysis tries to show, there were two factors which limited the role of consultants in this process: (1) the existence of large-scale trust-based networks among the entrepreneurs and industrialists in a given country, which enabled a direct exchange of new management ideas; and (2) the availability of other diffusion channels, which provided alternatives to the use of consultants. The underlying idea is that a view which examines consultant in market terms, as paid suppliers of new management ideas, has only limited validity, especially in a European context where networks and relationships play a crucial role. Nor is an overly critical approach, which sees consultants as manipulators, more convincing since it largely leaves out managers from the process.

In the literature on management innovation, consultants have long been seen as important actors in the diffusion process (for an early example, see Hagedorn 1955; more recently Alvarez 1998; Kipping and Engwall 2002; Sahlin-Andersson and Engwall 2002). On the whole, business historians have tended to see their involvement as unproblematic or even as outright positive. Thus, in his study on the adoption of the multidivisional form of organization in U.S. industrial firms, Chandler highlighted 'the very significant role' that certain management consulting firms 'had in bringing about the adoption of the new structure as well as introducing many other administrative innovations and practices' (1962, 381–382). More recently, based on the case of the medium-sized steel producer Lukens, McKenna concluded that

> consultants permitted a small, flexible manufacturer to remain competitive in a cutthroat industry over a sixty-year period by acting as the institutional conduits for new ideas. (2006, 79)

He argues that, while expensive, the consultants provided good value for money.

By contrast, a majority of the popular business press and, more importantly, a significant share of the relevant academic literature has taken a rather critical view of consultants and their impact (e.g., for the former, see Pinault 2000; Craig 2005; for the latter, see Clark and Fincham 2002). Stressing the discursive dimension of the consultants' activities, several authors have argued that their 'success' is largely based on managing clients' impressions (e.g., Clark 1995; Clark and Salaman 1998) and 'the process of definition and presentation' (Røvik 2002, 143). Others go even further, suggesting that consultants and gurus have created a kind of addiction, turning managers into 'marionettes on the strings of their fashions' by exploiting their control needs (Kieser 2002, 176; see also Ernst and Kieser 2002). These views have not remained without criticisms. In particular, it has been pointed out that these critical perspectives imply a rather simplistic view of managers as 'gullible' victims of the consultants (Sturdy 1997; Fincham 1999). But an important contribution of this literature has been to put consultants into a broader context of the 'management knowledge industry' (Micklethwaite and Wooldridge 1996) or the 'fashion-setting community' (e.g., Abrahamson 1991, 1996) which is seen to includes gurus, consultants, business schools and the popular management press.

What neither the efficiency-oriented nor the critical literature on management consultants has done so far is put the role of consultants into another context, namely, the (national) institutional context in which they are operating. This is somewhat surprising, since there is a large body of literature which has identified the role of the national context in the diffusion of innovation in general (e.g., Lundvall 1992, Whitley 2000) and of management innovation in particular (e.g., Whitley 1999; Guillén 1994, 2001; Hall and Soskice 2001). There are some exceptions—for example, Guillén (1994), who examined the adaption of major management innovations in different countries during the twentieth century and identified consultants as an important actor in this process. But he neither problematized their role in general nor tried to explain the variation in terms of their involvement in the different countries. Kipping (1996) did use the idea of national innovation systems, but looked at growth of the management-consulting industry in different countries rather than the involvement of consultants in the dissemination of new management ideas.

This chapter tries to fill some of this gap by examining the role of consultants in the dissemination of an organizational innovation in a selected range of countries. The chapter consists of four major sections. The first section gives a brief overview of the history of the consulting industry and explains why 'scientific management' was chosen for the subsequent in-depth analysis. The next three sections examine its dissemination in three different European countries, Britain, Germany and Spain, focusing on the role of consultants in this process. The chapter concludes with a discussion of the results and their broader implications for the diffusion of new management ideas in Europe.

MANAGEMENT CONSULTING: A BRIEF OVERVIEW

Since its modest beginnings towards the end of the nineteenth century, the management-consulting industry has expanded significantly and has also undergone a pattern of discontinuous change, both in the kinds of services that are delivered to clients and in the dominant service providers (for the following, see in more detail Kipping 2002). Using these two characteristics, the development of the industry can be subdivided into three successive and overlapping waves (see Table 4.1). The dominant consultancies in the first wave provided services related to the 'scientific' organization of individual work and the productive process in factories and offices. By contrast, the most successful consultancies in the second wave concentrated on advice to top management in terms of corporate strategy and structure. Finally, those in the third—and still emerging— wave focus on the use of information and communication technologies to control far-flung and extensively networked client organizations.

To analyze the influence of the country-based context on the dissemination of management innovations, it seems most appropriate to look at the first wave, scientific management. Its main ideas are very similar to and independent of the particular consultant or consulting firm selling it under its own 'brand' (for detailed comparisons of the different available systems, see, among others, Sanders 1926; Rochau [1939] 1952). Also, it spread quickly around the globe (see Merkle 1980; Guillén 1994), which makes

Table 4.1 Three Waves of Consultancy Development in the 20th Century

Consultancy Focus (Service Type)	Client Firm Type (Locus of Action)	Overall Duration Period of Dominance	Prominent Consultancies
Scientific Management	Production Unit	1900s–80s 1930s–50s	Emerson, Bedaux, Big 4 in the UK, Maynard
Strategy & Structure	Corporation (M-form)	1930s–?? 1960s–80s	Booz Allen, McKinsey, AT Kearney, ADL, BCG
Information & Communication	Network Organization	1950s–?? 1990s–??	IBM, Accenture, Capgemini, Deloitte

Source: Kipping 2002.

international comparisons about the role of consultants in this process both interesting and feasible.

Most of the literature credits Frederick W. Taylor with the invention of scientific management, or 'Taylorism' (e.g., Nelson 1980; Kanigel 1997). Generally, he is also characterized as the (grand)father of management consulting (e.g., Tisdall 1982). But neither he nor his followers actually ever established large-scale consulting firms (Nelson 1995). The two consultancies that actually played a crucial role in the introduction of scientific management in a large number of companies around the globe, respectively before and after World War II (WWII), were Bedaux and H. B. Maynard (Kipping 1999a). Both made important modifications to the organizational innovation and, more importantly, created elaborate and geographically widespread consulting firms to disseminate it.

The French immigrant Charles E. Bedaux (1886–1944) created his own consultancy in the American Midwest in 1916, after having himself worked as a manual labourer and then as a translator for an Italian efficiency engineer (Christy 1984). His system of scientific management was fairly unique in that it standardized all human efforts according to a single unit of measurement, the so-called 'B' value, defined as a fraction of a minute of activity plus a fraction of a minute of rest, always aggregating to unity (Sanders 1926; Rochau [1939] 1952). Workers were expected to achieve a minimum of 60B per hour and received a bonus for higher B values. From its modest origins, the Bedaux consultancy spread quite rapidly, first in the United States, then—from the mid-1920s onwards—also abroad (Kipping 1999a). Even after Bedaux's suicide in 1944, the consultancy continued to thrive, many of the country offices now working independently, some under a changed name.

Harold B. Maynard founded his consultancy in 1934 under the name Methods Engineering Council (MEC). Maynard had developed the so-called methods-time-measurement (MTM) system which allowed establishing optimum motions and 'normal' times under laboratory conditions, thus considerably improving accuracy compared to previous methods and provoking less resistance from the workers (see Maynard, Stegemerten and Schwab 1948). MEC installed the MTM system not only in the United States, but also at a large number of European companies. By the late 1960s, Maynard had become one of the largest service providers from the United States in Europe with about 330 consultants and offices in eight countries (Kipping 1999). Given their dominance of the industry during this wave and their geographic extension, Bedaux and H. B. Maynard therefore seemed ideal cases for international comparisons.

A first proxy for the role of consultants in the dissemination of scientific management in different European countries can be found in Table 4.2, which shows the number of plants using the Bedaux system during the 1930s.

Table 4.2 The International Expansion of the Bedaux Consultancy during the 1930s

Country	Office Opened	Plants with the Bedaux System	
		1931	*1937*
United States	1916	52	500
British Isles	1926	30	225
Germany	1927	5	25
Italy	1927	21	49
France	1929	16	144

Sources: See Kipping 1999a: 198.

Particularly striking is the difference between Britain and Germany with respect to the application of the Bedaux system. This seems surprising given that the consultancy had opened offices in both countries at about the same time and that both were highly developed economies with similar industrial structures. If anything, according to Chandler (1990) the prevalent 'personal capitalism' in the United Kingdom should have been less open to organizational innovation than its more managerial counterpart in Germany (see, with a somewhat contrasting view, Cassis 1997). Spain is another interesting case. It is absent from the table, since the Bedaux consultancy entered the country only after WWII, as did Maynard's MEC (Kipping and Puig 2003). Despite being latecomers, many Spanish companies rapidly and readily espoused scientific management during the 1950s and 1960s (Guillén 1994, 1 78–183).

Given these significant differences, this chapter therefore focuses on the role of Bedaux, Maynard and other consultancies in these three European countries, examining why they were present and influential in Britain, were present in Germany but with little apparent influence and appeared only late—but with a bang—in Spain.

BRITAIN: EARLY AND (ALMOST) EXCLUSIVE

As seen in Table 4.2, the application of the Bedaux system in the United Kingdom expanded significantly during the 1930s, outpacing even the United States—relative to the size of the two economies. The consultancy had established an office in London in 1926 following work for the British subsidiary of a major U.S. client, B. F. Goodrich (Kipping 1999a, 199). But it almost immediately started working for local firms, and by 1933 its number of annual assignments had reached 40, with a cumulative total of 170 (Kipping 1997, 72).

Not only did British Bedaux expand its own list of clients, but it also became the progenitor of a consulting industry through a number of spin-offs, which led to the formation of Urwick, Orr and Partners (UOP) and Production Engineering (P-E) in 1934 (for this and the following, see Tisdall 1982, 28–35, 55–59; Kipping 1997, 1999a; Ferguson 2002, 80–83). From 1938, British Bedaux called itself Associated Industrial Consultants (AIC), in order to remove any association with the Bedaux name. Bedaux also gave up his majority shareholding in the consultancy. He had become increasingly unpopular in Britain after hosting the wedding of the Duke of Windsor in his chateau in the Loire valley and, most importantly, organizing the Duke's controversial trip to Nazi Germany (Kipping 1997, 74). All these firms offered similar services and grew rapidly during the second half of the 1930s. It is therefore safe to assume that the number of British companies using some form of scientific management is significantly higher than indicated in Table 4.2, which focuses only on the Bedaux system.

The importance of consultants and their role in the dissemination of scientific management grew rapidly during WWII (Tisdall 1982, 35–41; Tiratsoo and Tomlinson 1993; Ferguson 2002, Ch. 5). Concerned with the need to increase output with a labour force made up of more and more unskilled workers (many of them being female), the British government, and in particular the minister of aircraft production, Sir Stafford Cripps, employed them in its own factories and encouraged their use in the private sector. Consultants were among the few employment categories exempted from military service. An indication of the soaring demand was the fact that yet another member of AIC, Ernest Butten, left in 1943 to set up his own consultancy named Personnel Administration (PA).

The consultancy boom continued unabated during the first post-war decade, again with considerable support from the British government (Kipping 1997, 75–76, Ferguson 2002, 128–136). Thus, consultants were closely associated with the efforts to increase productivity and improve living standards. Norman Pleming, managing director of AIC at the time, was seconded to the Anglo-American Council on Productivity (AACP) as 'Honorary Consultant'. Consultants also became involved in the British Institute of Management (BIM) where business and labour representatives could discuss ways to improve management methods. Sir Stafford Cripps, who had become chancellor of the exchequer in 1947, actively promoted its creation in 1947–1948 (Tiratsoo 1999). Lyndall Urwick and three other consultants were invited to become members of the BIM council.

During this period the British consultancy market grew at an unprecedented pace, both in terms of fee income and staff. By 1962, AIC, UOP, P-E and PA—or, as they were widely referred to, the 'Big Four'—together employed 1,100 consultants in the British Isles, making it the most developed consulting market in Europe (Tisdall 1982, 9, 41). In 1956 they had formed the Management Consultancies Association (MCA)—partially to fend off some form of government regulation to address the quality control problems in this growing market (Kipping and Saint-Martin 2005).

Despite this uninterrupted growth from the 1930s through the 1950s, the installation of scientific management systems did not always go smoothly, in particular at the beginning of the period. There were a number of highly publicized strikes against the installation of the Bedaux system in the early 1930s, mainly due to resistance against the associated speed up and deskilling (Littler 1982, Ch. 9). In a number of other cases, namely the automobile supplier Lucas and the electrical producer Ferranti, the Bedaux consultants had to pretend to be company employees in order to continue with the installation (Kipping and Armbrüster 2002). However, the Rover automobile company is the only known case where the attempt to install the system had to be abandoned completely (Downs 1990). In the vast majority of cases the Bedaux system was implemented without any problems (Kreis 1990); unions actually saw possible advantages in these systems, namely, an increase in wages and a better bargaining position. And neither the war effort nor the post-war productivity drive left much room for dissent anyway.

Thus, the main question is why consultancies ended up playing such an important part in the diffusion of scientific management in Britain. The answer is fairly simple: consultants thrived in Britain because there were few, if any, alternatives for the introduction of scientific management. A good illustration for the lack of such alternatives is the career of Lyndall Urwick. He was one of the most influential British and European management thinkers of the twentieth century (Witzel 2003, 299–306). From 1928 Urwick directed the International Management Institute in Geneva. What is significant is that upon its closure in 1933, he chose a consultancy to promote his ideas in Britain, co-founding UOP in 1934. This decision was probably driven by his previous experience. During the 1920s he had been heavily involved in the establishment and functioning of the so-called Management Research Groups (MRG). Following a U.S. example, the MRG were intended to provide a forum where member companies could confidentially discuss a wide range of management problems, including the application of scientific management. Several nationwide and regional groups were set up, but their overall appeal and their membership remained rather limited (Kipping 1997).

Nor did other institutions play a more important role in Britain. Thus, the different engineering bodies had grown significantly during the interwar period but served at best as a forum for the exchange of experiences and were in general rather sceptical towards scientific management. The National Institute of Industrial Psychology, created in 1921 with the support of leading industrialists, conducted a number of studies into the effect of these methods. However, in line with the interests of an influential group of British employers, such as Seebohm Rowntree, it shifted its attention more and more towards human relations and motivations (Guillén 1994, 205–253; Whitston 1996, 52–60). This contrasts with the German situation, where an institution played a dominant role in the dissemination of scientific management, all but crowding out the consultancies.

GERMANY: COOPERATION, NOT CONSULTANTS

As shown in Table 4.2, the Bedaux consultancy played a very limited role in the dissemination of scientific management in Germany. Part of the reason for this pattern can be found in the specific historical development of the country. When the Nazis came to power in 1933, they initially outlawed the Bedaux consultancy and seized its assets. In 1937, however, possibly as a reward for organizing the Duke of Windsor's trip to Germany (as previously stated), Bedaux was authorized to re-establish a consultancy together with German partners under the name Gesellschaft für Wirtschaftsberatung. At the start of WWII, he was again forced to withdraw, but the consultancy continued to operate under German control and was re-established after the war under yet a different name (Kipping 1997). In any case, during none of the periods that Bedaux actually operated in Germany was the consultancy particularly successful—and nor were other foreign or domestic consultancies until the 1970s, when McKinsey made significant inroads (Kipping 1999a).

One possible reason for the limited role consultancies played in the introduction of scientific management in Germany can clearly be excluded: the industrial structure. The country was actually among the first to develop large-scale managerial enterprises—natural users for this type of management tools—not much different from Britain (Chandler 1990; Cassis 1997). The real difference lies in the fact that between the 1920s and the 1950s German companies introduced scientific management *internally* rather than using outside consultants. These efforts were supported by an association of German manufacturing companies, the National Committee for Work Time Determination, REFA (Reichsausschuß für Arbeitszeitermittlung). Established in 1924, REFA developed its own method for the calculation of standard piecework times as a basis for the 'fair' remuneration of workers. It disseminated this method through a detailed handbook, published for the first time in 1928, and, more importantly, through the training of work-study engineers. By 1933, its courses had already attracted over ten thousand participants from the whole spectrum of German industry (for this and the following, see in more detail Kipping 1997, 2004).

REFA's activities increased during the Nazi period. After some initial hesitation due to their proclaimed hostility towards 'rationalization', the new rulers soon recognized the usefulness of these kinds of institutions for the rearmament and war efforts. The Nazis replaced some of the existing REFA leadership, changed its name to National Committee for Work Studies (Reichsausschuß für Arbeitsstudien) in 1936 and expanded its role considerably. Thus, between 1933 and 1945, REFA trained an additional thirty thousand engineers. These efforts continued unabated after the war. By the mid-1950s the number of trained engineers had more than doubled (to about one hundred thousand) and REFA itself had around thirteen thousand members. A representative survey carried out by the Munich-based ifo Institute for Economic Research (ifo stands for, in English, information and research) in March 1956 shows that among those German companies which applied work study, over 80 percent used the REFA system.

It is important to note that the predominant role of REFA cannot be explained by the 'technical' superiority of its system—a conclusion shared by several German observers. For example, Rochau ([1939] 1952), who compared the REFA and Bedaux systems in detail, evaluated the latter quite positively and saw it as especially appropriate for industries with a high content of manual rather than machine labour. The major advantages of REFA can be found in its cost, in the ease of implementation and in the standardized terminology, which in turn facilitated the exchange of experiences.

First, with respect to cost, the REFA approach—that is, sending engineers on training courses and exchanging information between member firms—was far cheaper than hiring a group of consulting engineers for periods which lasted at least six months and sometimes several years. Second, upon their return the *internal* work-study engineers usually found it easier to overcome the suspicion and a negative reaction from the workers (see some of the resistance towards the Bedaux system in Britain, as already mentioned). Third, and probably most importantly, as a result of the REFA dominance, the vast majority of work-study engineers in Germany used the same methodology and terminology, which made it much easier to compare and exchange experiences. The association actually organized frequent meetings among REFA engineers for such exchanges. Similar meetings also took place on a regular basis in large German companies. Combined with the frequent REFA publications, these meetings made it possible for improvements to spread quickly through this network. By contrast, consultancies such as Bedaux and MEC tend to treat their methods as a way to differentiate themselves, making it difficult for companies to exchange experiences.

Not surprisingly, a German REFA engineer, who had participated in a productivity mission to the United States in the spring of 1951, reached a similar conclusion:

> [In the United States] anyone who feels competent or sees a commercial opportunity, develops his theories, his methodology and, which is the worst, his own terminology . . . Because of this situation, those American engineers who are involved in our field out of interest are envious of our REFA organisation. (quoted by Kipping 1999b, 31–32)

For all these reasons the vast majority of German companies preferred to rely on REFA for the introduction of scientific management, leaving little room for consultancies to develop. REFA's dominance was such that it actually decided which new management ideas, developed outside Germany, were to be transferred and which were not. This becomes apparent from the fate of the MTM system—and, as a consequence, the Maynard consultancy. After WWII, REFA examined a number of systems that determined standard work times under laboratory conditions rather than on the shop floor, including MTM and the so-called Work Factor system. Their relative advantages and disadvantages were debated at length in the association's newsletter. REFA finally decided in favour of the Work Factor system and acquired the licence for its distribution in Germany. However, it apparently never became very popular, and REFA probably did little to promote it against its own system, which was constantly being updated and improved. As a result, these new techniques never made major inroads into German industry, unlike other countries, where H. B. Maynard and his MEC had a considerable success.

The question then remains why British companies insisted on using consultancies and failed to rely more on cooperative associations such as the MRG despite the obvious advantages of the latter. Before returning to this question, the chapter examines the role consultancies played in the Spanish case.

SPAIN: LATE, BUT INTENSE

In Spain, some limited diffusion of scientific management had already taken place during the 1920s and 1930s (Guillén 1994, 158–164). Taylor's book was translated quickly, and Spanish representatives participated regularly in the congresses of the international scientific-management movement. The Spanish national engineering association promoted the diffusion of scientific management, and a few engineers apparently worked as consultants for certain companies. After World War I, public engineering schools introduced courses on industrial engineering, which laid the ground for future developments. Many of the industrial engineers trained in these schools worked in the country's medium-sized manufacturing companies, which created organization departments in the 1940s. Thus, scientific-management ideas spread—albeit slowly—and opened up these companies for the consultancies when they eventually arrived in the 1950s (for this and the following, see in more detail Kipping and Puig 2003).

To a certain extent, this delay in the development of the consultancy market and, more importantly, in the introduction of scientific management was due to factors unrelated to the business system. In the 1930s, when many companies in other parts of Europe readily espoused the new methods to cut costs in the wake of the Great Depression, Spain was engulfed in a bloody civil war. Since it remained neutral during WWII, the country did not participate in the related drive for increased efficiency. So it was only in the 1950s, when Spain reversed its previous autarky policy, opened up to foreign—namely, U.S.—influences and gradually developed a consumer society, that Spanish companies saw a need for greater productivity to respond to a growing demand (very similar to what happened in other developed countries) and that foreign suppliers of these organizational innovations became readily available.

Nevertheless, probably the most important reason for the delay can be found in the fact that Spain lagged in terms of industrial development and in particular with respect to the existence of large-scale manufacturing enterprises (Carreras and Tafunell 1997). Here, the specific historical path taken by Spain made a bad situation for the consultancies even worse. Thus, the victorious fascist movement under General Franco decided to recombine many of the natural resources and manufacturing activities in a state-owned holding, the Instituto Nacional de Industria (INI). Due to the nature of their activities and their size, the INI industries were 'natural' clients of the consultancies who did not fail to offer their services. These were rejected, however, in particular by those sectors where military engineers wielded a significant influence. Only from the 1960s did these public-sector companies gradually start to be concerned about the introduction of systematic accounting and management methods—first under political pressure, then under growing competitive and client pressure—finally creating a ready market for the scientific-management consultancies.

All of these structural and serendipitous factors combined meant that the Spanish consulting market only took off from the 1950s onwards, as can be seen in table 4.3.

Table 4.3 The First Consultancies in Spain

Consultancy	Founded	Main foreign partners	Main Spanish partners
Ingeco-Gombert	1952	Georges Gombert (Belgian; former Bedaux engineer)	Ramón Rey Gabriel Barceló Francisco J. de Calonge
Técnicos Especialistas Asociados (TEA)	1952	Cegos (from the 1960s) French consultancy	Javier Benjumea Roberto Cuñat
Bedaux Ibérica	1953	Fern Bedaux Marcel André Grolleau (Bedaux France)	Jaime Díez de Rivera José María Rovira Francisco Donato
Central de Racionalización, Estudios y Aplicaciones (CREA)	1953	Adalbert Laffon de Gorse (French consultant)	José María de Zavala Dimas Menéndez José Ignacio de Isusi Juan Ségala Jeanjean
MEC (Methods Engineering Council) de España	1953	Harold B. Maynard John W. Hannon Donald E. Farr	Carlos Paz Shaw

Sources: See Kipping and Puig 2003.

What Table 4.3 also shows is a French, or rather francophone, dominance. For example, the Spanish Bedaux consultancy was directed from France, by his brother Gaston and his widow Fern. As in most other European countries, Bedaux turned out to be the most popular choice for the introduction of scientific management in Spanish companies. In 1960 the consultancy employed close to one hundred consultants and had offices in Barcelona, Bilbao and Madrid, where it also operated its own training centre. Bedaux's success continued during the 1960s and 1970s, but subsequently it started to decline and was eventually bought by the German consultancy Roland Berger in 1985. The French connection was relevant not only for the service providers, but also for the new management ideas. Thus, in Spain the work of the French engineer Henri Fayol on *General and Industrial Management*, first published in 1916, rivalled Taylor's influence.

However, the United States gradually started playing an ever more important role from the 1950s onwards. While Spain remained excluded from the Marshall Plan, it participated in the so-called Technical Assistance and Productivity programme (Maier 1977; McGlade 1995), which aimed at disseminating a U.S.-style efficiency and human-relations mentality. Rather than promoting a cooperative thinking and a sense of (collective) duty, it tried to motivate people individually—something clearly apparent in the payment-by-results system of scientific management. Like the British and the Germans, the Spanish also organized trips to the United States, where managers, engineers and workers could gain a first-hand impression of the U.S. model and its superiority.

One of the first Spanish engineers to visit the United States in 1946–1947, with a scholarship from the National Institute of Work Rationalization (Instituto Nacional de Racionalización del Trabajo), was Fermín de la Sierra. Among the firms and institutions he visited was H. B. Maynard's MEC in Pittsburgh. Subsequently, Fermín de la Sierra came to play an important role in the diffusion of scientific management in his home country. He became the secretary general of the Spanish Productivity Centre, CNPI (Centro Nacional de Productividad Industrial), and as such helped the consultancy establish an office in Spain in 1953. He was also instrumental in the creation of the first public school of industrial engineering in Spain, the Escuela de Organización Industrial (EOI) in Madrid in 1955 (Puig and Fernández Pérez 2001). Together with the engineers from the CNPI, EOI became an important launch pad for Maynard and the MTM system in Spain.

What also set the Spanish case apart was the fact that both the French and the U.S. consultants were faced with a strong local tradition of management, in the form of the catholic social doctrine—which forced them to make adjustments to their ideas in order to succeed in this context. It should be noted here that the Spanish were not only passive partners in this diffusion process, forcing some form of adaptation. They also played an active role in inviting various foreign recipients, probably in an effort to modernize Spanish management. They were particularly active in the creation of a significant number of industrial engineering and business schools. EOI has already been mentioned. Unlike this state-sponsored school, most of the others were inspired by the catholic social doctrine and sponsored by different catholic groups.

With hindsight, two of the most important ones were founded in Barcelona towards the end of the 1950s: the Instituto de Estudios Superiores de Empresa (IESE) in 1958 and the Escuela Superior de Administración y Dirección de Empresas (ESADE) in 1959 (for this and the following, see in more detail Puig and Fernández Pérez 2001 and 2003). The latter was instigated by the Jesuits, while the former was set up by the conservative catholic organization Opus Dei, acting through its own Universidad de Navarra. Consultants and engineers from Catalonia and the Basque Country also supported the foundation of IESE. Initially the school drew on resources from French business schools, but the U.S. influence once again quickly became more important. First, the representative of Opus Dei in the United States sent programme outlines and teaching material from the Harvard Business School (HBS) and Carnegie Mellon in Pittsburgh. Then, IESE received more direct assistance from HBS in terms of cases, guest professors and teacher training.

These schools probably played at least as important a role as the consultants in the diffusion of scientific management and subsequent organizational innovations in Spain. They did so not necessarily in competition with these consultancies, but in close collaboration. Several consultants had been involved in their establishment, taught scientific-management ideas and methods at these schools and recruited both future collaborators and clients there. At the same time, as in Britain, there was an absence of associations and cooperative ventures—which is equally striking—with a few exceptions confirming the rule such as the Asociación para el Progreso de la Dirección (APD), founded by Gabriel Barceló and Roberto Cuñat, who had previously been associated with competing consultancies, Gombert and TEA, respectively.

Overall, therefore, the Spanish 'backwardness' should not be overestimated, at least in terms of the availability of organizational (rather than technical) innovations. As noted previously, Spain was one of the first European countries to successfully develop U.S.-style business schools (see also Kipping, Üsdiken and Puig 2004), and from the 1950s onwards its consultancy market was on a par with many other developed European countries.

DISCUSSION AND CONCLUSION

When comparing the diffusion of scientific management and the role of consultants in this process, Britain, Germany and Spain show three very different patterns. Thus, in Britain consultants clearly played the most important role in the introduction of this organizational innovation from the 1920s through the 1950s, often with the support of the British government. While the pioneering firm came from the United States, its arrival sparked the development of a highly successful domestic consulting industry. During the same time period, German companies relied almost exclusively on the REFA association for the development of the actual scientific-management methods and the training of their internal work-study engineers. They also exchanged experiences both at the firm and the national level, the latter again mainly through REFA. In Spain, the diffusion of scientific management took off much later, in the 1950s, and saw a combination of consulting firms and newly founded business schools involved in the process—usually cooperating rather than competing with each other. The other difference, in addition to the timing, was the content of the ideas, with the catholic social doctrine exercising a strong influence.

The explication for these patterns can be found in both serendipitous and structural factors. In Britain, the systemic context favoured consultants since the available institutions and associations (1) showed little interest in scientific management—focusing instead on human-relations approaches in general—and (2) in any case, did not command a widespread appeal among companies (Guillén 1994). Consultants were able to fill this void first with the help of U.S. multinationals, which acted as a bridge for the Bedaux consultancy, then with support from the U.K. government, which tried to promote rapid productivity improvements, especially during and after WWII. In Germany, by contrast, an association formed by companies in the 1920s clearly dominated the dissemination of scientific management in the subsequent decades. Between 1933 and 1945, the Nazi government strongly supported these efforts in the interests of war preparations and war. It also complicated the operations of the Bedaux consultancy, which dominated most other European countries. But even before and after the Nazi period, Bedaux and other consultancies generated little interest among German employers.

Serendipitous factors played an even more important role in Spain. The civil war and the early, autarkist period of Franco's fascist dictatorship significantly delayed the introduction of scientific management. From the 1950s onwards, however, the country caught up with the more developed European economies, with consultancies and business schools equally important in the process. Both were heavily influenced initially from France and then increasingly from the United States, reflecting the geo-political importance of Spain. Two systemic factors influenced these developments: (1) the absence of large-scale enterprises outside the realm of the state, especially since companies in the INI holding were initially rather hostile towards consultants; and (2) the role of the Catholic Church, which meant that scientific management became imbued with ideas from the Catholic social doctrine. It also led to the establishment of different business schools by the competing denominational groups, namely, Opus Dei and the Jesuits, in addition to the public ones. These religious divisions, together with fairly strong regional rivalries, probably prohibited the formation of strong national associations like in Germany.

In terms of the success of these different patterns, reflected in the percentage of companies actually implementing some method of scientific management, the available evidence suggests that the associative channel was clearly superior. Thus, the previously mentioned representative ifo survey from March 1956 showed that an overwhelming majority of German companies (71 percent) considered work study as indispensable and that 78 percent had their own internal work-study department. By contrast, the available statistics from British industry reveal that at the beginning of the 1950s less than 30 percent of all workers were paid using some system of work study. It appears that most of them were actually working under straight-piece rates rather than a sophisticated payment-by-results system such as Bedaux or REFA. (Kipping 1999b)

This is not surprising. As mentioned previously, by the mid-1950s REFA counted thirteen thousand members and had trained about one hundred thousand internal work-study engineers. By comparison, at the same time the number of consultants in Britain came hardly close to one thousand, not all of which were actually involved in the implementation of work study. While these consultants acted as a kind of multiplier, they could never achieve the same penetration in British industry as the REFA engineers did in Germany. Similar statistics are not available for Spain, but one can probably assume that the number of companies employing some form of scientific management grew significantly from the 1950s onwards—driven by consultancies as well as industrial engineering and business schools.

If the advantages of institutions for the dissemination of management knowledge were so important and rather obvious, why then, we have to ask, did other countries not espouse them to the same extent? The answer to this question probably revolves around the importance of trust-based relationships within a given economy. Chandler (1990) has characterized German capitalism as cooperative. While he referred mainly to the cooperation of German companies in the form of cartels (compared to the—alleged—predominance of competitive markets in the United States), this also applies to the exchange of information and the dissemination of organizational innovations. Along similar lines, a comparative study has highlighted the importance of long-term trust relations between buyers and suppliers in Germany—compared to short-term power-based relations in the British case (Lane and Bachmann 1996). The trust-based relations formed the basis for a sharing of information which proved to be of mutual benefit. In this respect Spain might occupy some middle ground, with religion acting as a potential basis and as an obstacle for cooperation due to the struggle for influence among different Catholic groups.

In terms of broader implications, therefore, the comparison presented in this chapter has confirmed the importance of national business and innovation systems. The institutional environment played a significant role when it came to the diffusion of innovation in all three countries studied. Thus, for the diffusion of scientific management the associative route taken in Germany proved more effective than the reliance on consultants in the British and, to a lesser extent, Spanish cases. Without the trust-based networks within and among firms, this would not have been possible. At the same time, the lack of such trust in Britain and the rivalries between regions and religious groups in Spain prevented the formation of similar networks in these countries—at least not to the same extent. Put differently, strong intra- and inter-firm networks provided external consultants with few access points. Their absence, by contrast, made it much easier for them not only to gain access, but also to actually become nodal points in these networks—as can be seen from the role they played in the post-WWII productivity efforts in Britain and, to a lesser extent, Spain. Strong government support for consultancy activities was another facilitating factor in the former case, whereas government hostility or reluctance held consultants back in Germany and—at least temporarily—in Spain.

What the analysis also shows is that another context factor, the predominance of 'big business', had a less than expected influence. In much of the existing business history literature (e.g., Chandler, Amatori and Hikino 1997), large-scale managerial enterprises are seen as a crucial driver for the introduction of 'modern' management methods and organizational forms, since they tend to pioneer innovative practices and/or become primary clients for the consultancies. Our three country cases provide little evidence for this. Thus, despite similarly broad levels of development and numbers of large-scale firms, Britain and Germany exhibited vastly different patterns in the diffusion of scientific management. And in the Spanish case medium-sized firms seemed equally if not more keen to introduce management innovations than their large-scale counterparts (see also the contributions by Fernández Pérez and Puig in this volume).

What should also be noted is the influence of historical contingencies or serendipity as an explanatory variable in addition to possible systemic context factors. Again, Spain and, to a lesser extent, Germany provide examples for how specific circumstances influenced the adoption of organizational innovations and might have also contributed to shaping the systemic context.

Finally, regarding the broader debate about the role of consultants, the three country cases presented here support neither the market-based view, which sees consultants as an expensive but efficient way for companies to access new management ideas, nor the critical perspective, which explains consulting 'success' as the result of their ability to manipulate managers at will. The German and, to a lesser extent, Spanish cases clearly showed that strong associations and business schools provided equally if not more effective and, at the same time, less expensive ways of disseminating scientific management.

In all cases, managers and their preferences had significant influences on the overall scale of the consultancy involvement in the diffusion process and on the content of the ideas themselves, which is most apparent in the Spanish case with the influence of the Catholic social doctrine. If consultants had any influence on their own 'success', it was through their ability to access and become central actors in the existing networks of entrepreneurs, managers and—important to note—governments (see also Kipping 1999a; Kipping and Saint-Martin 2005). As noted previously, this ability was in turn constrained by the nature of these networks in the different countries. Given that all three countries were located in Europe, only future research can tell whether this importance of networks and networking skills was a typically European phenomenon.

REFERENCES

Abrahamson, E. 1991. Managerial fads and fashion: The diffusion and rejection of innovations. *Academy of Management Review* 16 (3): 586–612.

———. 1996. Management Fashion. *Academy of Management Review* 21 (1): 254–285.

Alvarez, J. L., ed. 1998. *The diffusion and consumption of business knowledge.* London: Macmillan.

Carreras, A., and X. Tafunell. 1997. Spain: Big manufacturing firms between state and market, 1917–1990. In *Big business and the wealth of nations*, ed. A. D. Chandler, Jr., F. Amatori and F. Hikino, 277–304. New York: Cambridge University Press.

Cassis, Y. 1997. *Big business: The European experience in the twentieth century.* Oxford: Oxford University Press.

Chandler, A. D., Jr. 1962. *Strategy and structure: Chapters in the history of the industrial enterprise.* Cambridge, MA: MIT Press.

———. 1990. *Scale and scope: The dynamics of industrial capitalism.* Cambridge, MA: Belknap Press.

Chandler, A. D. Jr., F. Amatori and F. Hikino, eds. 1997. *Big business and the wealth of nations.* New York: Cambridge University Press.

Christy, J. 1984. *The price of power: A biography of Charles Eugène Bedaux.* Toronto: Doubleday.

Clark, T. 1995. *Managing consultants: Consultancy as the management of impressions.* Buckingham, U.K.: Open University Press.

Clark, T., and R. Fincham, eds. 2002. *Critical consulting: New perspectives on the management advice industry.* Oxford: Blackwell.

Clark, T., and G. Salaman. 1998. Creating the 'right' impression: Towards a dramaturgy of management consulting. *The Service Industries Journal* 18 (1): 18–38.

Craig, D. 2005. *Rip-off!: The scandalous inside story of the management consulting money machine.* London: Original Book Company.

Downs, L. L. 1990. Industrial decline, rationalisation and equal pay: The Bedaux strike at Rover Automobile Company. *Social History* 15 (1): 45–73.

Ernst, B., and A. Kieser. 2002. In search of explanations for the consulting explosion. In *The Expansion of Management Knowledge: Carriers, Flows, and*

Sources, ed. K. Sahlin-Andersson and L. Engwall, 47–73. Stanford, CA: Stanford University Press.

Ferguson, M. 2002. *The rise of management consulting in Britain.* Aldershot, U.K.: Ashgate.

Fincham, R. 1999. The consultant-client relationship: Critical perspectives on the management of organizational change. *Journal of Management Studies* 36 (3): 331–351.

Guillén, M. F. 1994. *Models of management: Work, authority, and organization in a comparative perspective.* Chicago: University of Chicago Press.

———. 2001. *The limits of convergence: Globalization and organizational change in Argentina, South Korea, and Spain.* Princeton, NJ: Princeton University Press.

Hagedorn, H. J. 1955. The management consultant as transmitter of business techniques. *Explorations in Entrepreneurial History*, 1st ser., 7 (February): 164–173.

Hall, P. A., and D. Soskice. 2001. *Varieties of capitalism: The institutional foundations of comparative advantage.* Oxford: Oxford University Press.

Kanigel, R. 1997. *The one best way: Frederick Winslow Taylor and the enigma of efficiency.* New York: Viking.

Kieser, A. 2002. Managers as marionettes? Using fashion theories to explain the success of consultancies. In *Management consulting: Emergence and dynamics of a knowledge industry*, ed. M. Kipping and L. Engwall, 167–183. Oxford: Oxford University Press.

Kipping, M. 1996. The U.S. influence on the evolution of management consultancies in Britain, France, and Germany since 1945. *Business and Economic History* 25 (1): 112–123.

———. 1997. Consultancies, institutions and the diffusion of Taylorism in Britain, Germany and France, 1920s to 1950s. *Business History* 39 (4): 67–83.

———. 1999a. American management consulting companies in Western Europe, 1920 to 1990: Products, reputation and relationships. *Business History Review* 73 (2): 190–220.

———. 1999b. British economic decline: Blame it on the consultants? *Contemporary British History* 12 (3): 23–38.

———. 2002. Trapped in their wave: the evolution of management consultancies. In *Critical consulting: New perspectives on the management advice industry*, ed. T. Clark and R. Fincham, 28–49. Oxford: Blackwell.

———. 2004. 'Importing' American ideas to West Germany, 1940s to 1970s: From associations to private consultancies. In *German and Japanese business in the boom years: Transforming American management and technology models*, ed. A. Kudo, M. Kipping and H. Schröter, 30–53. London: Routledge.

Kipping, M., and T. Armbrüster. 2002. The burden of otherness: Limits of consultancy interventions in historical case studies. In *Management consulting: Emergence and dynamics of a knowledge industry*, ed. M. Kipping and L. Engwall, 203–221.

Kipping, M., and L. Engwall, eds. 2002. *Management consulting: Emergence and dynamics of a knowledge industry.* Oxford: Oxford University Press.

Kipping, M., and N. Puig. 2003. Entre influencias internacionales y tradiciones nacionales: Las consultoras de empresa en la España del siglo XX. *Cuadernos de Economía y Dirección de la Empresa* 17 (October-December): 105–137.

Kipping, M., and D. Saint-Martin. 2005. Between regulation, promotion and consumption: Government and management consultancy in Britain. *Business History*, 47 (3): 449–465.

Kipping, M., B. Üsdiken and N. Puig. 2004. Imitation, tension, and hybridization: Multiple 'Americanizations' of management education in Mediterranean Europe. *Journal of Management Inquiry* 13 (2): 98–108.

Kreis, S. 1990. The diffusion of an idea: A history of scientific management in Britain, 1890–1945. Ph.D. diss., University of Missouri-Columbia.

Lane, C., and R. Bachmann. 1996. The social constitution of supplier relations in Britain and Germany. *Organization Studies* 17 (3): 365–395.

Littler, C. R. 1982. *The development of the labour process in capitalist societies: A comparative study of the transformation of work organization in Britain, Japan and the USA*. London: Heinemann.

Lundvall, B.-Å., ed. 1992. *National systems of innovation: Towards a theory of innovation and interactive learning*. London: Pinter.

Maier, C. S. 1977. The politics of productivity: Foundations of American international economic policy after World War II. *International Organization* 31: 607–633.

Maynard, H. B., G. J. Stegemerten and J. L. Schwab. 1948. *Methods-time measurement*. New York: McGraw Hill.

McGlade, J. 1995. The illusion of consensus: American business, Cold War aid and the reconstruction of Western Europe 1948–1958. Ph.D. diss., George Washington University.

McKenna, C. D. 2006. *The world's newest profession: Management consulting in the twentieth century*. New York: Cambridge University Press.

Merkle, J. A. 1980. *Management and ideology: The legacy of the international scientific management movement*. Berkeley, CA: University of California Press.

Micklethwait, J., and A. Wooldridge. 1996. *The witch doctors: What the management gurus are saying, why it matters and how to make sense of it*. London: Heinemann.

Nelson, D. 1980. *Frederick W. Taylor and the rise of scientific management*. Madison, WI: University of Wisconsin Press.

———. 1995. Industrial engineering and the industrial enterprise, 1890–1940. In *Coordination and information: Historical perspectives on the organization of enterprise*, ed. N. R. Lamoreaux and D. M. G. Raff, 35–50. Chicago: University of Chicago Press.

Pinault, L. 2000. *Consulting demons: Inside the unscrupulous world of global corporate consulting*. New York: Harper Business.

Puig, N., and P. Fernández Pérez. 2001. Las escuelas de negocios y la formación de empresarios y directivos en España: Madrid y Barcelona, 1950–1975. Paper presented at the VIIth Congress of the Spanish Economic History Association (AEHE), Zaragoza, 19–21 September.

———. 2003. The education of Spanish entrepreneurs and managers: Madrid and Barcelona business schools, 1950–1975. *Paedagogica Historica* 39 (5): 651–672.

Rochau, E. [1939] 1952. *Das Bedaux-System: Praktische Anwendung und kritischer Vergleich mit dem Refa-System*. 3rd ed. Würzburg: Triltsch.

Røvik, K. A. 2002. The secrets of the winners: Management ideas that flow. In *The Expansion of Management Knowledge: Carriers, Flows, and Sources*, ed. K. Sahlin-Andersson and L. Engwall, 113–144. Stanford, CA: Stanford University Press.

Sahlin-Andersson, K., and L. Engwall, eds. 2002. *The expansion of management knowledge: Carriers, flows, and sources*. Stanford, CA: Stanford University Press.

Sanders, T. H. 1926. Wage systems—an appraisal. *Harvard Business Review* 5 (1): 11–20.

Sturdy, A. 1997. The consultancy process—an insecure business. *Journal of Management Studies* 34 (3): 389–413.

Tisdall, P. 1982. *Agents of change: The development and practice of management consultancy*. London: Heinemann.

Tiratsoo, N. 1999. High hopes frustrated: The British institute of management as an agent of change, 1947–63. In *Deindustrialization and reindustrialization in 20th century Europe*, ed. F. Amatori, A. Colli and N. Crepax, 143–154. Milan: FrancoAngeli.

Tiratsoo, N., and J. Tomlinson. 1993. *Industrial efficiency and state intervention: Labour 1939–51*. London: Routledge.

Whitley, R. 1999. *Divergent capitalisms: The social structuring and change of business systems*. Oxford: Oxford University Press.

———. 2000. The institutional structuring of innovation strategies: Business systems, firm types and patterns of technical change in different market economics. *Organization Studies* 21 (5): 855–886.

Whitston, K. 1996. Scientific management and production management practice in Britain between the wars. *Historical Studies in Industrial Relations* 1 (March): 47–75.

Witzel, M. 2003. *Fifty key figures in management*. London: Routledge.

5 Uncovering the Bottom of the Iceberg

Innovation and Large Family Firms in Spanish Metal Manufacturing

Paloma Fernández Pérez

INTRODUCTION

Innovation studies often deal with leading industrialized countries, corporations and sectors. They do not deal so often with late industrialized countries, technologically mature sectors and family firms. However, these are the dominant categories in which economic activity takes place in the world. This chapter is a contribution towards a better understanding of how innovation takes place in southern Europe, in medium and large capital-intensive firms highly characterized by technological transfer from abroad, where innovation takes place above all in services. It is also a contribution towards a better understanding of how personal networking within and among firms has been a key feature of the advance of the second technological revolution in Europe, as important as the creation of big modern corporations, as seems to have been the case also in the United States (Galambos 2005, 11–13).

As the chapter in this book on Spanish chemical firms also indicates, Spanish innovation in capital-intensive sectors was highly conditioned by its political history during the twentieth century. Two military dictatorships (1923–1929 and 1939–1975) blocked for five decades the process of integration into the world economy, during a period in which the second technological revolution developed in western Europe. Besides, regional elites were able to lobby with regional and national political administrations in a more stable and successful way than in other OECD (Organization for Economic Cooperation and Development) countries, in order to reduce the participation of outsiders in their market niches and to be able to maintain their dominance among Spanish consumers (Fernández Pérez and Puig 2007; Hernández and Fernández Pérez 2008).

In this context medium and large family firms have been able to transfer innovation and develop successful innovative strategies in the creation of intangible assets (distribution channels, reputation, brands) and services, particularly in some regions like Catalonia (Genescà and Salas 2007). Accepted traditional measures for comparing innovation among countries over time rely on indicators, such as patents, that provide data on product and process innovation, but not so much on innovation in services, which is a key intangible value of family firms (Galve and Salas 2003; Ortiz-Villajos 1999; Sáiz 2000). The evidence about this kind of innovation, so important to explaining the competitiveness of the largest Spanish family firms, rarely appears in official sources, and researchers need to dig in private archives and a wide variety of unorthodox sources (press, corporate documents and websites, oral interviews) in order to obtain relevant information.

This chapter uses this kind of source material and focuses on a capital-intensive industry typical of the first technological revolution, which is metal manufacturing. The documentary evidence comes basically from private archives and belongs to five family firms. Three of them were established in the late nineteenth century and lost independence and merged with a new firm in the 1980s or 1990s (Moreda, Quijano and Rivière). The fourth is the new firm which bought these three firms, established in the late 1960s (Compañia Española de Laminación S.A., or 'CELSA' - S. A. is Sociedad Anónima in Spanish, a joint stock company). And the fifth is a firm established in the mid-nineteenth century which successfully diversified into sanitary-equipment manufacturing activities during the twentieth century and sold its original metal branch to British investors three years ago (Roca). The evidence from these firms shows the complex economic, institutional and social context in which innovation took place during the second technological revolution. The cases of Roca and CELSA in particular also confirm some recent ideas about the competitive advantages which some dynastic family firms in the metal industries have shown in Europe, provided they have a flexible organization and are ready to diversify (James 2006). Roca and CELSA, like other European metal dynastic firms such as Wendels, Haniels and Falck, have been able to survive foreign competition after 1959 through diversification, connection with foreign markets, professionalization of the firm's management and successful and useful associationist networking in regional and transnational lobbies.

The chapter also shows how innovation alone is not a guarantee of company success: an inefficient interplay between family issues and business issues, and the lack of a real professional management in a large family firm, can lead to failure, as indicated by the case of Rivière—a pioneer in the introduction of Bedaux methods in Spain and a model of steel-wire factory lay-out in the 1960s. The iceberg metaphor of the title symbolizes, in this sense, the importance of social and cultural factors in the study of innovation, so crucial to understanding international differences. Technology and economic growth is the structure, the visible top of the iceberg, whereas social and cultural elements are at the bottom below sea level and may have a larger impact than expected on innovation (Brown and Ulijn 2004, 2–3).

Many definitions of innovation are available, but there is a bare minimum which would be that 'innovation is creating something new and implementing it successfully at a market' (Cumming 1998; Brown and Ulijn 2004, 2; Escorsa and Valls 2003, 20–21). There are two major approaches to innovation from the various disciplines that deal with the subject. One studies 'the innovation process', what we would call internal factors that transform creative ideas into successful products and services, within a firm or a group of firms. Existing innovative 'internal' models such as those from the London Business School, Rothwell and Kline stress as a common feature the outstanding importance of leadership, human relations and well-connected teams in the transformation of a creative idea into a possibly successful product, process or service (Escorsa and Valls 2003, 31). Recent literature also considers ownership structures, particularly when a firm or group of firms have a long history and avoid external financial capital in their control (Ortega-Argilés et al. 2004). The second major approach to innovation is about the 'innovative environment', including basically external or environmental aspects that have a history, an accumulated evolution, that makes such elements difficult to change in the short-run and thus influences innovation processes considerably. This long-term approach to innovation considers start-up costs, the role of government, informal and institutional knowledge-transference processes between markets and firms, regional or/and ethnic cultures, professional cultures and cross-national networks of technology and entrepreneurs (Lavoie and Chamlee-Wright 2000; Fonseca, López García and Pissaride 2001; Ulijn, Nagel and Tan 2001; Fornahl and Brenner 2004).

This essay combines aspects from both approaches. On the one hand, family ownership of firms has an influence on, and is influenced by, broader developments such as inheritance traditions, gender definitions of business activity and legal and cultural definitions about social reproduction (Colli, Fernández Pérez and Rose 2003). Recent perspectives about the factors that explain the rapid adoption of innovative ideas stress the importance of human networks that collaborate over common goals (Martínez Fernández 2004). According to these ideas, inter-firm projects are often short-run; however, interpersonal relations can often be long-run and may have more positive innovative results (Maskell and Lorenz 2003, 11). From this perspective, medium and large family firms seem to be a particularly good type of firm that may favour long-term personal networking and thus potential innovative processes in a long period. Size allows economies of scale, relatively decreased risk, a larger market and greater opportunities, while age would represent accumulated organizational resources such as leadership, experience, knowledge and learning capacity (Ortega, Moreno and Suriñach Caralt 2004, 9; Gallo and Amat 2003). Also, family-firm studies stress the key importance that good personal relations have on such critical moments of the firm's existence as generational succession or merging with other firms in an internationalization process (Colli, Fernández Pérez and Rose 2003; Goula 2004). Spanish family firms have historically designed a wide range of mechanisms, associations and institutions to create 'friendly' local and regional innovative environments, often in spite of political obstacles. These 'friendly' environments include professional associations, travel, private institutions for managerial education and personal stable relations with entrepreneurs and politicians at different territorial levels (Fernández Pérez and Puig 2004; Puig and Fernández Pérez 2003; Torres 2000; Cabana 2006).

This chapter pays attention to these mechanisms and how the formal and informal groups, which family firms have created in their regions, have contributed to the creation of positive 'innovative environments' within and outside firms which have helped change and growth. This process is analyzed through the study of five relatively medium and big family firms with more than two hundred employees that were founded in the mid-twentieth century or before and are still active: Trefilería Moreda (1879, Asturias), Grupo Roca (first workshop 1830 in Catalonia), Rivière S.A. (first workshop 1854/1860 in Madrid, moved to Barcelona in 1880s), Quijano (Forjas de Buelna factory started in 1873 in Cantabria) and CELSA (constituted in 1965 in Catalonia). These firms work mostly in the metal-transformation sector, or have worked there (Roca´s bathroom division started in 1929 and is now the main specialty, whereas the original radiator/heater production branch of the firm was sold to the British Baxi company in 2005) (*El País* 2005, 76).

THE CASES OF TREFILERÍA MOREDA AND GRUPO ROCA: THE STRONG ROLE OF PROFESSIONAL MANAGEMENT SINCE THE 1970s.

The legal origins of Trefilería Moreda (TM) need to be placed in the Spanish region of Asturias in 1895, when the firm was registered in Oviedo. TM was initially part of another firm, the steel and mining producer Sociedad de Minas y Fábrica Moreda y Gijón (Paris, 1879, with factories near the Asturian harbour of Gijón), whose initial owners were a consortium of French industrialists and bankers. TM's owners changed in 1899 when the Basque José Tartiere Lenegre, of French origins—and owner since 1895 of the Asturian Sociedad Industrial Asturiana Santa Barbara (SIASB)—bought S.A. Fábrica de Moreda y Gijón (Fábrica Moreda y Gijón: MG [Fábrica Moreda y Gijón] 1954). Tartiere was the leader of a group of Asturian entrepreneurs interested in 'regionalizing' the ownership and management of the wireworks. This was a group of people linked by strong friendship and a common local outlook. The industrial group remained under the Tartiere family's control until the early 1960s. In 1961 three Asturian metal companies were incorporated in the new Unión de Siderúrgicas Asturianas (UNINSA) made up of Duro Felguera, Fábrica de Mieres and SIASB. In this agreement, the wireworks of SIASB remained outside the association together with the copper workshops until 1982, when the wireworks became a new legally registered independent firm: Trefilería Moreda S.A. The Tartiere family controlled the strategic decisions of the wireworks for almost a century between 1895 and 1990—when CELSA bought the firm.

Between 1997 and 2002 CELSA invested 5,000 million pesetas (30 million euros) in the TM factories and made TM leader in the incorporation of technological and organizational innovations of the CELSA wire division. The goal was to reinforce the international expansion of TM, which sells 40 percent of production in the E.U. markets and is initiating sales in U.S. markets, and to intensify diversified specialty production in fences (Fernández Pérez 2004, 195–208). In 2002 TM secured 44 million euros in sales and employed 240 people, before absorbing the steel-wire firms Trenzas y Cables and Rivière (bought by CELSA in 2002).

From a technological point of view TM was at the very beginning adapting French and British technologies to Asturian possibilities. In the difficult post-war years of the 1940s TM started a new line of products (wires for cables, tubes and pipes, welded chains, can keys, sewing flat wires, shoe wires) and re-organized in a massive way all the machinery and production processes, including the installation of a new mill and furnaces and a new laboratory. The innovation in processes and products of course was very meagre and poor compared to other European firms such as the Belgian firm Bekaert that were adopting technological, marketing and managerial innovations after the Second World War (Van Houtte et al. 1992; Roig and Pou 1975), but it was quite considerable when compared to many industrial Spanish regions—such as Catalonia— that were suffering in the 1940s from serious difficulties in obtaining energy resources and even in buying second-hand imported machines, due to Franco's restrictive industrial and commercial policies (Catalan 1995). Besides, the firm was specializing in a few new products that were adapted to the scarcities of the time and also to the existing clients of the Spanish markets. TM served the specialized needs of two sectors that would later become leading Spanish export industries: canned food and the shoe industries.

Moreda's archive suffered flood damage, and information regarding the evolution of the firm in the important years between the 1960s and 1980s was lost. Since the 1990s the strategy of the new professional managers of TM (not related to family ownership at all) has been to drastically reduce manufacturing of low-added-value products and to specialize in a smaller range of superior added-value products: fences and related products. The potential markets are construction and residential sectors, industry and agrarian and cattle businesses, as well as infrastructure (protection for railways, highways, etc.), warehouses and sport areas. Because between 35 and 40 percent of production was going to foreign European markets in the early years of the twentieth century, and because the most important intermediary in Spanish markets is the hardware dealer, the marketing department leads product innovation, particularly through incremental innovations required by these intermediaries: new materials, new finishings, better presentation and more security in handling, with a strong dialogue with consumers' needs.

Also, due to Moreda being since 2002 the head of wire-working factories that include Asturian and Catalan centres (the old TM, Rivière S.A., TYCSA), organizational and managerial innovations have been needed in order to coordinate market expansion with internal innovation and growth. The CEO has a team of five managers responsible for five departments or specialized areas: commercial, finances, human resources, products and industrial processes. The commercial manager has five subsidiaries in the Spanish cities of Madrid, Seville, Vitoria, Gijón and Barcelona (the last two the most important ones), and commercial networks in Galicia, Castile-Leon, Canary Islands, Almeria and Portugal. Gijón is the commercial centre that manages the English-speaking markets, whereas the Catalan factory of Cerdanyola (formerly Rivière S.A.) manages the French, Italian and German markets. The industrial department has one factory manager for each productive centre, and the responsibilities of this department include process and quality engineering, methods and times, maintenance and environmental issues. The human-resources department has implemented a very important philosophy of team work and participative dialogue, as well as stability in the working place. This policy is indeed important to avoid union strikes in centres with an average of two hundred employees each, but is also important in the Catalan factory, which is now experiencing an increase in the number of qualified personnel coming from eastern European countries (particularly from Rumania, Ukraine and Bulgaria). The product- and process-development department of Moreda Rivière Trefilerías S.A. is located in the Gijón factory and is composed of commercial technicians with experience in marketing and new-product and applications development, who study the requirements of the market to design new products and develop marketing and communication strategies. This group of commercial people works closely with system technicians who apply the commercial ideas and make the final projects. In the last five years the Asturian centre has invested mainly in new-product development (like the plasticized electro-welded meshes) whereas the Catalan factory of Cerdanyola has received investments to improve organization, management and production processes due to inherited problems which blocked not only innovation but also any sort of profitability, as we see in the next section about Rivière.

Roca's historical evolution is better known than TM's (Fernández Pérez 2000, 278–283). The origins of the firm lie in a blacksmith workshop that also repaired artisan tools, in the small Catalan village of Manlleu in 1830. The workshop continued with Matías Soler and, after his death in 1880, with his son-in-law Pedro Roca, a blacksmith's son. The fourth generation of the family, the four surviving children of María Soler Serra and Pere Roca, inherited the business after Roca's death in 1910, at a critical time. Steam power was declining and electricity was taking over, together with 'new' materials such as steel, thus leading to a major restructuring of the industry in Catalonia, as elsewhere. Pere Roca's workshop had specialized in products and services which were disappearing, such as repairing steam machinery and iron stoves. The demise of the workshop was avoided with new specialized products and processes and new organizational strategies based on team work. Two brothers (Matías and Martín) went to France and worked in the French subsidiary of the U.S. American Radiator Co. (ARCo.) in Dôle, which manufactured iron radiators. With their own family resources and with support from the local bank Banco de Préstamos y Descuentos de Vic they secretly produced the first successful radiator in the Catalan village of Manlleu in 1914. The collapse of imports due to the First World War provided a great opportunity to control the Spanish markets and to lead the sector in competition with Asturian and Basque producers (such as Ara Hermanos, Marcelino Ibáñez, Fundaciones Alsasua and Casa Aurrerá of Bilbao). The expanding demand of radiators during the war made Roca Soler expand their old factory and finally build a new one in the city of Gavà near Barcelona, with better communication and transport systems. Production started here in 1917, under the name Talleres Roca S.A. Though technologically speaking it was a completely different world compared to metal working, from a market point of view it was a good strategy to sell more standardized and cheap products to the same clients, a revolutionary idea that was spreading in the marketing strategy of the big U.S. mass producers during these years. The Roca Soler family initiated conversations with ARCo. to bring the new technology to the Spanish market, which they concluded with the agreement signed in Paris on 7 March 1929. The name was changed to Compañía Roca Radiadores S.A., the capital tripled from 2 to 6 million Spanish pesetas and the family lost their majority in ownership (ARCo. had 51 percent of the shares) and management (ARCo. controlled all the council boards). The new firm was registered in Madrid in 1929. The U.S. technology arrived in manufacturing and marketing. Management also completely changed regarding the former company, with the introduction of rationalization techniques and the division of the company in three areas with three different managerial teams in which the Roca family had little presence.

The years of Franco's dictatorship between 1939 and 1975 were characterized in the Roca firm by the removal of the U.S. partners (due to new laws against foreign ownership of Spanish firms), with control of ownership and management being taken by Roca Soler family members, and the expansion of the firm in the Spanish market under monopolistic conditions protected by state laws. Because of raw-material and energy scarcities, during the 1940s the family was forced to reduce radiator production (metal was scarce and expensive) and increase sanitary equipment (cheaper to produce), which unexpectedly would be the successful 'shining star' section of the firm from then onwards. In 1948 the firm opened new furnaces, and in 1953 a factory, to manufacture small metal items for bathroom equipment. The expansion of the firm in the 1950s and 1960s also brought new needs in terms of human resources. At the workplace, a human-relations approach to managing employees was introduced. At the top, the family started to get away from managerial positions between 1969 and 1974: family managers reduced their numbers (Matías Roca died in 1959 and Angela in 1960), while at the same time more managers and a more complex organization were required due to the expansion of the Gavá factory and the creation of new factories in other Spanish regions or cities. Josep Roca Soler, the leader of the family in the Francoist period, was one of the first entrepreneurs who supported the creation of a special business school well connected with the outside—IESE—for the special needs of Catalan family firms during Franco's dictatorship and was of the first to attend and obtain advanced managerial education in that school (Puig and Fernández Pérez 2003). No wonder he soon recognized the need to professionalize management in the early 1970s. His brother Martín died in 1969, and in January 1974 Antonio Roca Portet, Martin's son, retired as CEO, and the council appointed as new CEO 'a man of the house', the production chief manager Salvador Gabarró Serra. With Gabarró the 1970s economic crisis that hit public firms and family small and medium enterprises (SMEs) hard in Spain was successfully overcome, and the potential conflicts of a family succession were avoided: the family decided as a whole to retire from management. Gabarró achieved an outstanding international expansion of the firm. By the end of the twentieth century the Roca group had factories and a significant market share in eighteen countries: Spain, Portugal, China, Morocco, Turkey, Poland, Italy, Argentina, Peru, Dominican Republic, Switzerland, Austria, Czech Republic, Slovakia, Bulgaria, Brazil, the United States and, since mid-2005, China. Group sales in 2005 reached 1,660 million euros, and cash flow amounted that year to 290 million euros (Fortuny 2002).

The success of the internationalization strategy of the 'Gabarro era' (1974–2000) in the history of the Roca group was above all the result of a complex process of managerial and organizational innovation in the firm, more than a result of technological innovation. It was also the result of a process of network building with providers that enabled within the firm not radical innovations in the Schumpeterian meaning of the term, but rather incremental innovations. To start with the managerial innovation, Salvador Gabarró organized the firm in departments with professional managers who received a relatively strong degree of independence (Fortuny 2002). He attached great importance to human-resources management. When he inherited CEO responsibilities he had to deal with a ninety-day strike in 1974 in which the 7,400 employees of the Roca group participated. It really was an advanced training course for him. He had to reduce over-employment, and by 1981 the company had already reduced its workforce by 40 percent, to 4,400 workers and managers. As in other big corporations with thousands of employees from different cultural backgrounds, Gabarró recognized the need to favour policies of stability, to define clear rules of internal promotion and to create a common corporate identity and culture around which employees could build a sense of belonging and loyalty. The psychologist Francisco Javier Martin helped Gabarró in building this identity and culture to be shared by all employees, named 'roquismo'. Regarding network building, Gabarro worked in two directions. First, he connected as CEO with the political and industrial top circles of Catalonia and Spain. He participated in the councils of the Círculo de Economía from 1974 (president in 1999) and Cambra de Comerç, Indústria i Navegació from 1979, and contributed to the creation of the Unió Patronal Metal.lúrgica and the Confederación Española de Organizaciones Empresariales (CEOE). Second, he connected with innovative providers to introduce external technological innovations in the factories through a process of internal adaptation to the different markets the company served. This adaptation of foreign technologies had a precedent in the transfer of U.S./French iron-smelting technology to produce radiators that Matias and Martin Roca Soler had realized after their stage in Paris in 1913. A similar case was his efforts to replace iron radiators by light steel radiators made with German technology, in a move supported by Josep Roca Vilaseca and Salvador Gabarró 'against' the opinion of Josep Roca Soler, probably in the early 1960s. Burners for water heaters in those years came from Italy, and French managers were hired to maintain the management of a bathtub factory in Gavà in the 1970s. Also in the 1970s a new air-conditioning division started with technological transfer agreements being established with the U.S. firm York and with SANYO.

Innovation in the Roca group, thus, has historically been incremental innovation of radical foreign technological innovations and management adapted to local realities. The history of Roca shows the existence of strong leaders like Pere Roca at the end of the nineteenth century, Josep Roca Soler in the Francoist period and Salvador Gabarró Serra between 1974 and 2000. It also shows the importance of team work at the top (between 1913 and 1921, the four Roca Soler brothers and sister) and between managers and employees (particularly during Francoist period, and afterwards as the corporation took shape). And finally, it shows the importance, for survival and information-cost reduction, of networks established with economic and political interests, and networks of trust and loyalty.

The cases of Moreda and Roca are evidence of how strong leadership, team work, dialogue between managers and employees and close cooperation between the marketing and technical functions are features that have allowed both firms to survive and maintain a relatively innovative identity in their activities. Innovation in these firms was often based on transfer and adaptation of technology and management from abroad. In the case of Moreda, the available evidence indicates that Tartière family ownership was completely lost in the 1980s, to be replaced by dominant Rubiralta family ownership. The Roca group is still basically owned by the Roca family. In both cases professional non-family management of factories was soon introduced (from the beginning in Moreda, after 1940s in Roca) as the technological complexities of metal manufacturing increased. Family relatives specialized in the commercial and 'external relations' areas of the firm. This division of functions is significant in explaining how both firms survived the civil war and innovated during the interventionist period of Franco's dictatorship. The ability to professionalize top managerial responsibilities and the external-relations area of the firm could help explain why the Tartière family had to leave and why the Rubiraltas continued management in Moreda; also, why the Roca group avoided loss of family ownership and obtained a leading market position in Europe in bath-equipment manufacturing.

THE CASES OF RIVIÈRE S.A. AND QUIJANO: INNOVATION IN TIMES OF BACKWARDNESS AND PROTECTION

Rivière and Quijano are two cases of firms that efficiently managed innovation projects while the external institutional environment protected their activity. (Fernández Pérez 2007a) However, when they had to face, without this institutional umbrella, the challenge of the 1970s global crisis and the final participation in the European market after 1986, family interests were unable to deal efficiently with business needs. Because both firms belonged to a very specialized market niche in the wireworks industries, it was, predictably, another specialized family firm in this field (CELSA) that became the new family owner from the 1980s and 1990s (Fernández Pérez 2004). Quijano was founded in 1873, and Rivière in 1854. Their sizes were relatively smaller than Roca's, but similar to Moreda's. Comparing employment in 1896, Quijano had 276 employees and Rivière 147; in 1930 the numbers were respectively 2,076 and 316; in 1970, 1,300 and 1,100; and in 1989, 700 and 421 (Quijano 1998; Laguillo García-Bárcena 2001; Fernández Pérez 2004). Both firms made incremental technological innovations in products and processes that were observed or bought abroad during the nineteenth and twentieth centuries. Standardization and mass production slowly took place only in the twentieth century.

In both firms the founders had no previous experience or training in the businesses they started but enjoyed excellent personal relations with networks of people within and outside Spain who provided capital, labour and technology transfer. Before they became leading regional and national entrepreneurs in the wireworks industries of Spain, José María Quijano y Fernández-Hontoria (born in Los Corrales de Buelna in Cantabria in 1843) was a lawyer, and François Rivière Bonneton (born in Issoire, France, in 1835) worked for a textile workshop in Paris and for a French railway company managing resources operations. Quijano enjoyed particularly good political connections in the Spanish capital—which may explain many of the favourable conditions Quijano enjoyed in terms of raw materials and market control in critical times like the post-war periods (after the First

World War and after the Spanish civil war). Rivière did not, but had strong and stable connections with French providers during three generations, which helped overcome critical periods such as the Spanish civil war and the scarcities of the 1940s and 1950s.

The second generations of Quijano and Rivière improved their formal education to cope with the technological changes of the first third of the twentieth century in a different way. Several Quijano sons obtained engineering degrees in Belgium and adapted Bedaux methods, and Rivière sons, in the traditional way, received training in the factory next to their father. It was, on the other hand, a logical decision due to the different markets their firms wanted to conquer: Quijano specialized in mass production of relatively easy to standardize metal products for large clients in the energy and transportation markets, while Rivière specialized in specialty production for a diversity of clients in the Spanish market. In the first case, production almost required mass techniques, while in the other, artisan-like approaches. When Rivière's market grew in size after the civil war, then mass-production techniques and Bedaux-Gombert methods of time control and productivity were also introduced, in the late 1940s and early 1950s. In the 1920s the third generation of Rivières received professional technical education in engineering schools (in Barcelona, Madrid and Germany), and in the 1950s, advanced managerial education in private business schools (IESE in Barcelona). The 1960s witnessed a profound re-organization of the production process in Rivière, with the closing of three old factories in the centre and outskirts of Barcelona and the building of a new factory with Belgium technology and lay-out. This new factory, in Cerdanyola del Vallès, included a laboratory to experiment with new materials and tools, though it could not be considered a modern R&D department.

During the 1950s and 1960s Quijano hired as professional managers outsiders who had good contacts with the ministry of industry in Madrid and diversified in manufacturing cars in partnership with foreign firms. In Rivière production rocketed due to market expansion of traditional products, but little was done in terms of diversification or serious professional management, as it would be the case in Moreda or Roca or Quijano. Strong family characters blocked strategic business decisions, and the traditional innovation character of the firm was lost in the process (Fernández Pérez 2004). The firm was bought by CELSA, much more aware of organizational issues and market developments in this market niche, in the late 1990s.

THE CASE OF CELSA: INTERNATIONALIZATION FROM THE START AND PROFESSIONAL MANAGEMENT

CELSA (Compañía Española de Laminación, S.A.) is the youngest of the five firms of this chapter, just beginning a succession process to achieve the second family generation, though it is the largest in turnover of our sample.

It was founded in 1967 in Sant Andreu de la Barca, near Barcelona, by the twenty-six-year-old entrepreneur Francisco Rubiralta Vilaseca, son of an entrepreneur specialized in the commercial distribution of scrap iron and metal products (Anselm Rubiralta) who had good relations with metal providers and clients of the Manresa area and with the nearby Vallès and Barcelonès industrial districts.

Francisco Rubiralta initiated CELSA with inherited knowledge in the distribution of the business from his father and with the financial support of the other owner of CELSA, his brother Josep Maria. Both brothers shared ownership (until 2007 when they began the separation of the firm) but not management, probably to avoid leadership problems, so Josep Maria concentrated in the management of another firm (Grupo Izasa-Werfen, specialized in clinical equipment), and Francisco in the management of CELSA. In thirty years the growth that the two brothers had achieved in their two firms has been spectacular: in 2004 Jose Maria's Izasa-Werfen had a turnover of 600 million euros and employed 2,000 people in different countries of Europe and America, whereas CELSA's figures that year were 2,559 million euros and 5,694 employees in Spain, the United Kingdom and Poland.

Francisco Rubiralta i Vilaseca obtained a Ph.D. in industrial engineering at the public Universidad Politécnica de Barcelona in 1963 (Fernández Pérez 2007b: 151–162). Instead of moving fast to work in his father's business—as other heirs of Catalan metal entrepreneurs such as the Rivières were just doing—he decided on a quite uncommon and innovative approach for those years and travelled far away—to Pittsburgh, an area of innovative industrial metal tradition—to follow postgraduate studies during two years (1964–1965), specializing in industrial administration at Carnegie Mellon University. In 1967 he was in Spain and created CELSA; in 1969 he attended a course at IESE (a private business school whose courses were enthusiastically attended in the same years by other young members of Catalan metal family firms like Roca or Rivière). In 1973 Rubiralta registered in the PMD programme of business administration of Harvard Business School and followed courses in the Californian Stanford Business School in 1984, 1985 and 1986. The experience in the U.S. centres inspired Rubiralta to create in Barcelona locally rooted centres of global-learning experience and qualified marketing. Between the late 1980s and the early 2000s Rubiralta financed chairs of research and study (named after his father and his firm) in industrial and globalization strategies in the public and private institutions where he had been educated in Barcelona. The creation of these chairs has contributed to improving Barcelona's innovative environment for industrial engineers. At the same time, it allowed the establishment of long-term networks with qualified Spanish and Latin American technicians and professionals who can potentially choose, improve—and sell—CELSA's services and products in the big corporations where they work. These are located in the transcontinental Spanish-speaking markets, therefore also contributing to CELSA's priority strategy of globalization through innovation in international markets.

It is always difficult to demonstrate the direct links between the influence of training and personal contacts and innovation, but in Rubiralta's case available evidence shows that the bigger the net of personal contacts and the diversity of accumulated experiences and knowledge, the more global and successful the strategic-innovative direction of the firm. In the case of CELSA we have more data about production and strategic changes in production than about leadership, team work or other internal organizational aspects that could have provided more information about internal-innovation processes. Taking this into account, we know that the original activity of CELSA during its first ten years (1967–1977, years of economic expansion before the oil crisis hit the Spanish economy hard) was second- and third-stage working of metal products, not manufacturing of primary products. The main specialty in these ten years was corrugated bars used in construction, a field which was living a strong expansion during the golden age of the 1960s in Spain, with the strong push of urban growth and infrastructure building. Clients were Spanish steel producers such as ENSIDESA and Torras that needed intermediaries in the transformation and commercial distribution of their large-scale steel production. CELSA performed as a middle-sized firm that charged a fee for the transformation of a semi-finished product. Also, CELSA specialized in looking for new export markets for the products of the big Spanish steel producers, ENSIDESA and Torras. Therefore, CELSA was, in its first ten years, a family firm with knowledge of the commercial distribution of steel products in Spain, with a leader trained in industrial organization at the best public and private universities of Spain and the United States, that combined experience, knowledge and contacts to do something very few metal firms in Spain were doing in the expanding years of the 1960s: to export. Innovation in these years seemed to be taking place more in the marketing area than in other areas of the firm. CELSA spent time and effort doing precisely this, winning foreign clients for other Spanish firms that risked their products and money, and in the process learning about the diverse European metal markets and firms. This knowledge was, in combination with the knowledge of the Spanish market, the key internal aspect that allowed CELSA to survive the 1970s crisis and the European integration/reorganization of the metal sector. CELSA did not drastically diversify production in other sectors, as Roca had done to survive with the bathroom and tiles divisions, but specialized in a particular production niche in Europe: corrugated bars for construction, the most dynamic sector of the Spanish economy in the last decades.

CELSA reinvested accumulated profits in 1977 to achieve vertical integration of metal manufacturing, thus reducing dependence on steel providers and at the same time increasing production capacity of existing factories. There soon followed in the 1980s a phase of acquiring steel-manufacturing firms from among those in crisis due to the public policy of re-organizing the steel sector after 1988. CELSA bought at a cheap price century-old firms which had not only strategic locations near expanding cities and infrastructure networks (in Catalonia, Cantabria and Basque Country), but also a loyal net of clients and providers in the diverse Spanish regions and sectors (Fernández Pérez 2007b). Thus, in 1987 CELSA bought 100 percent of the old steel producer Torras Herrería y Construcciones S.A. (THC)—which included the furnaces of the main CELSA competitor in Catalonia, Altos Hornos de Catalunya, S.A. (Hospitalet, Barcelona)—with special tax benefits regulated in 1980s legislation (the final absorption took place in 1990—see Cabana and Feliu 1987). In 1988, and in the context of the Spanish industrial crisis, CELSA bought the Cantabrian firms Nueva Montaña Quijano S.A. (presently Global Steel Wire) and Trefilerías Quijano. A year later in 1989 the new acquisition was the Basque Nervacero, a small steel factory in Vizcaya specializing in bars for construction, which doubled the total annual steel production of the group and made CELSA the leader of the Spanish market in corrugated bars for construction mesh. Finally, in 1991 the Catalan commercial-steel-bar producer Industrias del Besós S.A. (San Adrián del Besós, Barcelona) was bought, and in this way CELSA became the only Catalan metal group of real importance at the end of the twentieth century. CELSA closed the original factory of Sant Andreu de la Barca and concentrated all the production in Castellbisbal. (CELSA. 2000)

The next growth strategy of the firm was to diversify production and increase added value with technology that allowed more and new transformation processes. Wireworks was the line of specialty production that was the management priority in the 1990s. CELSA bought Trenzas y Cables de Acero, S.A. (TYCSA) in Barberá del Vallés and Trefilería Moreda S.A in Gijón; in 1999 Rivière S.A., in Cerdanyola del Vallés. At the very beginning of the twenty-first century CELSA was the largest Spanish producer of wire-rod and wire manufactures, with an enormous distance between it and the other much smaller Spanish competitors.

To reduce domestic competition once more, and to avoid dependence on raw-materials provision and price increases (due to rise of energy prices, the U.S./E.U. 'steel battle' and Chinese steel consumption), CELSA started in the 1990s to acquire Spanish scrap-iron factories: in 1990 Corporación Siderúrgica, S.A. (Sabadell, Barcelona) and Compañía Fragmentadora Valenciana, S.A. (Sollana, Valencia); in 1994 Hierros y Desguaces, S.A. (Reus, Tarragona); in 1995 Reciclatges d'Osona, S.L. (Vic, Barcelona); in 1997 Reciclatges del Maresme, S.L. (Mataró, Barcelona) and Reciclados Metálicos, S.L. (Hospitalet de Llobregat, Barcelona); and in 2005 Ferimet, S.L. (Granollers, Barcelona).

Diversifying production and vertical integration have required technological and organizational innovations. First, technological innovations (one's own, or bought from others) are introduced only if technology reduces production costs and favours flexibility and diversification in response to

changing and flexible client requirements. Staff in the marketing departments are very influential in the initial selection of a particular product or
process, as in Trefilería Moreda. Often production lines are designed to be
short to respond to client requirements. Second, production centres (old
and new) are located near the big consumption markets but also frequently
have at the same time extraordinarily attractive locations which, due to the
effects of the real-estate bubble, offer the prospect of profitable disposal
should the need arise. Third, there is a strong philosophy of small-team
work and strict hierarchical obedience to responsible managers of every
section, firm and division of the group: hierarchy works because there are
mechanisms for frequent dialogue among responsible persons of the groups
and the commitment to make such a dialogue an efficient way to respond
to employees' requirements and needs.

The addition of new markets, clients, qualified employees, inputs and
firms with the integration of new eastern members to the European Union
has definitely constituted an opportunity and a challenge to CELSA from
an organizational point of view to. In the early 2000s a factory in Cardiff
in the United Kingdom and another in Poland were bought. The internationalization process needs new networks with entrepreneurs and politicians, and this is indeed a good explanation for CELSA's membership in
the 'Iron and Steel Institute (IISI)'—where Francisco Rubiralta belongs to
the executive committee—'EUROFER', the Spanish metal-entrepreneurial
association 'UNESID' and the Spanish family-firm association 'Instituto de
la Empresa Familiar'.

CONCLUSIONS

Spanish family firms have historically designed mechanisms to create local
and regional innovative environments, often in spite of political obstacles.
(Fernández Pérez and Puig 2008. Instituto de la Empresa Familiar 2004).
The existing literature has outlined training programmes, professional
associations, travel, private institutions for managerial educational and
stable personal relations with entrepreneurs and politicians. Our five case
studies show that, in sectors and regions dominated by large family firms,
innovation is normally generated through the strong interaction between
the marketing and production functions of the firm in order to create intangible assets such as reputation and brands. In family-owned firms this process requires a strong coordination between professional management and
family interests.

Innovation in a long-term perspective meant in the five case studies the
ability to adapt radical or incremental innovations in technology and management usually created abroad to particular conditions of their market
niches. This adaptation meant, in all the cases, intensive technology transfer

from abroad, but also innovation in services and in human-resources management and professionalization of the CEOs.

ACKNOWLEDGEMENTS

This chapter has received at different stages funding from Fundación BBVA and the Spanish public research projects SEJ2005–02788 and ECO2008–00398/ECON.

REFERENCES

Brown, T. E., and J. Ulijn, eds. 2004. *Innovation, entrepreneurship and culture: The interaction between technology, progress and economic growth.* Cheltenham, U.K.: Edward Elgar.

Cabana, F., ed. 2006. *Cien empresarios catalanes del siglo XX.* Madrid, LID.

Cabana, F., and A. Feliu. 1987. *Can Torras dels Ferros 1865–1985. Siderúrgia i Construccions Metàl.liques a Catalunya.* Barcelona: Tallers Gràfics Hostench.

Casson, M. 1999. The economics of the family firm. *Scandinavian Economic History Review* 47 (1): 10–23.

Catalan, J. 1995. *La economía española y la segunda guerra mundial.* Barcelona, Ariel.

Cebrián, M. 2005. La regulación industrial y la transferencia internacional de tecnología en España (1959–1973). *Investigaciones de Historia Económica* 3:11–42.

CELSA. 2000. *Catálogo CELSA. Un compromiso global.* Barcelona, CELSA.

Colli, A., P. Fernández Pérez and M. B. Rose. 2003. National determinants of family firm development? Family firms in Britain, Spain and Italy in the nineteenth and twentieth centuries. *Enterprise & Society* 4 (1): 28–64.

Cumming, B. 1998. Innovation overview and future challenges. *European Journal of Innovation Management* 1 (1): 21–29.

Escorsa Castells, P., and J. Valls Pasola. 2003. *Tecnología e innovación en la empresa.* Barcelona: Edicions UPC.

Fernández Pérez, P. 2000. Ángela, Matías, Martín y Josep Roca Soler. In *Los cien empresarios españoles del siglo XX,* ed. E. Torres, 278–283. Madrid: LID.

———. 2004. *Moreda (1879–2004) y Rivière (1854–2004). Un siglo y medio de trefilería en España.* Barcelona: MRT-Trivium.

———. 2007a. Small firms and networks in capital intensive industries: The case of Spanish steel wire manufacturing. *Business History* 49 (5): 647–667.

———. 2007b. CELSA. In *El sello de la excelencia. Empresas, emprendedores y dirigentes,* ed. F. Ribera, 151–162. Barcelona: Doblerre.

Fernández Pérez, P., and N. Puig Raposo. 2004. Knowledge and training in family firms of the European periphery: Spain in the eighteenth to twentieth centuries. *Business History* 46 (1): 79–99.

———. 2007. The Spanish Mittelstand: A long learning process of survival and success. Paper presented at the colloquium 'The European Mittelstand Since 1900 to the Present'. Lake Como, Italy, 29–31 October.

———. 2008. Bonsais in a wild forest: A historical interpretation on the longevity of large Spanish family firms. *Revista de Historia Económica. Journal of Iberian and Latin American Economic History* 25 (3): 459–497.

Fonseca, R., P. López García and C. A. Pissaride. 2001. Entrepreneurship, start-up costs and employment. *European Economic Review* 45:692–705.

Fornahl, D., and T. Brenner, eds. 2004. *Cooperation, networks and institutions in regional innovation systems.* Cheltenham, U.K.: Edward Elgar.

Fortuny, J. 2002. *Conversaciones empresariales con Salvador Gabarró.* Barcelona: ESADE-Mobil Books.

Galambos, L. 2005. Recasting the organizational synthesis: Structure and process in the twentieth and twenty-first centuries. *Business History Review* 79:1–38.

Gallo, M. A., and J. M. Amat. 2003. *Los secretos de las empresas familiares centenarias. Claves del éxito de las empresas familiares multigeneracionales.* Barcelona: Deusto.

Galve, C., and V. Salas. 2003. *La empresa familiar española.* Bilbao, Spain: Fundación BBVA.

Genescà, E., and V. Salas. 2007. La competitividad de la empresa catalana. In *Economía catalana: Retos de futuro,* ed. J. L. Escrivá, 275–292. Barcelona: Generalitat de Catalunya-FBBVA.

Goula, J. 2004. Fusiones y adquisiciones. Procesos rigurosamente analizados. *La Vanguardia* 26: 47–49.

Instituto de la Empresa Familiar. 1992–2004. *IEF.*

Hernández, A., and P. Fernández Pérez. 2008. Family firms and tax policies in Spain in the long run. Paper presented at the European Business History Conference, Bergen, Norway, 21–23 August.

James, H. 2006. *Family capitalism: Wendels, Haniels, Falcks and the continental European model.* Cambridge MA: Belknap Press.

Laguillo García-Bárcena, P. 2001. *Los Corrales de Buelna: Siglo XX.* Resumen Histórico. Santander, Spain: Excmo. Ayuntamiento de Los Corrales de Buelna.

Lavoie, D., and F. Chamlee-Wright. 2000. *Culture and enterprise: The development, representation and morality of business.* London: Routledge.

Martínez Fernández, M. C. 2004. La capacidad innovadora de las redes de desarrollo regional: El valor añadido de la colaboración, la competitividad y la difusión del conocimiento. *Información Comercial Española* 812:55–69.

Maskell, P., and M. Lorenz. 2003. The cluster and other current forms of market organisation. AEGIS Working Paper Series 2003/4, University of Western, Sydney.

MG (Fábrica Moreda y Gijón). 1954. *Fábrica Siderúrgica Moreda 1879–1954.* Bilbao, Spain: Editorial Vasca.

Ortega-Argilés, R., R. Moreno and J. Suriñach Caralt. 2004. Ownership structure and innovation: Is there a real link? *Documents de Treball de la Facultat de Ciències Econòmiques i Empresarials, Collecció d'Economia* (E04/111).

Ortiz-Villajos, J. M. 1999. *Tecnología y desarrollo económico en la historia contemporánea: Estudio de las patentes registradas en España entre 1882 y 1935.* Madrid: Oficina Española de Patentes y Marcas.

Puig Raposo, N., and P. Fernández Pérez. 2003. The education of Spanish entrepreneurs and managers: Madrid and Barcelona business schools 1950–1975. *Paedagogica Historica* 39 (5): 651–672.

Quijano, T. 1998. *125 Aniversario de Trefilerías Quijano, S.A. (1873–1998).* Cámara Oficial de Comercio, Industria y Navegación de Cantabria, Santander.

Roig, B., and V. Pou. 1975. *Bekaert SA. Documento de Trabajo núm. 465.* Barcelona: IESE.

Rothwell, R. 1994. Towards the fifth-generation innovation process. *International Marketing Review* 11 (1): 7–31.

Saiz, P. 2000. *Invención, patentes e innovación en España (1759–1878)*. Madrid: UAM.

Torres, E., ed. 2000. *Cien empresarios españoles del siglo XX*. Madrid, LID.

Ulijn, J., A. P. Nagel and W.-L. Tan. 2001. The impact of national, corporate and professional cultures on innovation: German and Dutch firms compared. Special issue on 'Innovation in an international context', *Journal of Enterprising Culture* 9 (1): 21–52.

Van Houtte, J., N. Maddens, R. Vandeputte, J. Deloof, L. Kympers, N. Maes, J. Meert and M. Naessens. 1992. *Bekaert 100. Développement économique dans le sud de la Flandre Occidentale*. Tielt, Belgium: Editions Lannoo and N.V. Bekaert.

6 Patterns of Innovation, Strategies and Structures in the Italian Chemical Industry, 1973–2003

Andrea Colli

INTRODUCTION: BROADENING (A BIT) THE CONCEPT OF INNOVATION

As theory recognized long time ago (Schumpeter 1934), innovation is a complex and articulated process, in which *product* innovation—that is, the introduction of new or improved goods—is only one aspect. Schumpeter mentioned other important 'areas' in which innovation takes place: methods of production (processes), supply sources, exploitation of new markets and, finally, organizational structures. The strong theoretical framework provided by the Austrian economist (Fagerberg 2005, 7–8) was able to shape the subsequent research in the field, which, however, tended to focus mainly on product and process innovation. In this way, entrepreneurs able to introduce new products or to innovate the process of production—inventing, for instance, new techniques capable of saving labour or enhancing energy productivity—have been commonly considered as 'Schumpeterian entrepreneurs', able to gain through their strategies a (temporarily) stable competitive advantage.

This powerful framework is however broad enough to include other innovative patterns, which are more specific but relevant as well, even if scarcely mentioned both in empirical research and in theory. New products can be generated, for instance, not only by a creative effort pursued by teams in laboratories or by individuals, but also by mixing well-established techniques with other, additional elements as, for instance, in the case of *services* (an analogue perspective, even if not exactly the same, is provided by von Tunzelmann and Acha 2005). 'Service' is, in its turn, a very broad conceptual category, which includes elements such as quickness in delivering, flexibility in producing and the capability to design, develop and adapt customer-oriented specific solutions (generally starting from general-purpose technologies), to maintain 'in stock' a wide range of specific-purpose products ready for use, as well as to be able to provide the customers themselves with the technologies and the knowledge necessary to utilize the products they need (e.g., machine tools). Service component(s) can be expected to include a relevant, and growing, proportion of the 'new' product value added; this explains why increasingly the most dynamic and 'innovative' firms are moving towards the inclusion of service contents into their products (von Hippel 2005, esp. Ch. 9).

This kind of innovation strategy has relevant, further implications. For instance, it makes it, if not obsolete, at least difficult to apply the well-established taxonomy of sectors and industries. In other words, by 'enlarging' the borders of its products to include tangible or intangible services, a single firm can go quite beyond its own industry 'boundaries' (with consequent and not negligible problems for the researcher). This approach to innovation is not typical of a single sector, or of high-tech/low-tech industries, or of the final or intermediate goods producers. It is adopted by *single* firms, or groups of firms (Porter 1979).

Second, the firms involved in this process of innovation have to reshape their whole organization, their competitive strategies and, in general, their capabilities and internal-learning processes in order to cope with the new 'products' designed. The service content, as a relevant proportion of the added value and a key asset in the market strategy of the firm, is a very *specific* resource that (as stressed by transaction-cost theory) has to be kept strictly under control (i.e., appropriated) by the firm itself. In other words, the production and development of the service content attached to the product are firm-specific, that is, are not easily (both for the customer and for the supplier itself) available on the market and have to be developed internally through an appropriate investment policy. Moreover very often the service content is also *customer specific*, and this implies for the customer the necessity to establish and maintain very close and stable relationships with the producer, giving it a secure competitive advantage.

A third, more general, effect is on the *process of innovation*, which becomes more complex and articulated. Product—and process—innovations *stricto sensu* cannot be enough to compete, in the absence of other innovations in the tangible and intangible components of the product itself. The innovation process is to be seen as a *multiple* one inside the firm, and its effectiveness is largely determined by the ability of the firm to carry on and improve all the processes of innovation. In some sense, even if not exactly, the process of innovation becomes *modular*; the final product is decomposable into different subsystems (e.g., physical parts, tangible services, intangible services), each one characterized by a specific innovative pattern (Baldwin and Clark 1997). The final effectiveness of the innovative policy, as well as the effect at a micro level on the firm's performance, is determined by the ability of the firm management's to carry on effectively the innovation process at each level. I try to summarize in Figure 6.1 this idea of *complex modular innovative product* (CMIP).

CMIPs: Size and Age of the Firm

Generally speaking, there is no reason for limiting this kind of innovative behaviour in respect of the *size* and of the organizational complexity of the firm. Experience, however, shows a close relationship between this kind of innovation strategy and defined dimensional features. Small or very small firms, which can be highly craft oriented, generally lack the necessary degree of integration and the necessary resources to sustain an effective innovation process like that just described. CMIPs are in this case the outcome of a collaborative process among separate independent small firms, each specializing in a single or a few phases of the production process. This is a situation which is quite common in areas such as the industrial districts, but which is extremely difficult to replicate outside them. Also, when industrial districts are considered, the service component of the added value, if outsourced, is not particularly relevant as a competitive tool. On the other side, overly large firms have a degree of rigidity and scale-oriented investments which rarely enable them to pursue innovative strategies like those here discussed. CMIPs can be probably more easily found in large organizations which succeed in adopting network-type fragmented structures (Bartlett and Goshal 1993) or in business groups made by medium-size independent entities.

As for size, it is possible to advance some hypotheses about the relationship between the CMIPs-based strategies and the life cycle of the firm, suggesting that the supply of additional products/services tends to increase with the age of the firm, for many reasons. First of all, a generational-entrepreneurial effect: first-generation entrepreneurs tend to be more committed to productive aspects. They often start their ventures making available very specific products for well-defined market niches and users, emphasizing cost-reducing strategies. The evolution of their products' content comes with the following generation of entrepreneurs, who start to make use of differentiated competitive tools. Second, the complex processes of innovation based upon services and intangibles occur more frequently in well-established companies with a long-standing knowledge of the market dynamics and of the users' needs.

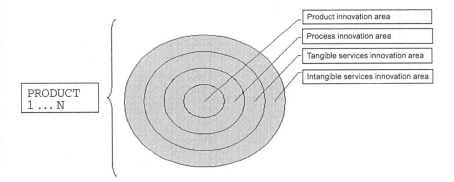

Figure 6.1 Product 1 N.

CMIPs: Final Demand and Design Process

As it is for all the *stricto sensu* products, the evolutionary patterns of the potential customers' needs are extremely relevant for CMIPs as well. Complex products made of physical and services components are very often *intermediate* goods required by other firms and not by final consumers. The nature and structure of the intermediate-goods production is obviously influenced by the evolutionary patterns in the final demand. In a situation of relative stability of the model of final consumption (e.g., a trend towards standardization), the user has fewer incentives to search for sophisticated intermediate products which are generally non-specific and quite easily found on the market at a cheap cost. However, a reverse situation can be found when users' needs start to become variable and to differentiate themselves, given a correspondent evolution in the final demand. This will probably have a direct effect on what von Hippel calls 'willingness to pay for new improvements' by the customers (2005, 40) and an incentive for entrepreneurs to invest in CMIPs. In this case, innovative patterns in products, processes and tangible/intangible improvements are heavily conditioned by the context provided by the final demand. The readiness of an entrepreneur to provide appropriate CMIPs or to update existing ones according to users' needs is a crucial and powerful competitive tool. In the same way, the extent to which CMIPs are introduced also depends on crucial innovations in the final markets, innovations which can obviously concern products, processes, design, marketing and so on. The crucial capability of the innovative entrepreneur is to provide the necessary CMIPs, but also to develop them looking at the same time at the evolution of the final-consumption market. This means that the intermediate producer is subject to innovative stimuli coming from two sources, directly from the user and from the final market as well.

I try to summarize this analysis in Figure 6.2

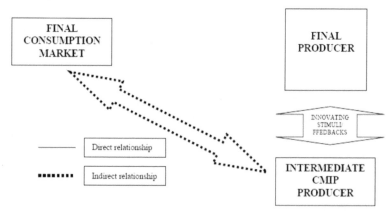

Figure 6.2 Final-consumption market.

Modular innovative intermediate products come from a vast array of sources, since the process of innovation in the way previously described can equally be performed by suppliers of raw materials and semi-finished goods, and also by machine-tool producers. A crucial notion is that evidence shows that the process of innovation is more efficient when information asymmetries between CMIPs users and producers are reduced—for instance, through co-design and continuous information flows. Borrowing from von Hippel,

> in the specific case of product development, this means that users as a class will tend to develop innovations that draw heavily on their own information about need and context of use. Similarly, manufacturers as a class will tend to develop innovations that draw heavily on the types of solutions information in which they specialized. (2005, 70)

A second key point is that the co-design activity reveals an important body of information and knowledge to CMIPs makers, mainly in the service-innovation area, information which it is possible to codify and use for different purposes (von Hippel 2005, Ch. 7).

In light of this framework, in the following sections of this chapter I examine the evolutionary patterns in the Italian chemical industry during the last three decades. This case study proves to be particularly interesting for many reasons. Taken as a whole, the Italian chemical industry is, for many reasons, characterized by a structural weakness in comparison to other advanced industrial countries. This weakness is revealed by a huge deficit in the foreign-trade balance, as well as by the absence of large-scale producers active on an international scale. Notwithstanding these deficiencies, some 'sub-sectors' show an above-average performance level in terms of innovative activity, profits and returns, sales and international activity in well-defined production niches. A large number of firms in these 'sub-sectors' are medium-sized producers of intermediate goods and develop innovative solutions for their customers through a process which is modular in the way previously described, with abnormal results, as said, in terms of performance. This chapter investigates the dynamics of this innovative activity through extensive use of a vast number of case studies. The analysis, however, goes beyond the study of innovation processes, examining also the strategies and structures at a firm's level to understand the links with the specific patterns of innovation. In paragraph two, I provide a brief account of the recent history of the Italian chemical industry. Paragraph three deals with strategies, structures, patterns of innovation and performances at a micro level. In a fourth, conclusions are drawn.

THE EVOLUTION OF THE CHEMICAL INDUSTRY IN ITALY (1970s–2000)

Taken as a whole, the Italian chemical industry has shown a steady decline, in both the internal and international markets. The standing of the largest

Italian chemical corporations has been constantly declining, directly affecting the trade balance, which is today almost negative (nearly 8.5 billion euros in 2002), mainly due to raw chemicals. The decline has also affected the employment levels: the number of employees in chemical sector decreased from 171,000 in 1991 to nearly 134,000 in 2001.

In a recent article Vera Zamagni (2006) analyzes what can be labelled the 'rise and fall' of the Italian chemical industry. Zamagni identifies two main structural causes for the decline of the sector. First of all, during the 'economic miracle' (in the 1950s and 1960s), mainly due to political reasons, a strategy of expansion of the industry based upon the building of as many petrochemical plants as possible took place. Both state-owned and private groups (which enjoyed the financial support of the state) were involved in this strategy which was undertaken without planning and coordination. All this emphasized the weaknesses of the whole sector which became apparent later, during the oil crisis. Second, an entrepreneurial failure took place during the 1980s, when Montedison, the largest Italian chemical company, failed to unify the Italian chemical industry under its control after having unsuccessfully merged with the chemical activities of ENI (Enichem), creating Enimont (Lanzavecchia, Saviotti and Soru 1996).

The Present Structure of the Italian Chemical Industry

The crisis of the major corporations during the last ten years has fostered the diminution of the concentration rate, which was historically low in comparison with that of other industrialized countries. The Italian chemical industry is today dominated by small and medium enterprises to a greater extent than in the other European countries, and more than elsewhere the large dimension is lacking. Defining as 'small' firms with 10 to 99 employees and 'medium sized' those with 100 up to 250 employees, the situation which emerges is that depicted in Tables 6.2 and 6.3.

The small- (and also medium-) sized firm is anyway diffused among the chemical industries of all the European countries, confirming the global trend towards the reduction of the firm's average size. This is

Table 6.1 Trade Balances of Chemical Products (bln Euros)

	Germany	France	UK	Belgium	Netherl.	Italy	EU	Japan	USA
1980	8.3	1.8	3.2	2.2	3.7	-2.2	26.4	0.4	8.7
1998	24.2	7.8	6.5	7.5	9.0	-7.8	41.2	5.7	12.0
*1985									

Source: CEFIC, National Statistics; the table is borrowed from Zamagni 2007.

Table 6.2 Number of Enterprises in the Chemical and Pharmaceutical Sectors in Various European Countries, by Employees

	Germany	France	Italy	UK	EU 15
10–19	422	351	833	428	3211
20–99	689	727	906	639	4666
100–249	289	257	219	232	1466
SME	1400	1335	1958	1299	9343
250–499	132	127	67	124	697
>500	164	126	69	102	621
TOTAL	1696	1588	2094	1525	10661

Source: Eurostat, SBS database (year 2000).

Table 6.3 Distribution of the Workforce in the Chemical Sector, by Size of the Firm

	Germany	France	Italy	UK	EU 15
10–19	2.3	3.7	11.9	5.8	5.6
20–99	7.0	11.8	18.8	12.1	12.7
100–249	9.0	14.1	17.2	14.5	13.7
SME	18.3	29.6	47.8	32.4	31.9
250–499	9.3	16.0	11.5	17.2	14.3
>500	72.4	54.4	40.6	50.4	53.7
TOTAL	100.0	100.0	100.0	100.0	100.0

Source: Eurostat, SBS database (year 2000).

only partially due to technological evolution; in general, the small and medium scale of production means a specialization in some sub-sector characterized by a very differentiated final market of consumption, mainly 'specialized' chemical products and specialties (industrial gases, paints, special inks, glues and adhesives, phytotherapics, detergents and cosmetics) where the scale effect is less important. This effect is obviously relevant in the Italian case as well (last column of table 6.4).

According to the last census data (2001), small- and medium-sized enterprises account for a significant proportion of the production value, added value and other indicators. They also confirm the relevance of the specialized subsectors (Table 6.5).

During the last twenty-five years, in sum, a double dynamic affected the industry as a whole: on the one side, a growing relevance of specialties and

Table 6.4 Workforce Distribution (%) in the Italian Chemical Industry

	1–99	100–249	SMEs	250–499	500 and over	Total
Chemical Industry	**84.7**	**66.6**	**78.2**	**65.1**	**51.2**	**65.7**
Raw Chemicals	20.4	25.4	**22.2**	22.5	30.7	25.7
Fibers	2.0	1.8	**2.0**	12.5	4.6	4.3
Specialties:	62.2	39.4	**54.0**	30.0	15.9	35.7
Paints, Adhesives and inks	17.5	10.4	**14.9**	9.0	3.1	9.5
Detergents and cosmetics	19.5	11.0	**16.4**	12.4	7.1	12.2
Phytotherapics	1.6	1.6	**1.6**	1.2	0.7	1.2
Other chemical prod.	23.6	16.4	**21.0**	7.4	4.9	12.9
Pharmaceuticals	**15.3**	**33.4**	**21.8**	**34.9**	**48.8**	**34.3**
Chemicals and Pharmac.	*100.0*	*100.0*	*100.0*	*100.0*	*100.0*	*100.0*

Source: ISTAT Instituto Nazionde Di Statistica (year 2004).

Table 6.5 Relevance of the SME (up to 250 employees) in the Italian Chemical Industry.

	Production Value (%)	Added Value (%)	Gross Margin (%)	Investments (%)	Workers (%)
Chemical Industry	**46.8**	**50.1**	**52.7**	**39.3**	**56.9**
Raw chemicals and fibers	31.2	35.3	38.7	20.4	38.6
Others, of which:	63.9	63.2	64.7	75.6	72.3
Paints, adhesives and inks	71.7	69.5	71.6	86.4	75.5
Detergents and cosmetics	50.8	50.1	50.6	54.7	64.6
Other chemical products	72.0	72.2	76.7	81.1	76.8
Pharmaceuticals	**26.4**	**26.3**	**29.2**	**39.5**	**30.4**
Chemicals and Pharmac.	*40.9*	*40.6*	*44.1*	*39.3*	*47.8*

Source: Census 2000.

final products such as paints and cosmetics (rising from 28.1 percent of the total employment in the chemical industry in 1981 to the 38.2 percent in 2001), which are also the sole sub-sectors with a slightly positive trade balance and the only ones which succeeded in increasing the Italian market share in the European Union in the period from 1998 to 2002.

On the other side, the growing importance of small- and medium-size enterprises: in 2001 the firms with less than 250 employees accounted for nearly 60 percent of the total employment of the chemical industry (this percentage was about 44 percent ten years before), gaining in ten years about 4,000 employees in absolute terms. The size classes mostly responsible for the decline were those from 250 to 499 employees and, above all, that over 500 employees, which alone lost nearly 33,000 employees in the period between 1991 and 2001.

A third, relevant characteristic is the role played by the foreign-controlled firms. According to the data recently published by the National Census (ISTAT 2004, 176–178), at the beginning of the new millennium foreign firms accounted for 44 percent of the industry's total workforce, 50 percent of the total sales and an outstanding 55.5 percent of the total value added. A relevant feature of the foreign investment in the chemical sector is the tendency to cluster in the medium- and above all large-size class. Foreign firms are comparatively bigger than the Italian ones (this is a situation which is similar to other capital intensive industries). Not so easy to analyze is the role of foreign capital in the long period, even if some evidence is available. For instance, from 1985 to 1995 the number of foreign chemical firms present among the top two hundred Italian corporations rose from 10 to 14, the workforce employed from 14,500 to over 19,000, and the percentage of total sales of the top two hundred Italian corporations increased from 10 to 14 percent. As can be expected, the crisis in the Italian chemical industry brought about a further consolidation of the foreign presence, which remained mainly clustered in raw chemicals and pharmaceuticals, confirming a trend started during the 1960s.

Less easy to understand is the relationship between the presence of the foreign capital and the nature, structure and evolution of the national SMEs in the chemical industry. In the absence of a systematic exploration, only some hypotheses can be suggested. First of all, the presence of foreign multinationals was (and this is confirmed by the qualitative evidence deriving from interviews with some practitioners) a strong incentive to specialization. As a corollary of this, the national SMEs tended from the beginning to emphasize non-price competition and to develop niche productions with a high service content. Entrepreneurs learned from the beginning to specialize as the sole way of surviving in these market conditions. This effect, which was mainly indirect, was associated with another, namely, the fact than some of the new, specialized ventures were actually spin-offs from the main corporations, both national and foreign.

Third, the presence of foreign firms was a strong incentive for national entrepreneurs to update their know-how. Even if this is very difficult to demonstrate, there is some evidence of at least two ways in which this knowledge diffusion took place. First of all, some of the specialized firms were involved in some form of collaboration (through joint ventures) with the largest ones, the most common of which was that the former commercialized some of the latter's products alongside their own. Second, when the founders had been salesmen or had some technical role *inside* a large multinational firm during the start-up phase (and later), they maintained in general some relationship with the 'parent' firm, and above all with a network of colleagues which facilitated the flow of information.

In synthesis, in nearly a quarter of a century the Italian chemical sector has been increasingly dominated by dynamic small- and medium-size specialized firms adopting niche-oriented strategies and very active in the international markets. These firms show a degree of dynamism which exceeds the average of the industry, with better results in economic and financial terms, as for employment levels as well.

An important point which has to be stressed is that the growing relevance of medium, specialized and internationalized firms is common to other Italian sectors and is a part of a more general evolutionary trend in the country's industrial demography, due mainly to the decline of the 'small firm economy' of the industrial districts occurring for two reasons. The first one is the decline in the competitiveness of Italian exports due to a currency effect. The rise in the export trade of products made in Italy, achieved by frequent devaluations of the currency and a favourable exchange rate, could not longer be sustained with the introduction of the euro. A more 'structural' cause is the (often unfair) competition of very recently industrialized countries, such as China and other Far East economies.

This situation has renewed a never-ending debate on the industrial decline of the country, essentially stressing the lack of entrepreneurship and investment, especially in technological and research-intensive industries. Many commentators focussed their attention on the failure of the 'modern' industries in Italy—that is, consumer electronics, computers, chemicals and energy—due both to entrepreneurial reasons as well as to the lack of suitable economic policies, and forecast the future industrial decline of the country. According to a different analysis, the manufacturing sector is transforming its structure into something different (and maybe more balanced) than was the case in the past.

MICRO-LEVEL ANALYSIS: PERFORMANCE, STRATEGIES AND STRUCTURES

Performance and profitability

According to a very recent research study, the small- and medium-sized enterprises in the Italian chemical industry show a better performance (in terms of profitability) than the average of the manufacturing sector. In a European comparison, the specialized Italian chemical companies were able to generate higher margins than their E.U. counterparts, while their relative weakness in terms of value added reflected their specialization in non-raw chemicals (see Table 6.6).

Table 6.6 Added Value and Profitability in the Italian Chemical Industry

	Gross Margin/ Added Value (%)		AV/worker (000)	
	Italy	Europe	Italy	Europe
1–99	54.3	45.7	57.9	59.2
100–249	44.1	39.4	73.6	73.3
SME	50.6	42.9	62.7	64.7
250–499	39.8	46.8	72.3	90.0
>500	47.3	36.7	86.4	89.5
TOTAL CHEMICALS	48.1	40.0	71.3	80.9
Raw chemicals and fibers	47.2	40.7	73.6	90.3
Others of which	49.0	39.0	69.4	71.9
Specialties	45.7	38.0	65.2	72.3
Chemicals for consumption	54.3	40.7	77.6	71.2
Pharmaceuticals	42.4	44.5	90.1	96.9
Chemicals and Pharmaceuticals	*45.8*	*41.4*	*77.7*	*85.4*

Source: Federchimica (Italian Federation of the Chemical Industries); Istat 2004, Eurostat.

Looking Inside

But where does this structure come from, who are the actors and what are their strategies? Moving to a qualitative level of analysis, the researcher notes two elements. The first is the variety and fragmentation of the sub-sector niches in which the Italian chemical industry can be disaggregated, from fibres to coatings and paint, from phytotherapics to intermediate productions for pharmaceutical industry and many others. Each niche is composed by hundreds of different products, sold on the international markets.

The second is that, even if the presence of many small firms is important in absolute terms, these niches are characterized by the presence of a number of medium-sized corporations (with total sales from 100 to 400 million euros), which occupy the next place in the national ranking just after the main integrated and diversified groups in basic chemicals.

In these and several other cases, an aggregative perspective (sector level) seems to be scarcely adequate to give a full account of the success of these medium-sized companies, which can be better understood by adopting a 'micro' perspective focussed upon the single actors' evolution.

The growing importance of the *Mittelstand* in the Italian economy is not limited to the chemical industry. Medium-sized, international-ized companies, specialized producers often relying on a wide network of sub-contractors, are now present in several sectors, mainly in those where Italy shows a strong and enduring leadership on the world market. 'Pocket multinationals' can be found in clothing and textiles, footwear, light mechanics, food, jewellery, tiles and ceramics and many other 'Made in Italy' sectors.

The aim of this chapter is to analyze the nature and the structure of these medium-sized companies in the chemical industry in comparison

Table 6.7 The Main Italian Chemical Companies, 2002

Company Name	Main activity	Sales, Euro /000	Rank among the main Italian companies	Workers
ENICHEM (Syndial)	BASIC CHEMICALS	4762000	N.A.	12154
POLIMERI EUROPA	BASIC CHEMICALS	1457063	65	1457
RADICI GROUP	FIBRES, DIVERSIFIED	1423130	67	8604
GRUPPO SNIA	FIBRES, DIVERSIFIED	957164	104	5638
M&G FINAZIARIA	PLASTICS, PET, PVC	943054	108	1069
MAPEI	ADHESIVES	583130	176	2646
MONTEFIBRE	FIBRES	529867	201	1745
COIM	PVC PRODUCTS	385000	N.A.	N.A.
AQUAFIL	FIBRES	335770	N.A.	2412
ACS DOBFAR	INTERMEDIATE PHARMAC.	254403	N.A.	759
LAMBERTI	SPECIAL CHEMICALS	292475	367	1052
IVM GROUP	PAINTS FOR WOOD	275000	N.A.	N.A.
SOL GROUP	INDUSTRIAL GASES	235731	444	1180
SIPCAM OXON	PHYTOTHERAPICS	166857	599	519
INDENA	INTERMEDIATE PHARMAC.	156709	632	886
COLOROBBIA	PIGMENTS FOR CERAMICS	105139	865	325
LECHLER	PAINTS	98500	N.A.	N.A.
BOERO	COATINGS	86435	988	363
ISAGRO	PHYTOTHERAPICS	80545	1038	741
INVER	SPECIAL COATINGS	56965	1295	249

Source: Mediobanca, *Le principali società italiane 2002* and *Federchimica, Annual Report.*

with those present in other sectors.[1] This can be done by adopting a methodology of analysis which focuses upon the single cases in a historical and comparative perspective.

Evolution

According to the available evidence, the emerging companies in the Italian chemical industry have a relatively consistent history. The only recent start-up is Isagro (phytotherapics), founded through a Management Buy Out (MBO) in 1993. Before this date, however, Isagro was a division of Montedison, the largest Italian chemical company, so that also in this case the history of the company dates back to the immediate post-war period. The foundation of Acs Dobfar (intermediate products for the pharmaceutical industry) took place at the beginning of the 1970s. Anyway, also in this case the entrepreneurial activity originated from a spin-off. In all the other cases, the origin of the company goes back to the inter-war period, or immediately after the Second World War. Frequently there were spin-offs—for example, sometimes, in the case of COIM (polyurethane) or Sipcam-Oxom (phytotherapics), the initiative was taken by technicians who decided to became independent and associated themselves with other people with commercial skills. In general, looking at the histories of these companies it is possible to identify three phases of growth: (1) during the late 1950s and the 1960s, (2) in the second half of the 1970s and (3) starting from the 1990s.

As far as marketing and production techniques are concerned, from the beginning differentiation, specialization and niche strategies prevailed. In many cases these firms started as spin-offs and their founders were well aware that it was necessary to differentiate their products from those of the 'mother' firm to survive. Working as laboratory technicians as well as commercial agents they also became conscious of the availability of a wide range of intermediate and finished goods for particular purposes and of the fact that there was a huge potential market for specialties (see next). In other cases the firm was from the beginning concerned with the supply of specialized products for large industries. In the case of SOL (oxygen and other gases for industrial uses) the main customers were from the 1950s onwards the main steelworks and the firm specialized in building facilities and pipelines near their main customers.

This process also took the form of an 'unconscious' differentiation policy by adding value to the supply mainly through close contact with the final customer (customization and tailored production). One striking point in all these company histories is that the development of an efficient network of selling agents was a relevant part of the competitive strategy from the very beginning. This point is extremely important since the same strategy was replicated during the internationalization process which in general took place during the second half of the 1970s, when the enterprises began to enlarge the scale of their activities and consolidate their presence on the world market using the same strategies employed in Italy, that is, differentiation and customization of their products.

The Production Strategy: What Do They Do?

The policies of production specialization developed as competitive strategies over time and, especially during the last thirty years, more and more consciously. From the 1970s onwards, in fact, independently from the typology of the product, it is possible to discern a process of focusing the activity of these firms, which increasingly specialized in the supply of 'families' of goods (sometimes 'large families', with catalogues made up of several thousands of items) aimed at satisfying every aspect of a particular market. This is, for instance, the case of ink and paint producers: the IVM group specialized in the production of paints for wooden products; Boero in coatings for the shipping industries; Lechler in coatings for automotives; and Inver in special paints for the mechanical industry. In the case of intermediates for the pharmaceutical industry, IdB Group has specialized in the production of every kind of natural intermediates obtained from plants and vegetables, while Sicor produces a wide range of intermediate principles for antithumorals. In the case of Mapei, which is committed to the production of adhesives for the building industry, there are more than six thousand products aimed at covering almost every necessity of the market. It is anyway important to note that this process of specialization has accelerated during the last fifteen/twenty years also under the pressure of the main competitors (namely, the largest multinationals) which themselves started a strategy of product differentiation.

The strategy of specialization has been carried out not only through a 'deepening' of the niches—this has gone side by side with a transformation of the concept of product itself, which has been progressively embedding immaterial components and services for the customer. In all the cases considered, the emphasis on the productive side of the competitive strategy (i.e., to develop a niche production free from pressure by the main competitors through production and process innovation) has been associated with the development of an ever-closer relationship between the enterprise and its customers culminating in the production of on-demand specific chemical products. In the case of producers of pharmaceutical intermediates, this has increasingly been the preferred strategy, while it seems to be less important (even if not irrelevant) in the case of, say, producers of paints and coatings.

Over time all this has had an important effect on the internal and organizational structure of the enterprise.

First a growing emphasis has been put on the sales network and on the formation of skilled human capital able to perceive and immediately transmit the changes in demand. Second, the flexible organizational structure of these middle-sized enterprises plays an important role, especially with regard to the nature of the innovation process. The specialization and niche strategies are consistent with a flexible organizational structure in which decisions have to be taken very quickly.

Third, corporate forms aimed at emphasizing the collaborative perspective and custom orientation are often developed, as for instance joint ventures, while common features are network arrangements and a close relationship with institutions such as universities and technical institutes.

Contexts of Production

Given their size and organizational structures, these enterprises are heavily influenced by the context—or better, the *contexts*—in which their activity takes place.

Even if the innovative chemical firms tend to concentrate their headquarters and the most important production facilities in the northwestern area of the country (about 50 percent of the industry workers are employed in Piedmont, Liguria and Lombardy), it is not possible to talk of an 'industrial district' for chemicals, given the typology of the production process (based upon high-throughput flows) and the nature of the production unit (integrated).

Anyway, the majority of these firms have a history of long-standing relationships with the industrial districts and local production systems. 'Made in Italy' products—from textiles to footwear, from furniture to machine tools, from ceramics and tiles to other household goods—are sometimes largely dependent on chemicals to differentiate their products. Maybe the most significant is the case of Mapei, which during the 1960s and the 1970s developed a close relationship with the tile producers located in Sassuolo (near Modena, in the Emilia Romagna region), even if its headquarters and production facilities remained in Milan. The learning paths of many of these firms are closely linked to the needs expressed by the districts' producers, who in turn perceive the change in market demand. This is, for instance, the case of COIM, which produces polyurethane soles for almost all the footwear districts of the country and frames for the ski-boot manufacturers clustered in Montebelluna (in the alpine area of the Venetian region); as well as that of the Radici Group in Bergamo, which sells fibres to the stocking producers located in Castelgoffredo, near Mantua, in Lombardy. The relationship with the small firms of the industrial districts sometimes drives the process of innovation in terms of products. The link with local systems of production proves to be strategic, especially in the early phases of the activity, providing an initial amount of marketing and technical knowledge. In the following period—mainly from the 1980s onwards—however, the relationship with local production systems started to evolve due to the acceleration of the *internationalization process.*

With very few exceptions, the internationalization process started in the second half of the 1970s. The flow of exports was almost immediately replaced by the opening of selling agencies abroad. This was an important precursor to the next step, which was during the 1990s an increasing multinational activity culminating in the opening of production facilities both on the eastern Europe and Asian markets. In general these initiatives are not taken, as happens in other sectors (e.g., textiles), to enjoy localization advantages such as, for instance, low labour costs. The internationalization process is linked to other variables—for instance, transport costs (this is, for instance, the case of Mapei), or alternatively the fact that the main customer (a steelwork in the case of Sol) started to produce abroad. As previously stressed, however, both the process of internationalization and the decision to invest abroad tends to replicate the strategy of focalization, specialization and deepening of the niches refined on the internal market.

How Do They Do

At a micro-economic level the organizational and ownership structure of the firm, notwithstanding the specificity of the industry concerned, seems not to be radically different from that characterizing other enterprises in other sectors which are part of the Italian *Mittelstand.* Moreover, some organizational features—such as, for instance, family ownership—seem to be consistent with the kind of competitive advantage which these firms can enjoy given the possibility of taking quick decisions in a lean and flexible context. Notwithstanding the rapid growth experienced in the last few years in terms of turnover, employees and number of subsidiaries both in Italy and abroad, almost all these companies are directly owned by the founding families whose members are also in key managerial positions. This is reflected in a financial structure which is based mainly on self-financing—given not negligible returns on investments and equities—with a limited access to financial markets and above all to the stock exchange (in the very rare case of a listing, however, the floating capital is at a very low level).

CONCLUDING REMARKS: CMIPS AND THE COMPETITIVE ADVANTAGE OF THE ITALIAN CHEMICAL INDUSTRY: IMPLICATIONS FOR FURTHER RESEARCH

In a pamphlet recently published and titled *Il declino dell'Italia industriale (The decline of the Italian industry),* the sociologist Luciano Gallino analyzes and comments on the crisis in Italian big business in several sectors, from energy to mechanics, to air transportation. The chemical industry is considered by Gallino to be one of the most relevant failures since the activities in basic chemicals represented once by Montedison and Enichem are now reduced in their relevance and are going to be sold or closed. As seen already, these poor results are reflected in a growing deficit in the sector's trade balance. However, the case of these 'pocket multinationals' shows the vitality of some branches of the industry, a vitality which is countered by the decline in the basic chemicals. As is happening to other industrial sectors, the decline of large firms is leaving room for middle-sized internationalized firms which tend to replicate, on a larger scale and with a stronger tendency towards internationalization, the flexibility and custom orientation typical of the small-firm model characterizing the Italian experience.

In synthesis, three are the main sources of this competitive advantage: (1) specialization, (2) internationalization and (3) innovation. This chapter has tried to demonstrate that the origins of the present competitive advantage are firmly rooted in these firms' past history.

Specialization (i.e., coverage of almost every aspect of a niche of production) was from the very beginning of the life of these enterprises a strategy pursued to survive cost competition. Specialization involves intense cooperation with customers as well as a high rate of innovation.

R&D and *innovation* were in this way from the beginning conceived as among the most important strategic functions. Formal and informal R&D serve product and also process innovation. Often, the innovation of the production process is carried out by means of in-house built machinery.

The specialization and innovation strategy of focalization creates a strong competitive advantage. The national market was, however, too small to fully enjoy the advantages of scale, scope and distribution, so that after a certain point a process of *internationalization* took place which culminated in the realization of foreign direct investments at the beginning of the 1990s.

Innovation, specialization and internationalization are behaviours, or strategies, which are adopted by the firms to very different extents. A general and common characteristic is, however, the fact that these competitive behaviours are based on a wide array of CMIPs developed by the firms through dynamic and complex innovative strategies which frequently include the appropriation of some knowledge base from the customers. The impression—which at this stage is to be corroborated by further research—is that the innovative patterns in which the enterprises are involved (and which give them a considerable advantage in terms of dynamism, growth and competitive strength) are to be seen as the result of an exchange of knowledge between the innovative firm itself and the customer. The innovative behaviour, in this specific case, takes the form of a (partially) open process involving at least two subjects, and the 'Schumpeterian' process of creation mainly concerns the ability of the producer to maximize the efficiency of knowledge flow by incorporating them in CMIPs.

Just as a final word, this is a tale of transformation more than a story of decline. The crisis of the 'traditional' chemical industry has brought some other actors to emerge, whose dynamism and competitiveness are the result of a complex historical process of evolution. Another relevant point to stress is that these enterprises in general participate in articulated networks of cooperation among firms of different sizes, active in different sectors of the manufacturing industry. The sectoral linkage becomes in this way more articulated and flexible thanks also to the enhancement of interdependencies which are essential for the welfare of the whole national economy.

NOTES

1. According to the available research, and also taking into account the international perspective, a medium-sized company in the chemical industry can be considered one with total sales from 100 to 500 million euros. In this qualitative study also the case of M&G Finanziaria is taken into account since the growth in the size of turnover, which now is about 1 billion euros, is very recent.

REFERENCES

Baldwin, C. Y., and K. B. Clark. 1997. Managing in an age of modularity. *Harvard Business Review* 8 (4): 576–587.

Bartlett, C. A., and S. Goshal. 1993. Beyond the M-form: Toward a managerial theory of the firm. *Strategic Management Journal* 14 (Winter): 23–46.

Fagerberg, J. 2005. Innovation: A guide to the literature. In *The Oxford handbook of innovation*, ed. J. Fagerberg, D. C. Movery and R. R. Nelson, 1–26. Oxford: Oxford University Press.

Federchimica. 2003. *L'industria chimica in Italia: Rapporto 2002–2003*. Milan: Federchimica.

ISTAT. 2004. *Rapporto sulla situazione economica del Paese 2003: 176*. Rome: ISTAT.

Lanzavecchia, P., G. Saviotti and A. Soru. 1996. *La Montecatini-Montedison e l'industria chimica italiana*. Chapter 6 of *L'evoluzione delle industrie ad alta tecnologia in Italia*, ed. C. Bussolati, F. Malerba and S. Torrisi. Bologna: Il Mulino.

Mediobanca. 2003. *Le principali società italiane (2002)*. Milano: Mediobanca.

Porter, M. 1979. The structure within industries and companies' performance. *Review of Economics and Statistics* 61 (2): 214–227.

Schumpeter, J. A. 1934. *The theory of economic development*. Cambridge: Cambridge University Press.

von Hippel, E. 2005. *Democratizing innovation*. Cambridge, MA: MIT Press.

von Tunzelmann, N., and V. Acha. 2005. Innovation in low-tech industries. In *The Oxford handbook of innovation*, ed. J. Fagerberg, D. C. Movery and R. R. Nelson, 407–432. Oxford: Oxford University Press.

Zamagni, V. 2007. The rise and fall of the Italian chemical industry, 1950–1990. In *The global chemical industry in the age of petrochemical revolution*, ed. L. Galambos, T. Hikino and V. Zamagni, 347–367. Cambridge: Cambridge University Press. 2006

7 Competitive Behaviour and Business Innovations in the Forestry Industry

Family Firms and Listed Firms in Comparison

Jari Ojala, Juha-Antti Lamberg and Anders Melander

INTRODUCTION: BUSINESS INNOVATIONS AND OWNERSHIP STRUCTURE

In the literature originating from the Carnegie-school tradition (e.g., Cyert and March 1963), company behaviour has been defined as 'innovative if it differs significantly from current or recent activities' (Greve and Taylor 2000, 55). An evolutionary perspective on company behaviour assumes that the usual way firms evolve is via incremental changes in the routines and procedures which eventually cause systemic changes over relatively lengthy periods of time (Nelson and Winter 1982). Recently, both evolutionary (Augier and Teece 2006) and behavioural (Becker, Knudsen and March 2006) researchers have suggested that the entrepreneurial acts of individual actors may also be a source of novelty. Indeed, as Winter suggests, a historical account of a firm means that 'the existence of a multiplicity of unobservable factors that shape firm behaviour would be explicitly recognized' ([1968] 2006, 140).

A related question is the influence of the ownership structure (Williamson 1985) of a firm. For example, in strategic management (Mintzberg and Waters 1982) it has been assumed that some firms are per se more 'novelty driven' than large organizations, which rely heavily on formal planning and other types of bureaucracy. According to Mintzberg, family firms or other types of organizations in which the power is centralized and which have a lean organizational structure tend to adopt more novel strategies than larger systems. Also, according to the standard Schumpeterian (Schumpeter 1947) assumption, business innovations by definition emerge as a result of firm heterogeneity. This said, it is often assumed that this should be the case, at least to a certain extent, with family firms, which are often (but not always) regarded as 'entrepreneurial' by comparison with listed firms (Kreiser et al. 2006).

Despite the increasing number of claims that firms are different in terms of their level of novelty, the literature is silent about the actual impact of the ownership structure. Especially, we have only a scattered knowledge of business innovations, in particular those that are not necessarily technical in nature. In business history, too, Chandler's (1990) view that only large corporations are able to adopt the complicated marketing and organizational structures required by the modern economy can be criticized. Thus there is an urgent need to study firms in their historical contexts with the aim of finding similarities and differences vis-à-vis their ownership structures. Thus the purpose of this chapter is to investigate whether management in family firms is more innovative than in other ownership structures and how the level of novelty may be analyzed.

As strategic-management researchers have suggested, the actions realized by firms over time eventually build their competitive position and thus lead to a certain level of business performance. Mintzberg, for example, defines strategy as a pattern of actions: strategies emerge through activity in time rather than in the structural properties of a firm. Following Miller and Chen, we use 'action' to mean a specific and observable competitive move, such as the introduction of a new product, an advertising campaign, or price cut, initiated by a firm to improve or defend its relative competitive position. (1994)

Thus the nature and content of actions can be seen as a fundamental building block in company history. With regard to the level of innovation (Baden-Fuller 1995), we suggest that an operational difference be made between strategic actions that aim to follow rivals in the industry (catch-up actions) and business innovations. Catch-up actions, even though they are strategic for the individual company, are often of a second-best nature as the industry leaders are already moving on. Business innovations are, on the other hand, strategic actions that force rivals to make costly responses. Business innovations thus break boundaries and introduce new ideas in the industry. If successful, a business innovation will pave the way for future successes, that is, industry leadership, but failure can be equally important as an indicator of the innovative character of the organization. Business innovations thus incorporate the two dominant characteristics of entrepreneurial behaviour: pro-activeness and risk taking.

In this chapter, we identify strategic actions on the level of the individual company and compare patterns on the group level. This analysis is to be seen as the input for analyses at the next level, in which we aim to identify actions that can be classified as business innovations. The object of our empirical research is the forestry industry. The forestry-industry sector represents a group of relatively mature, large-scale industries that have gradually become 'more global' during the last couple of decades. Over the long term, the forestry industries have been one of the fastest growing lines of business. Since 1950, the average annual growth of the paper industry has been around 4 percent. For example, the growth exceeded GDP growth in Europe during the last decades of the twentieth century and grew three times faster than in the manufacturing industries on average (Diesen 1998; Huolman 1992; Lamberg and Ojala 2006; Rytkönen 2000).

CONCEPTUAL BACKGROUND

In the literature on strategic management, the governance structure has been seen as an important factor determining firms' responses in terms of business activities and thus, potentially, innovations. In the research tradition originating from Mintzberg's work ([1973] 1980, 1987, 1994), different governance structures are seen to have a tendency to emphasize different aspects in decision making. It is important to note that this kind of perspective can help researchers make sense of the complexity of the modern world. As Miller has emphasized,

> [Configurations] . . . are not intended to be exhaustive but merely illustrative of important relationships . . . one can begin to identify some central themes that orchestrate the alignment among a great many variables of strategy and structure. (1986, 505)

Thus the firms in this study are seen as a comprehensive set of structures and systems incorporating a particular way of taking stock of the organizational environment and making decisions. Hence, the underlying assumption is that different governance structures may include certain mental models that are by and large comparable in similarly structured organizations. Using Mintzberg's typology, the two most relevant firm types are the entrepreneurial and the diversified organization.

In this study investigating the link between ownership structure and business innovations, the basic assumption is that business innovations are more or less likely to occur as a result of the ownership structure. This implies that there is a link between ownership, strategic actions and business innovation. Consequently, our definition of family firms focuses on control and the opportunity to exercise this control. This control can be exercised by the owners either as 'outsiders' (for instance, as board members) or as managers involved in the daily running of the company. Hence, we define a family business as one in which the family is in control and wishes to retain this control (Chua, Chrisman and Sharma 1999).

Much attention has been paid to defining the family business in the relevant literature. Numerous different definitions still exist, which makes it more important than ever to state explicitly the definition that one is applying (Hall 2003). The definitions used range from those stating that a company is a family firm when the family has a voting control of the company to those in which it is stated that the company must be run by the family, with multiple generations being involved in its day-to-day operations (Sharma, Chrisman and Chua 1997).

It has been argued that an inherited business creates complacency and conservatism and delays the adoption of efficient administrative and organizational structures (Chandler 1977, 1990; Nicholas 1999). Family firms are accused of suffering from several disadvantages compared to listed companies. The limited-ownership structure constricts their growth capabilities. Although family firms may be dynamic in the beginning, they cannot grow as fast as listed companies because of financial factors. The willingness of the family members to invest more capital in the company may diminish when their family grows in size, and thus the owners are no longer able to involve themselves in the daily affairs of the company. A change of leadership is always problematic in industrial enterprises, but it is especially difficult in family firms, as the number of possible managerial candidates is relatively low if the manager can only be chosen from the immediate family or kin. Nepotism and, related to it, conflicts within the family are among the worst problems in family firms (Casson 1993; Rose 1993).

On the other hand, family firms are often described as having a number of advantages. The entrepreneurial attitude towards business activities is a breeding ground for dynamic, innovative behaviour in Schumpeterian terms (Casson 1982). However, while entrepreneurial management diminishes bureaucratic structures, it may also cause difficulties by disorganizing the modes of operation. In family firms, the needs of the family and firm are partly overlapping: what is good for the family is good for the business and vice versa (Hall 2003). Thus the owners' commitment to the company is typically much tighter than in other forms of enterprise. This is crucial in terms of their willingness to overcome crisis situations. The definition of family firms as entrepreneurial organizations, however, is rather simplistic and misleading. Although family firms may have characteristics typical of entrepreneurial organizations (such as innovativeness, risk taking and proactiveness), they are also quite often associated with rather non-entrepreneurial values, such as financial conservatism, security and family control over the firm (Hall, Melin and Nordqvist 2001; Kreiser et al. 2006).

On the basis of the preceding discussion, we can state our purpose in this chapter as follows:

1. To examine to what extent family firms as a group differ from listed firms in their competitive behaviour (strategic actions).
2. To study how identified differences in actions can be related to the level of business innovation in family firms and listed firms.

SAMPLE AND METHOD

Our sample consists of nineteen Swedish and Finnish forestry-industry firms (Table 7.1), all engaged in various branches of the sector, though during the last decades of the study most notably the paper industry. Of these companies, six are family firms, nine are listed (two out of those have been state controlled for some periods), and finally four are classified as cooperatives. In this chapter, we focus our analysis on the listed firms (including the state-controlled ones) and the family firms. It must be noted that this is an analysis of survivors, that is, companies that survived as independent companies for most of the post-war period. In the last decade analyzed, however, several mergers took place among the firms analyzed here.

Table 7.1 The Company Sample (1946–2000)

Company	Nationality	Founding year	1999 turnover (billion US dollars)	Original focus	Ownership structure
Ahlström	Finland	1851	2.7	Timber	Family firm
Schauman	Finland	1883	..	Timber, Plywood	Family firm (acquired by Kymmene 1988)
MoDo	Sweden	1872	9.1	Timber	Family firm
Korsnäs	Sweden	1855	0.7[1]	Timber	Family firm
Serlachius	Finland	1868	..	Paper	Family firm (acquired by Metsäliitto 1987)
Myllykoski	Finland	1892	1.1	Paper	Family firm
Enso-Gutzeit (Stora-Enso)	Finland	1918	11	Timber	Listed
Kymmene	Finland	1904	..	Paper	Listed (acquired by UPM 1995)
UPM	Finland	1920	8.8	Paper	Listed
SCA	Sweden	1920s	2.1	Pulp	Listed
Holmen	Sweden	1854	..	Paper	Listed (1988-1999 MoDo)[2]
Iggesund	Sweden	1876	..	Iron/Timber	Listed (Modo- Iggesund-Holmen 1988)[3]
Munksjö	Sweden	1862	0.67[4]	Paper	Listed
Stora	Sweden	1888	..	Iron	Family controlled (Stora-Enso 1998)[5]
Assi	Sweden	1942	..	Lumber	State-owned (Assi-Domän-NCB 1994)[6]
Metsäliitto	Finland	1934	4.5	Lumber	Cooperative
Norske Skog	Norway	1962	3[7]	Lumber	Cooperative
Södra	Sweden	1938	1.1[8]	Lumber	Cooperative

continued

Table 7.1 (continued)

Company	Nationality	Founding year	1999 turnover (billion US dollars)	Original focus	Ownership structure
NCB	Sweden	1959	..	Lumber	Cooperative (Assi-Domän-Ncb 1994)[9]

1. The turnover for Korsnäs is from 2000 and is 5209 million SEK
2. Holmen was a part of MoDo during the years 1988-1999
3. Iggesund became a part of Modo in 1988 as a result of a merger.
4. The turnover for Munksjö is 4854 million SEK.
5. Stora became Stora Enso in 1998.
6. Assi became AssiDomän after a series of mergers that started in 1994.
7. The turnover for Norske Skog is 18 500 million NOK.
8. The turnover for Södra is 8106 million SEK
9. NCB was acquired and became a part of AssiDomän in 1994.

Our methodology in the chapter is based on an event-data analysis that was developed in our previous research (Lamberg and Ojala 2006). The sources for this quantification-based analysis are historical events that are arranged chronologically and then coded by using a set of dichotomous variables. The idea of coded event data is that they can be analyzed by using different quantitative methods and that these systematic event series can be used in comparative studies (Van de Ven 1987; Van de Ven and Poole 1995). Our action database consisted of 1,694 company-specific strategic actions executed in the period 1946–2000. These actions were divided into different decades, so that we have altogether 210 actions for the period 1946–1960, 233 for 1961–1970, 377 for 1971–1980, 516 for 1981–1990, and 358 actions for 1991–2000.

All the strategic actions were coded according to a four-parameter framework (Lamberg, Laurila and Nokelainen 2006). First of all, we made an analysis of the general nature of the actions, divided according to the company ownership structures (family and listed). Then we analyzed the direction of the identified actions in the four parameters. The first parameter is industry invariant, showing the general nature of each action (e.g., acquisitions, investments, divestments). The second parameter is industry specific, focusing on specific actions in the product and resource market (e.g., actions related to raw materials, semi-finished products or marketing). The third parameter defines whether the actions were conducted independently or with other organizations, and the fourth parameter deals with the geographical focus of the actions (domestic or international). In this chapter we only include results for the first two dimensions.

RESULTS

The results are divided under two overall headings: activities and directions. Under 'activities' we present our results concerning the overall number and distribution of actions in family firms and listed firms. Under 'directions' we discuss the distribution of actions in the production chain, how actions reflect growth strategies and networking.

Activities

As Table 7.2 suggests, in terms of personnel, listed firms were larger than family firms over the whole period. The family firms' share of the combined labour force was around one-third during the 1950s but declined steadily thereafter, so that by the 1990s it was around a fifth. At the same time, the proportion of the listed firms' personnel rose from 50 to 57 percent. This implies that listed firms might have had scale advantages over other types of ownership. As Figure 7.1 shows, in terms of turnover the development was even more striking, as the productivity growth was substantial within the forestry industries. The figure for a sample of only eight companies suggests that listed firms and cooperatives outperformed family firms in the paper industry during the 1990s and the first years of the third millennium. However, as the number of cases is relatively low, these figures are only tentative. Even so, in our previous research, with a larger sample of companies, including U.S.-based ones, the pattern is similar, albeit not as dramatic as that presented in Figure 7.1 (Ojala et al. 2006).

The growth rate of family firms was lower than that of listed firms. The number of personnel in family firms has doubled, while in listed firms it has almost tripled. Cooperatives are interesting in this respect: although they arrived in the wood-processing sector rather late, they not only grew to be among the major players in all three Nordic countries by the turn of the third millennium, but they also became important global actors in the forestry industries.

The overall number of actions per year rose until the 1990s and then declined (Table 7.3). This decline is mostly due to mergers and acquisitions: there were simply fewer companies executing actions, although larger companies do execute more actions than smaller ones, as can be seen

Table 7.2 Average Number of Personnel in the Sample Companies, Divided According to Ownership Structure

	Family firms	Listed firms	Cooperatives	All
1946–1960	5399	6384	2844	5744
1961–1970	6837	8083	4394	7226
1971–1980	7536	8229	6922	7742
1981–1990	10481	10859	6602	9886
1991–2000	10823	17748	7561	13845
1946–2000	7959	9908	6049	8603

Source: Database compiled by the authors (http://research.jyu.fi/orgevolution/).

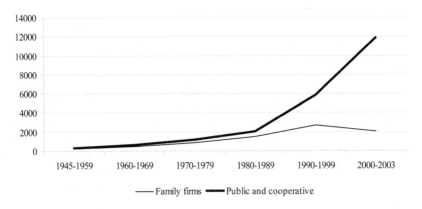

Figure 7.1 Average annual sales of Nordic family forestry-industry firms in comparison with listed firms and cooperatives, 1945–2003 (deflated to 2004 million US dollars) (Source: Annual reports).[1]

by comparing large, U.S.-based forestry-industry firms with Nordic ones (Ojala et. al 2006).

In terms of ownership structures, listed firms were more active than family firms (Table 7.3). This was mostly due to the larger size of these firms (for example, they were active and able to acquire relatively small-scale companies, paper merchants and production facilities, and to convert units).

Directions

Actions in production chain

Vertical integration and related diversification were typical features in the paper and pulp industries up to the mid-twentieth century (Ohanian 1994),

Table 7.3 Average Annual Number of Actions and Actions per Year / Average Personnel by Family Firms and Listed Firms, 1946–2000

	Number of actions, family firms	Number of actions, listed firms
1946–1960	5.9	7.6
1961–1970	9.2	10.8
1971–1980	12.5	16.8
1981–1990	17.7	24.0
1991–2000	10.0	10.7
1946–2000	10.5	13.3

Sources: see Table 7.2.

and unrelated diversification up to the 1980s. During the past few decades, companies have sought growth particularly through horizontal integration, that is, by concentrating on core business activities.

Upstream strategy actions are here classified as those related to raw-material acquisition and to semi-finished products (pulp and sawn timber). Midstream strategy actions are classified as those related to the production of paper and board, and downstream strategy actions those related to conversion and sales. Diversification strategies (both related and unrelated) are classified here separately. Multiple strategies refer to actions that concern several business areas simultaneously, as in the establishment of a production unit which produces several different end products. Typically, large-scale mergers and acquisitions are events that concern a variety of business areas.

The centre of gravity in the Nordic forestry industry companies has moved from raw materials and semi-finished production (sawmills and pulp) towards finished products such as paper—thus from upstream to downstream strategies (Galbraith 1988). Interestingly, upstream strategies played only a minor role when analyzed in terms of the number of actions. While from the 1940s up to the 1960s upstream strategies were dominant in both family firms and listed companies, this share had diminished clearly by the 1990s (Tables 7.4 and 7.5). However, here the analyses most probably underestimate the strong role played by the raw-material base. Both

Table 7.4 Strategic Actions in the Value Chain, Family Firms (Percentage of Strategic Actions per Decade, 1946–2000)

Years	Up-stream (1–3)	Mid-stream (4–5)	Down-stream (6–8)	Related and unrelated diversification (9 and 11)	Multiple categories (10)	Total	N
1946–1960	37	12	12	33	6	100	83
1961–1970	25	22	25	21	8	100	92
1971–1980	29	18	26	22	5	100	125
1981–1990	18	17	20	31	15	100	177
1991–2000	12	22	27	27	11	100	99
1946–2000	23	18	22	27	10	100	576
N	133	104	129	155	55	576	..

Source: see Table 7.2.

Table 7.5 Strategic Actions in the Value Chain, Listed Firms (Percentage of Strategic Actions per Decade, 1946–2000)

	Up-stream (1–3)	Mid-stream (4–5)	Down stream (6–8)	Related and unrelated diversification (9 and 11)	Multiple categories (10)	Total	N
1946–1960	24	27	12	25	11	100	107
1961–1970	26	32	12	21	9	100	207
1971–1980	28	22	21	22	7	100	165
1981–1990	20	27	18	26	9	100	235
1991–2000	19	25	23	14	19	100	105
1946–2000	23	27	18	22	10	100	719
N	168	194	127	156	74	719	..

Source: see Table 7.2.

in Sweden and Finland, the fear of diminishing timber in the 1960s led to a number of reforms throughout the industry (Kuusela 1999; Melander 1997). It is also important to remember that in Finland, cartels, in particular, made it possible to concentrate on mid-stream strategies, as it was these centralized associations that bore the marketing responsibilities until the 1980s and 1990s (Jensen-Eriksen 2007).

At the same time, midstream strategies—that is, paper and board production—gained more importance in strategic actions. This can also be seen from the export figures: in the case of Finland, sawn products were the most important export items from the early nineteenth up to the mid-twentieth centuries, when they were replaced by pulp. However, exports of pulp more or less disappeared in the 1970s, when it was more commonly refined into paper in domestic production units. Furthermore, a number of companies were also engaged in producing end products, such as United Paper Mills with laminates, and Stora-Enso and SCA with packaging.

The clearest trend from upstream to downstream strategies can be found in the case of family firms: altogether 37 percent of the actions concerned upstream strategies during the 1940s and 1950s, after which this share declined steadily and was only 12 percent in the 1990s (Table 7.4). The trend is not as clear in the case of listed firms, as the share of upstream strategies rose somewhat from the 1950s to the 1970s, but declined thereafter.

Midstream strategies, that is, actions related to paper and board production, grew throughout the post-war period. The largest proportion of midstream strategies can be found in the listed firms that integrated forwards in the production chain at a quite early point in time. Investments in paper production have always been expensive and thus difficult for family firms with limited access to outside financing to carry out (Ojala and Pajunen 2006). Family firms, for their part, were the most active in downstream strategies, for example, in the production of consumer products such as special papers and also in marketing. The proportion of both down- and midstream strategies in family firms rose at the expense of upstream strategies.

Vertical integration was a part of the related diversification that occurred within the forestry industries generally throughout the period. Though the proportion of related actions was reasonably low, their importance, especially for the Nordic companies, was crucial. Related diversification gave birth to the forestry clusters both in Sweden and in Finland. Most companies started to produce machinery for their own use, and later this mechanical-engineering industry developed its own branches and sub-industries (Haley 2000; Jääskeläinen 2001; Lammi 2000). In the 1970s, diversification was still the dominant strategy, but from the 1980s onwards the forestry-industry companies began to concentrate on their core businesses. While during the 1960s and 1970s forestry-industry firms diversified into several unrelated sectors, by the turn of the 1990s the Nordic forestry-industry firms had become considerably less diversified—the same phenomena had occurred in U.S.-based firms somewhat earlier (Davis, Diekmann and Tinsley 1994; Ojala et al. 2006).

The number of strategic actions related to diversification was, however, still high even in the 1990s, comprising around 18 percent of all actions taken by the sample companies. This is related to the divesting of unrelated businesses. Thus the share is composed mainly of actions that ended diversified businesses. The concentration on traditional core business activities led not only to the divestment of (unrelated) diversified businesses, but in some cases even to the closure of some branches of paper production. For example, MoDo relinquished the production of newsprint and magazine papers to a new company (Holmen) in 1999, Metsäliitto divested itself of tissue papers (1997) and Ahlström of all other but special papers (Melander 2006; Ojala and Lamberg 2006; Ojala et al. 2006; Ojala and Pajunen 2006; Siitonen 2003).

Growth strategies

The development of forestry-industry firms was mainly achieved either through organic growth—that is, by building new production capacity—or through mergers and acquisitions (M&A). M&A have led to growing consolidation within the industry, though there are significant differences between geographical areas and also in the lines of production. The top ten paper companies produced around a quarter of the top one thousand companies' production at the beginning of the twenty-first century (Ojala et al. 2006; Siitonen 2003). While organic growth clearly played a more significant role in the strategies of the Nordic companies from the 1940s up to the 1970s, the focus in strategic actions from the turn of the 1980s was on M&A (Table 7.6).

Family firms were especially eager to build new production facilities in the 1950s—a fact that seems quite at odds with the problems usually associated with family-owned companies with only limited possibilities for organic growth. However, the share of actions related to organic growth declined rapidly in the case of family firms, as it did with the listed companies, and the share of M&A grew correspondingly.

Closing actions, in the form of either selling out or ending production (Table 7.7), have only taken on more importance during the last few decades. In the 1940s and 1950s, only around 15 percent of strategic actions were related to the selling or divesting of units, while this figure was around 40 percent during the 1980s and 1990s. This is related to the dismantling of the diversified structures of the companies, when a number of units were either sold or closed down as companies concentrated on their core competences. Old and unproductive mills were also closed down at the same time (Barnett and Grier 1996; Gagne 1995). For example, Kymmene divested itself of its diversified lines of businesses in just a couple of years in the late 1980s, as United Paper Mills had already done in the 1970s.

Family firms were generally not as eager to sell or divest units as listed firms. This implies a certain amount of conservatism in their actions, or perhaps a family-related 'involvement' with the production. Throughout the period, only around one-fifth of the actions of the family firms were related to selling and divesting, while this figure was well over one-third for listed firms. Only in the 1990s did family firms apparently become active in selling off units. Ahlström, for example, sold off a number of its diversified units in this period and concentrated on producing special paper grades.

Table 7.6 Organic Growth, and Growth Through M&A (Percentages of Strategic Actions)

	Organic growth Family firms	*Organic growth Listed firms*	*M&A Family firms*	*M&A Listed firms*
1946–1960	74	63	8	23
1961–1970	55	46	28	27
1971–1980	50	43	28	30
1981–1990	33	23	36	34
1991–2000	20	28	45	31
1946–2000	44	37	31	30

Source: see Table 7.2.

DISCUSSION

Most studies of the Nordic pulp and paper industries focus either on individual firms or on comparisons at the sectoral or national level. Studies that focus on the sectoral level (e.g., Lilja, Räsänen and Tainio 1992; Melander 1997; Moen 1998; Peterson 1996, 2001) clearly show that sector-based innovation systems were firmly rooted at the national level. These studies take the national borders as a starting point. Either sector specifics are studied within a nation, or in a few cases sector specifics in different nations are compared. This approach creates a focus on differences between sectoral systems. From the data setup used in this chapter—that is, a comparison of family and listed companies from several countries—it is striking how similar the development has been throughout the Nordic countries. Companies, at a general level, have followed the same overall path.

However, when strategic actions are compared from an ownership-structure perspective, new findings surface, findings that will direct us in the next step of our research endeavour. Next we first summarize the findings of our initial study reported in this chapter. Then we discuss the results and suggest subjects for future research.

SUMMARY OF FINDINGS

Activity

1 Listed firms were far more active than family firms in terms of reported strategic actions.
2. Listed firms were larger in terms of personnel and grew more than family firms over the entire period.

Table 7.7 Selling and Divesting of Units Per Cent Share of Strategic Actions

	Selling Family firms	Selling Listed firms	Divesting Family firms	Divesting Listed firms
1946–1960	6	1	13	13
1961–1970	8	10	9	17
1971–1980	9	17	13	10
1981–1990	19	32	11	11
1991–2000	23	34	13	6
1946–2000	14	21	12	11

Source: see Table 7.2.

Direction

1. All companies had a similar overall pattern of growth strategies.
2. The clearest trend from upstream to downstream strategies can be found in the case of family firms.
3. Family firms were the most active in downstream strategies, for example, in the production of consumer products such as special papers and also in marketing.
4. The largest share of midstream strategies can be found in the listed firms that integrated forwards in the production chain at a quite early point in time.
5. Family firms were generally not as eager to sell or divest units as listed firms.

ACTIVITY

Earlier study on North American paper-industry firms (Ahola 2006) confirms our result that listed firms 'do more'. According to the general view, family firms take a longer perspective in their decision making and avoid activities that are trendy and spectacular. Following this, it is logical that family firms report a lower level of actions, both in total and adjusted for size, than listed firms. Supporting this assumption, neo-institutional literature (DiMaggio and Powell 1983) suggests that we would find a higher level of activity in listed firms, as they need to signal their legitimacy among their competitors and other stakeholders.

The first implication, following the obvious assumption that the frequency of actions is related to the size of the company, is that we have to extend our study in time and include at least the period 1900–1945. This will offer us a better understanding of how company growth is related to strategic actions. Is there a higher level of actions in certain phases of the company life cycle, or is there a structural difference between listed and family firms in the level of actions regardless of company size?

Secondly, we have to gain a greater understanding of the causality between strategic actions and business innovations. Building on Shaker Zahra's well-known study in 1993, one could speculate on how actions and business innovations developed over time. Zahra argues that industries characterized as having a narrow business focus and low level of price competition (the Nordic pulp and paper industry from the 1950s to the 1970s) correlate with few innovations. Further, he argues that industries characterized by concentration, vertical integration and higher price competition (the Nordic pulp and paper industry in the period 1980–2000) correlate with a high level of business innovation. So far, our data only verify this at the level of strategic actions, leaving the question of the correlation between actions and business innovations to be answered. Zahra's data are cross-sectional, making our longitudinal data valuable in analyzing the chronological aspects of the hypotheses. One of the few similar studies in the same vein (Craig and Moores 2006) takes a longitudinal perspective on the correlation between family firms and the level of innovation. Finding that family firms tend to be more innovative than generally assumed, they also conclude, thirteen years after Zahra's study, that the limited research in this area must be complemented with more longitudinal and chronological studies.

Thirdly, as stated previously, this discussion points to the need in future research to study the entire life cycle of family firms and listed firms in order to understand the pattern of strategic actions. But there is also a need to take the next step and qualify the study of strategic actions in order to be able to relate them to business innovations in a better way and thus to separate catching-up actions from real business innovations, which force rivals to initiate costly responses.

Strikingly, the data show that listed firms were bigger and grew faster than family firms. In 2006 only two family firms from our sample had survived, Myllykoski and Korsnäs. Our biased sample, which includes only long-time survivors, and our knowledge of the general industry context, leads us to the same conclusion. Family firms have lost ground in the Nordic pulp and paper industry. Why is this so?

Following Ojala and Pajunen's (2006) in-depth analyses of two family firms in Finland, we argue that ownership structures strongly influence access to capital markets. Listed firms are generally better suited to raise capital for major investments. Investments in paper production have always been expensive, and consequently the family-firm structure is at a disadvantage in this industry. This becomes evident in the 1980s and 1990s, when the paper industry was characterized by a wave of mergers and acquisitions. This happened at the same time as the width, speed and price of paper machines expanded tremendously. The result was that family firms lagged behind in terms of growth.

With regard to the specifics of the industry, one might ask why family firms actually survived as long as they did. The answer to this question probably lies in the specific features of the pulp and paper sector in Sweden and Finland. In both countries, the industry was traditionally organized in spheres, often with a bank as a controlling node. In Sweden, the Wallenberg sphere is one such example, making Stora Kopparberg one of the few family-controlled firms that survived until the end of the 1990s. It is also likely that the survival of the only remaining family firm in Sweden, Korsnäs, could be explained by the fact that it belonged to a wider group (the Stenbeck family group).

Direction

Why then did the companies act with such apparent similarity? We can offer at least two explanations. The first derives from the path-dependence principle: all the most important technical and business innovations originated before the 1960s. After the 1950s, competitive advantage was no longer created by means of technical innovations, but rather from solutions related to scale and scope (Chandler 1990; Melander 1997; Toivanen 2004). At this stage, the similarity resulted from the cognitive constraints of the organizational actors, which in turn were a direct result of historical experiences. Moreover, after the industry assumed its typical characteristics in the early twentieth century, the sunk-costs tied to the machinery and plants alone made it practically impossible to change the direction of the entire industry or even of particular companies. The diversification wave of the 1970s was clearly an attempt to change the basic determinants of the industry. Secondly, all the major alterations were caused by radical changes in the surrounding socio-economic environment. Thus it is no wonder that the sequence of strategic logic more or less follows the Chandlerian sequence of growth strategies (Cantwell 1989; Chandler 1990; Ojala et al. 2006).

We may state that the strategic logic was strongly dependent on history and the market environment, resulting in few 'strategic innovations' and consequent similarity in the repertoire of growth strategies. It is clear that the industry has not yet faced the kind of changes that inevitably create a radical rupture in the evolution of industries, namely, changes in the basic technology (such as the substitution of wood as the principal raw material) or in the market channel (for example, a radical marginalization of print media).

The overall strategy in the pulp and paper industry after the Second World War has been to integrate forwards (Peterson 1996, 2001). The pattern of strategic actions supports this conclusion. Family firms, however, tended to reduce costly investments in midstream activities (the production of paper) and focus more on downstream activities such as paper conversion, merchandising operations and marketing. From more qualitative studies we also learn that family firms tended to follow niche strategies more. Hence, specialization in niches featured by more intense customer contacts in product development (business to business) seems to be a prominent strategy in family firms.

The emerging picture is that listed firms aimed at products that supplied bigger markets and demanded a wider international presence. This strategy caused them to invest in large, technically advanced paper machines and undertake large acquisitions (forcing them in the next step to divest operations that did not match their chosen focus). When this happens, family firms concentrate on more specialized products with a narrow but still global market. These products require machines that are smaller, allowing for more incremental improvements with longer lifetimes. Further, because of their niche strategies family firms grow either incrementally or by making very precise acquisitions. The result is a lower need for large, one-off investments (see, for instance, Ojala and Pajunen 2006, a review of Ahlström's strategic development).

It may therefore be that the slower absolute growth of family firms in the 1980s and 1990s was the result of intentional decisions to allow active strategizing in smaller niche markets. Thus growth may be more important in listed firms, which are dependent on the opinion of the financial market, whereas other performance measures (profitability, longevity) may drive family firms to adopt specialized niche strategies. Again, this question requires more qualitative work in terms of analyzing the motivational aspects of company decision making.

CONCLUSIONS

Earlier literature has been divided into two opposite views on the effect of ownership structure on company behaviour. On the one hand, many scholars have seen family firms as innovative, risk taking and pro-active. The underlying assumption, thus, is that family firms embody certain properties which allow them to seek novel solutions during their evolution. On the other hand, family firms can be equally associated with rather non-entrepreneurial values, such as financial conservatism, security and family control over the firm.

In this chapter we report the first analyses of a research project addressing this complex issue. The analyses of strategic actions in listed firms and family firms provide us with interesting information opening the way for a number of reflections on the connection between ownership structure and business innovation.

In the next step of the project, we will closely analyze our data in order to separate actions of a catching-up nature from true business innovations. This will then be the starting point for more in-depth studies of the identified business innovations.

NOTES

1. The sample includes only seven companies: MoDo, Ahlström and Schauman as family firms, and Enso, Kymmene, UPM, and Metsäliitto as listed and cooperative companies.

REFERENCES

Ahola, A. 2006. Comparing the strategic evolution of Georgia-Pacific, Mead and Weyerhaeuser. In *The evolution of competitive strategies in global forestry industries: Comparative perspectives*, ed. J.-A. Lamberg, J. Ojala, J. Näsi and P. Sajasalo, 65–105. Dordrecht: Springer.

Augier, M., and D. J. Teece. 2006. Understanding complex organization: The role of know-how, internal structure, and human behavior in the evolution of capabilities. *Industrial and Corporate Change* 15:395–416.

Baden-Fuller, C. 1995. Strategic innovation, corporate entreneurship and matching outside-in to inside-out approaches to strategy research. *British Journal of Management* 6:51 page 53–516.

Barnett, D. J., and L. Grier. 1996. Mill closure forces focus on fines retention, foam control. *Pulp & Paper,* 70(4):89–93.

Becker, M. C., T. Knudsen and J. G. March. 2006. Schumpeter, Winter, and the sources of novelty. *Industrial and Corporate Change* 15:353–371.

Cantwell, J. 1989. The changing form of multinational enterprise expansion in the twentieth century. In *Historical studies in international corporate business,* ed. A. Teichova, M. Lévy-Leboyer and H. Nussbaum, 15–28. Cambridge: Cambridge University Press.

Casson, M. 1982. *The entrepreneur: An economic theory.* Oxford: Martin Robertson.

———. 1993. Entrepreneurship and business culture. In *Entrepreneurship, networks and modern business,* ed. J. Brown and M. Rose, 30–54. Manchester: Manchester University Press.

Chandler, A. D. J. 1977. *The visible hand: The managerial revolution in American business.* Cambridge, MA: Harvard University Press.

———. 1990. *Scale and scope: The dynamics of industrial capitalism.* Cambridge, MA: Belknap Press.

Chua, J. G., J. J. Chrisman and P. Sharma. 1999. Defining the family business by behaviour. *Entrepreneurship Theory and Practice* 23:19–39.

Craig, J., and K. Moores. 2006. A 10-year longitudinal investigation of strategy, systems, and environment on innovation in family firms. *Family Business Review* 19:1. 1–10.

Cyert, R. M., and J. G. March. 1963. *A behavioral theory of the firm.* Englewood Cliffs, NJ: Prentice-Hall.

Davis, G. F., K. A. Diekmann and C. H. Tinsley. 1994. The decline and fall of the conglomerate firm in the 1980s: The deinstitutionalization of an organizational form. *American Sociological Review* 59:547–570.

Diesen, M. 1998. *Economics of the pulp and paper industry: Paper making science and technology.* Helsinki: Fapet.

DiMaggio, P., and W. W. Powell. 1983. The iron cage revisited: Institutional isomorphism and collective rationality in organizational fields. *American Sociological Review* 48:147–160.

Gagne, P. E. 1995. Industry must evolve to sustain turnaround. *Pulp & Paper,* 69:144ff.

Galbraith, J. R. 1988. Strategy and organizational planning. In *The strategy in process: Concepts, contexts, and cases,* ed. J. B. Quinn, H. Mintzberg and R. M. James, 315–323. Englewood Cliffs, NJ: Prentice-Hall.

Greve, H., and A. Taylor. 2000. Innovations as catalysts for organizational change: Shifts in organizational cognition and search. *Administrative Science Quarterly* 45:54–80.

Hall, A. 2003. *Strategising in the context of genuine relations.* Jönköping, Sweden: Jönköping International Business School.

Hall, A., L. Melin and M. Nordqvist. 2001. Entrepreneurship as radical change in the family business: The role of cultural patterns. *Family Business Review* 14:193–208.

Haley, C. 2000. *Forest-based and related industries of the European Union: Industrial districts, clusters and agglomerations,* Helsinki: Taloustieto.

Huolman, M. 1992. *Metsäteollisuusyritykset Suomessa ja Ruotsissa: Kasvustrategiat vuosina 1973–1989.* Helsinki: Helsingin kauppakorkeakoulu.

Jensen-Eriksen, N. 2007. *Läpimurto: Metsäteollisuus kasvun, integraation ja kylmän sodan Euroopassa 1950–1973.* Helsinki: SKS.

Jääskeläinen, J. 2001. *Klusteri tieteen ja politiikan välissä: Teollisuuspolitiikasta yhteiskuntapolitiikkaan.* Helsinki: Taloustieto Oy.

Kreiser, P. M., J. Ojala, J.-A. Lamberg and A. Melander. 2006. A historical investigation of the strategic process within family firms. *Journal of Management History* 12:100–114.

Kuusela, K. 1999. *Metsän leiviskät: Metsäsuunnittelu ja saavutukset 1947–1996.* Jyväskylä, Finland: Atena.

Lamberg, J.-A., J. Laurila and T. Nokelainen. 2006. Competitive activities of forestry industry firms: A coding manual for event history analysis. In *The evolution of competitive strategies in global forestry industries: Comparative perspectives,* ed. J.-A. Lamberg, J. Näsi, J. Ojala and P. Sajasalo, 307–312. Dordrecht: Springer.

Lamberg, J.-A., and J. Ojala. 2006. Evolution of competitive strategies in global forestry industries. Introduction to *The evolution of competitive strategies in global forestry industries: Comparative perspectives,* ed. J.-A. Lamberg, J. Näsi, J. Ojala and P. Sajasalo, 1–29. Dordrecht: Springer.

Lammi, M. 2000. *Metsäklusteri Suomen taloudessa* [*The forest cluster in the Finnish economy*]. Helsinki: Taloustieto Oy.

Lilja, K., K. Räsänen and R. Tainio. 1992. A dominant business recipe: The forest sector in Finland. In *European Business Systems,* ed. R. Whithley, 137–154. London: Sage Publications.

Melander, A. 1997. *Industrial wisdom and strategic change: The Swedish pulp and paper industry 1945–1990.* Jonköping, Sweden: Jonköping International Business School.

———. 2006. Strategy formation in the Swedish forest industry: Comparing SCA and MoDo. In *The evolution of competitive strategies in global forestry industries: Comparative perspectives,* ed. J.-A. Lamberg, J. Näsi, J. Ojala and P. Sajasalo, 141–166. Dordrecht: Springer.

Miller, D. 1986. Configurations of strategy and structure: Towards a synthesis. *Strategic Management Journal* 7:233–250.

Miller, D., and M.-J. Chen. 1994. Sources and consequences of competitive inertia. *Administrative Science Quarterly* 39:1–17.

Mintzberg, H. [1973] 1980. *The nature of managerial work.* New York: Harper & Row.

———. 1987. Crafting strategy. *Harvard Business Review* 65 (4): 66–75.

———. 1994. *The rise and fall of strategic planning: Reconceiving roles for planning, plans, planners.* New York: Free Press.

Mintzberg, H., and J. A. Waters. 1982. Tracking strategy in an entrepreneurial firm. *Academy of Management Journal* 25:465–499.

Moen, E. 1998. *The decline of the pulp and paper industry in Norway, 1950–1980: A study of a closed system in an open economy.* Oslo: Scandinavian University Press.

Nelson, R., and S. Winter. 1982. *An evolutionary theory of economic change.* Cambridge, MA: Harvard University Press.

Nicholas, T. 1999. Clogs to clogs in three generations? Explaining entrepreneurial performance in Britain since 1850. *Journal of Economic History* 59: 88–713.

Ohanian, N. K. 1994. Vertical integration in the U.S. pulp and paper industry, 1900–1940. *Review of Economics and Statistics* 76:202–207.

Ojala, J., and J.-.A. Lamberg. 2006. The challengers: Kymmene, United Paper Mills, and Metsäliitto. In *The evolution of competitive strategies in global forestry industries: Comparative perspectives,* ed. J.-A. Lamberg, J. Näsi, J. Ojala and P. Sajasalo, 107–140. Dordrecht: Springer.

Ojala, J., J.-A. Lamberg, A. Ahola and A. Melander. 2006. The ephemera of success: Strategy, structure and performance in the forestry industries. In *The evolution of competitive strategies in global forestry industries: Comparative perspectives*, ed. J.-A. Lamberg, J. Näsi, J. Ojala and P. Sajasalo, 257–286. Dordrecht: Springer.

Ojala, J., and K. Pajunen. 2006. Two Finnish family firms in comparison: Ahlström and Schauman during the 20th Century. In *The ephemera of success: Strategy, structure and performance in the forestry industries*, ed. J.-A. Lamberg, J. Ojala, J. Näsi and P. Sajasalo, 167–189. Dordrecht: Springer.

Peterson, C. 1996. *Finsk ingerjörskonst och svenskt imperiebyggande: En jämförande studie av finsk och svensk skogsindustri.* Stockholm: SNS.

———. 2001. The development paths of two Nordic forest nations, 1950–1992. *Scandinavian Economic History Review* 49 (1): 23–44.

Rose, M. B. 1993. Beyond Buddenbrooks: The family firm and the management of succession in nineteenth-century Britain. In *Entrepreneurship, networks and modern business*, ed. J. Brown and M. B. Rose, 127–143. Manchester: Manchester University Press.

Rytkönen, A. 2000. Globaalija eusooppalainen toimintaympäristö. In *Suomen mestäklusteri tienhaarassa*, ed. R. Seppälä, 27–30. Helsinki: Wood Wisdom.

Schumpeter, J. A. 1947. The creative response in economic history. *Journal of Economic History* 7:149–159.

Sharma, P., J. J. Chrisman and J. H. Chua. 1997. Strategic management of the family business: Past research and future challenges. *Family Business Review* 10:1–35.

Siitonen, S. 2003. *Impact of globalisation and regionalisation strategies on the performance of the world's pulp and paper companies.* Helsinki: Helsinki School of Economics.

Toivanen, H. 2004. Learning and corporate strategy: The dynamic evolution of the North American pulp and paper industry, 1860–1960. Ph.D. diss., Georgia Institute of Technology.

Van de Ven, A. 1987. Four requirements for processual analysis. In *The management of strategic change*, ed. A. Pettigrew, 330–341. Oxford: Basil Blackwell.

Van de Ven, A., and M. S. Poole. 1995. Explaining development and change in organizations. *Academy of Management Review* 20:510–549.

Williamson, O. E. 1985. *The economic institutions of capitalism: Firms, markets, relational contracting.* New York: Free Press.

Winter, S. G. [1968] 2006. Towards a neo-Schumpeterian theory of the firm. *Industrial and Corporate Change* 15:151–170.

Zahra, S. A. 1993. New product innovation in established companies: Associations with industry and strategy variables. *Entrepreneurship, Theory and Practice* 18 (2): 47–69.

8 Networks, Cartels and Innovations in Finland, 1945–1984

Jani Saarinen

INTRODUCTION AND OBJECTIVE

Networks have always played—and still play—an important role in industrial and entrepreneurial life in Finland. Over the years, networks have been built up for various purposes, usually in order to rationalize the activities of the firms. However, over the years, a wide variety of new kinds of organizational arrangements has emerged to support innovation. It is not a big secret that the industrial development in Finland before the mid-1980s was characterized by large number of cartels. As cartels became less acceptable, later on even forbidden by law, other forms of networking increased their importance.

Innovative firms confront significant challenges in capturing value from new technology. Success in research and development does not automatically translate into a financial success, even if the technology developed meets a significant market need. To succeed financially, innovative firms must quickly position themselves advantageously in the appropriate complementary resources and technologies. If they are not already integrated, the best solution often involves bilateral and multilateral cooperative agreements (Jorde and Teece 1990).

The objective of this chapter is to examine changes in collaboration of new product-development projects during the period 1945–1984. In order to achieve the objective, data on some 1,600 Finnish innovations commercialized during the period 1945–1984 were used. The definition of an innovation used in this chapter is based mainly on the definitions provided in the Oslo Manual (OECD 1997). In addition to the changes in collaboration, this chapter explores the role of cartels, as one special form of collaboration, in innovation activities of companies. As collaboration takes place during the product research and development process, cartels play a central role on the market side of the innovation process, after the commercialization of innovation. The chapter argues that over the years, there has been a switch in the networking activities of the firms. As networks in the markets (=cartels) have decreased, R&D type of networking has become more popular. This change is illustrated in Figure 8.1.

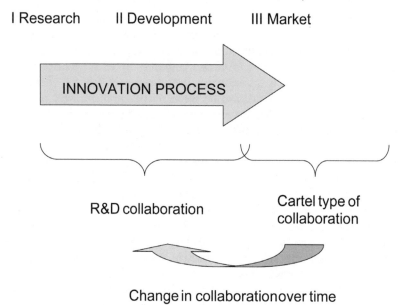

Figure 8.1 Change in collaboration over time.

The development process of innovation has been divided into three different parts, which are considered to follow each other chronologically during the process of development. The first phase is called 'Research'. During this phase, various types of knowledge bases are collected together for the development of a new product. During the second phase, called 'Development', innovation is going through a change from idea to a concrete product (from invention towards innovation). In this stage, decisions concerning the use of external knowledge in terms of collaboration are usually made. The last phase is called 'Market'. In that phase, the market introduction of a new product is made. This means that there exists a concrete product, which needs some marketing efforts to be made. Cartels make their entry usually at this phase, as there is a need to maximize the sales of the new product. In figure 8.1, the arrow going to the left illustrates the main argument of this chapter—change in collaboration over time from markets to R&D. With the help of two models, the chapter also tests which factors explain the changes in cartel and R&D collaboration as it affects networks of Finnish innovative firms.

HISTORY OF R&D COLLABORATION

Collaboration in the development of new products, as a phenomenon, has its roots far back in history. In Germany and the United States, there already existed some type of collaboration between large companies and universities at the beginning of the nineteenth century (Michelsen 1993, 14). Unfortunately, these early attempts turned into failures, due to the inability to organize research. After these failures, companies' interest evaporated, and universities and research laboratories continued research for themselves (14–15). As the direct connection between science and industry now was lost, this vacuum was filled by some great individual innovators, such as Thomas Edison, Alexander Bell, Alfred Nobel and others. They earned their living by selling patent rights to industry. The missing link between science and industry, but not with academia, was re-created.

The era of individual innovators lasted until the early twentieth century. After that, the large companies began to establish their own research units on an increasing scale, in order to solve new and complex technical problems. The research staff was hired basically from the university world, which indicated a new level in the science—industry relation. As competition in new markets, particularly in the high-technology industries, increased, large industries resorted more and more to the scientific solutions provided by the universities. Industries started to finance university research, which resulted in a strong link between these actors (Michelsen 1993, 15–16).

As this short historical overview illustrates, research collaboration changes as time goes by. Despite the long history of collaboration, it was not until the 1980s that different forms of collaboration emerged as a subject of academic studies. One of the pioneers, Chesnais (1988), divided collaboration into three different categories, on the basis of the distance to the market during the product-development process.[1]

Firstly, there is the category called 'science in innovation'. Firms increasingly view universities and government laboratories as key external sources of basic research even if they use suppliers and competitors as external sources of technology for product development (Brooks and Randazzese 1998). However, the role of universities is in transition towards more commercial types of activities (Kankaala et al. 2004).

Secondly, as many results of innovation studies show, innovation has become more of a networking (horizontal) process (see, e.g., Becker and Dietz 2004, 209–223). During the 1980s the number of horizontal strategic alliances and collaborative R&D consortia with competitors increased rapidly (Lemola 1994, 4–8; Lievonen 1998, 5–6). Companies realized that the use of external R&D can speed up new product development, as can buying or licensing-in existing technology (Gold 1987, 81–88). Another form of linkage in Finland is the so-called 'technology programme', which has become more popular among companies. This happened especially during the 1990s, when the strategic role of Tekes (the national technology agency) as a coordinator and financier increased. Collaboration has become a central activity in the Finnish technology policy.

Thirdly, there is a particular type of collaboration is called vertical collaboration, which includes close linkages with customers and sub-contractors during the development process of innovation (Rothwell 1994). Considering the role of customers, it seems to vary a lot during different periods of time and between countries. A comparative study of technical developments during the post-war period in the U.K. and West German machine-tool industries found major differences in customers' involvement in the product design. In British companies, customers were not involved in the development process until the product was on the market, whereas they were involved at an early stage in West Germany. These differences helped the West German machine-tool suppliers to become more successful than their British competitors (Parkinson 1982; see also Rothwell 1977, 191–206).

As regards sub-contractors, Japanese companies have been particularly successful in enrolling them for product development. The collaboration of leading Japanese vehicle companies with their own robotics suppliers and with electronic companies was an important factor behind their reduced development costs and increased development speeds in the 1970s (Free-man 1988, 330–348). In a Finnish study of collaborative R&D in thirty-four companies in the engineering and electronic industries, the role of subcontractors in the companies' 'key' development projects was found to be the most important model of collaborative R&D (Halme, Pulkkinen and Tiilikka 1999, 3–5). The importance of vertical collaboration in Finland was also highlighted in a comparative study on Austrian and Finnish collaboration behaviour. According to this study, the high share of collaboration in Finland could be explained by a 'national culture of co-operation', which is deeply rooted in the underlying innovation system (Dachs, Ebersberger and Pyka 2004, 2–4).

HISTORY OF CARTELS AND COMPETITION POLICY

Competition policy has a long history in Finland, as restraints on competition appeared from the outset of its industrial development. The earliest reported Finnish decision about industrial competition dates from 1837, when a court refused to enforce an agreement among mill owners because it put undue limitations on the economic freedom of the parties to the agreement and of their input suppliers, who were its victims. Around the turn of the twentieth century, Finnish firms in some export-oriented businesses, especially forestry products, combined to achieve economies of scale. In some cases, particularly involving the Russian market, they also entered agreements to maintain prices and limit production. Some of these combinations and agreements also had domestic effects, as Finnish firms discriminated against the home market, selling products more cheaply in St. Petersburg than in Helsinki.

Thirty years of debate preceded the first national competition law. The problem of industrial combinations appeared in policy debate in 1928, when the 'progressive cooperative' platform called for investigation and public control of 'rings and trusts'. This call was renewed in 1948, along with a proposal to ban unfair methods of competition. The government responded by appointing a committee representing industry, agriculture and trade interests to study the matter. The committee's report in 1952 endorsed in principle the protection of economic freedom to compete, but it suggested basing a competition law on information and publicity, rather than on control or prohibition. Two prohibitions were nonetheless included in the government's proposed bill, which was based on experiences elsewhere in Scandinavia. One, a blanket prohibition against resale-price maintenance, was refined in parliamentary committee to make it dependent on showing actual harmful effects in the particular case. Legislators evidently thought that agreements would help make prices uniform across the country and that uniformity would be desirable. The other, against bid rigging, was intended to encourage competition in the construction industry; however, joint bidding could be permitted if it would lead to cost savings. The bid-rigging prohibition was included because such conspiracies were secret. By contrast, ordinary cartels were not prohibited; rather, such unconcealed agreements would be registered with the cartel office. Cartels involving imports and exports were exempted, even from registration, in order to maintain the system of licence-base control over international trade. These were the basic provisions of the first, limited Finnish law about competition, which was adopted in 1958 (Virtanen 1998, 238–245).

A more comprehensive competition law, based on notification and control of abuse, was adopted in 1964 (1958 Act on Competition Restrictions Within the Economy). Finland's 1961 association agreement with the European Free Trade Association (EFTA) required Finland to prevent practices that would nullify the pro-competitive effect of tariff reductions. The 1958 law was inadequate for this purpose; moreover, the 1958 law had failed its own intended purposes of gathering information and shaming cartels through publicity. The new law provided for controlling cartels and dominant firms if they were abusive. It created a new competition authority, the Council of Freedom of Trade, to negotiate resolutions and grant exemptions. The law required associations to notify agreements, and more than eighty price agreements had been registered by 1967 (Virtanen 1998, 246–253).

The next major reform of competition law, in 1973, introduced an executive official, the competition ombudsman, who was empowered to represent the public interest in negotiations involving the (renamed) Competition Council. The ombudsman could refer matters to the Competition Council for action, as could consumer associations or union organizations. By 1982, the ombudsman had handled 183 cases, of which only 9 were referred to the council. Most were about refusals to deal, and much of the ombudsman's work was in aid of small-business interests. But in the 1970s, the principal policy concern was inflation, and the main objective of the institutional changes was controlling price increases. The Board of Trade and Consumer Interests was to administer both price regulation and competition policy. Price control proved unworkable, though. The system was progressively suppressed in the early 1980s, without repealing the law, by eliminating commodities from coverage. But as late as 1984, 40 percent of the consumer-price-index weight was still liable to price regulation, and 11 percent was in the stricter 'price confirmation' category. Meanwhile the ombudsman was recording information about the harm caused by restrictive agreements. As a result of an adoption of a new law in 1988, the Board of Trade and Consumer Interests was eliminated, and a new administrative agency was established (OECD 2003).

This new institution aggressively attacked the system of cartels. The powers of what was then called the Office of Free Competition (OFC) were broadly similar to those of the competition ombudsman. The OFC—which is now called the Finnish Competition Authority—was authorized to register and investigate restraints, negotiate about removing them and refer matters that could not be resolved to the competition council (Virtanen 1998, 260–265). The new agency enjoyed some advantages over its predecessor, though, notably more resources and government support for a more vigorous policy. The OFC immediately undertook a programme of eliminating the effects of price regulation, by systematically challenging the horizontal price agreements and recommendations that had been registered under the previous laws. It succeeded in dissolving about one hundred of them over the next five years (OECD 2003).

DATA

Innovation Data, 1945–1984

The innovation data were compiled using a combination of two different methodologies for the identification of innovations: reviews of trade and technical journals, and reviews of the company histories of forty-six large Finnish companies. The literature reviews were undertaken during the years 2001–2002. First, the population of journals that were eligible for innovation detection was defined. Journals were considered eligible if they were independently edited and regularly published; that is, mere product listings or announcements, irregular publications or journals directly controlled by companies were not considered eligible. This approach resulted in a population of forty-two trade or technical journals. In the next phase all such journals were selected that regularly published edited and non-paid material about innovations. The focus was on articles dealing with the introduction of new products which conformed to the definitions and criteria for an innovation. Listings of new products were avoided. Instead, more emphasis was paid on the editorial content of the journals. However, as it turned out, the number of journals was rather limited and not all journals, particularly during the first decades, contained information on innovations. After this selection process, the final list included thirty-six of the forty-two journals. The list of journals can be found in Appendix 8.4. Together, the selected journals ensure a proper sectoral coverage of the industrial life in Finland during this particular period.

This type of approach is in contrast to, for instance, the work of Kleinknecht and Bain (1993) or the OECD Oslo Manual's guidelines (OECD 1997) for literature-based innovation collection that also consider as eligible non-edited product announcements. However, this latter kind of approach contains a serious risk of high selection bias, as firms have incentives to announce even incremental design modifications, product differentiations and imitations that should not be considered as innovations. On the other hand, having trust in professional journal editors should reduce this risk substantially.

In the studies conducted by the Futures Group in the United States (based on the SBIDB—Small Business Administration's Innovation Data Base—data) (Edwards and Gordon 1984, 14–15) and by Acs and Audretsch (1990, 12), a common concern was the representativeness of large firms' innovations. In the study by the Futures Group, the over-representation of the large firms was seen as problematic:

> The material appearing in the new-product sections of the trade journals should only be weighted to the large firm to the extent that the small firm is not sophisticated enough, or does not have the necessary resources, to produce press releases. (Edwards and Gordon 1984, 14–15)

Learning lessons from the previous exercises, I decided to use annual reviews of large companies for the database. Unfortunately, the older reviews did not contain any information on new products or R&D activities. Instead, the economic development of the firm and market situation was well described. Information on products and production methods appeared for the first time in the early 1980s, which was close to the final year in my historical time period. Therefore, I decided to include company histories of forty-six large Finnish companies (listed in Appendix 8.5) as a complement to the annual reviews.

Altogether, after the reviewing of journals and company histories, the number of innovations reached 2,208. After a check for duplicates, the number of innovations over the period 1945–1984 was reduced by 615 to a total of 1,593. The list of collected variables as well as the distribution of innovations can be found in Appendix 8.3 (for more information about innovation data, see Saarinen 2005, 73–89).

Company Data

The next stage in data collection, after the identification of innovations, was to collect data about the commercializing firms. In order to analyze the relationship between innovations and the economic success of firms, a database including basic information (such as year of establishment, Standard Industrial Classification code, geographical location) and financial information (turnover, balance sheet, employee costs) of innovative firms was constructed.[2] According to the criteria and definitions during the innovation-identification process, an innovation was only included in the database if the name of the commercializing firm was also available. This was a starting point for the construction of the company data. Innovations opened up a window to the world of innovative companies, and since the names of 825 companies were known, a search for relevant data began. Soon it turned out that the list of companies also included cases, in which the company had changed the registered official name or the company had merged, been bought, split, re-organized itself and so on. After tracking histories and double-checking the list of 825 companies, the final list included 710 innovative companies, which had commercialized innovations during the years 1945–1984. Out of the 710 different companies, I was able to find financial time-series data for 626 (88 percent) of them. Basic information was found for 657 (93 percent) of the companies.

Cartel Data

The data on cartels were collected from various cartel magazines. These were *Kartellirekisteri* (*Cartel Register*) for the years 1959–1963 and *Kilpailunvapauslehti* (*Competition's Freedom Magazine*) for the years 1964–1984. The magazines presented all agreements starting from 1932, which companies signed about different types of arrangements on the market side. All cartel announcements were read, the names of all firms mentioned in the cartel agreements were collected and analyzed against the innovation data. For instance, if company A had built up a cartel agreement with companies B and C, commercialized innovations were searched from each of these firms around the year the cartel agreement was signed and for the period of its validity. If an innovation was found from some of these firms, the technical description of innovation was combined with the cartel-agreement data. If it turned out to be clear that the cartel agreement had major similarities with the description of innovation, a variable indicating CARTEL was added to the innovation data.

Considering the cartels, there were four different classes characterized by the type of cartel. However, in this chapter, all types of cartels have been united and analyzed as one bunch. In total, there were some 800 cartels made in Finland during the years before 1985. In 1969, there were 494 cartel agreements, which were active. Still in 1988, as the Competition Office began its activities, some 600 market agreements were valid (Purasjoki and Jokinen 2001, 100–108). The number of innovations, which involved the cartel type of collaboration, is 341 out of 1,593 (21 percent). These numbers illustrate well the importance of market-side collaboration between the Finnish firms during the studied period.

RESULTS

Collaboration

The increase in collaboration has evolved in different forms, as the preceding literature review described. The first time collaboration was included in an innovation study was in Austria around 1990. Company respondents were asked whether the firm had engaged in R&D cooperation when developing the innovation. Unfortunately, this question was poorly answered and any results on this issue were not published (Fleissner, Hofkirchner and Poh 1993, 85–112). In Finnish innovation data for the period 1945–1984, the only information comes from the technical magazines and is based on the facts mentioned there.

Collaboration for innovation has faced many changes and displayed different patterns during the period studied. The first two decades, the 1940s

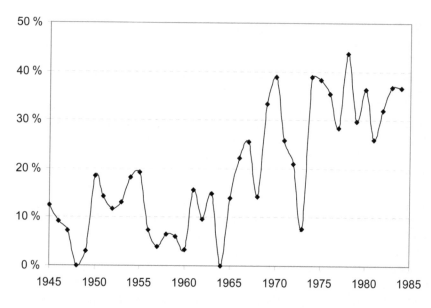

Figure 8.2 Share of innovations involving R&D collaboration (excluding collaboration with customers).

and 1950s, were a period of limited collaboration. The early 1950s witnessed a minor peak in collaboration due to the involvement of universities and research centres as collaborative partners, but then it fell back. A new increase started in the mid-1960s, as experience and knowledge from other countries reached Finland and were transferred into use. What also affected the growth was that the turnover tax was modified in order to encourage collaboration between companies. Previously, heavy taxation hindered the collaboration between various partners, mainly with sub-contractors, since it was cheaper for a company to have all production facilities in-house.

Since the 1960s, the variety of collaborative partners has rapidly increased. The role of customers, consultants, sub-contractors and competing companies increased. Joint research laboratories and firms were established, because it was realized soon after the Second World War that investment in R&D activities was essential for the success of firms. The common opinion in industry and the government was that these investments should be possible for all companies—either by having their own laboratories or by getting in touch with state-owned research centres (e.g., VTT and Keskuslaboratorio Oy). Otherwise, there was a risk of becoming only a raw-material producing and exporting country in the future (Unknown 1951, 410).

Moreover, collaboration with universities and research centres increased significantly with the typology of Chesnais' 'science in innovation'. The standard view is that universities conduct basic research, research centres do applied research and companies concentrate on R&D activities. The results of these activities are the increase in terms of knowledge as well as new products. After the wars, the situation in many Finnish companies was that they knew how to produce various items, but they did not have knowledge about the most recent technological trends in their particular business area. An indication of this 'backwardness' is the percentage of domestic patents granted compared to applications. During the 1940s and 1950s, this share was less than 10 percent. Due to the relatively low level of technological knowledge of the companies, the need for external knowledge was understood. Particularly those companies which focused on the international markets soon realized the importance of collaboration with universities and research institutions, domestic and foreign, in order to get some information about the latest knowledge available. Universities were mainly seen as a source of basic knowledge, whereas research institutions had their advantage in applied research, in testing and in practical issues.

In absolute terms, the 'scientific' collaboration became popular in the late 1960s or at the turn of the 1970s. Geographically, as a result of the foundation of new universities (see Lemola 2002, 468–475; Oksanen 2003, 15–17) all over the country, new regions and cities entered the collaboration map. In addition, VTT started to regionalize as well, by establishing new units in places such as Oulu and Tampere in 1974; Jyväskylä, Outokumpu and Lappeenranta in the 1980s; followed by Rajamäki, Raahe, Vaasa and

Turku in the 1990s. In geographic terms, scientific knowledge became easily available. Lastly, a characteristic of this period of growth was also the increase of foreign partners. In the mid-1980s, collaboration turned into a new era, by means of technology programmes by Tekes, followed by the framework programmes in the European Union in the 1990s.

In order to test the relationships between various characteristics of innovation in relation to R&D collaboration, I constructed a model. In recent academic articles, a large number of factors, which potentially might affect R&D collaboration during the innovation process, have been analyzed. Considering the novelty of the innovation, empirical studies have shown that deliberate sharing of technological knowledge is generated as a continuous flow of incremental technological improvements in products and production processes rather than a series of radical innovation occurring from time to time (Petit and Tolwinski 1996; see also Katz and Ordover 1990; Baumol 1992, 1993; Allen 1983; von Hippel 1988). This can be interpreted in the following way: as a result of technological collaboration during the development process of innovation, the novelty of innovation is more incremental-like. This means that there should be a positive coefficient for the variable *INCRE* in the collaboration model. Considering patents, I include the variable *PATENT* to capture innovations that have been patented prior to their commercialization. My expectation is that as firms are sharing technological information during the development process of an innovation, the information that transfers from one firm to another has to be protected. In this study, I use patents to capture this protection of the firms' technological knowledge.

Even though the occurrences of collaboration are relatively few during the first decades of the studied period, it is still valuable to look at the pioneering firms—for instance, the size of them—in more detail. A general opinion has been and still is that R&D collaboration depends on the size of the firm (Negassi 2004; Fritsch and Lukas 2001; Kamien, Muller and Zang 1992). Large firms have more resources to be invested in R&D collaboration, compared with small firms. However, even small firms might have their motives for R&D collaboration. If innovating firms, particularly small ones, do not have the necessary capabilities in-house, they may need to engage in various forms of restrictive contracts with providers of inputs and complementary assets (Jorde and Teece 1990, 77–80). Considering the model, I test the role of large firms in R&D collaboration, but I put a question mark regarding expectations about the result. The model has the following form:

$$\log(COLLA_t) = \alpha + \beta_1 \log(INCRE_t) + \beta_2 \log(PATENT_t) + \beta_3 \log(LARGE_t) + \varepsilon_t$$

in which

$COLLA$ = share of innovations, in which R&D collaboration is included;

INCRE = share of incremental innovations (+);[3]
PATENT = share of patented innovations (+);
LARGE = share of large firm innovations (?).[4]

Expected outcomes of the estimation are presented in parentheses. The model is estimated for the period 1945–1984 by the method of ordinary least squares (OLS). All variables are in logarithms.

Table 8.1 displays the model estimates. Coefficient *INCRE* is statistically significant at the 10-percent level of significance, whereas *LARGE* is at the 5-percent level and *PATENT* at the 1-percent level of significance. As expected, they all have a positive impact on the core R&D collaboration. A 1-percent increase in the entries will make the core technology of old firms decrease by 0.23 percent in year three. Putting this on the other way around, it means that when the number of entries decreases, old innovative firms rely increasingly on the commercialization of their core technologies. This means that the industry, or a particular technology, moves towards the phase of maturity.

Although the results strengthen the expectations, one has to bear in mind that time-series data do often have problems of serial correlation and heteroskedasticity. A common finding in time-series regressions is that the residuals are correlated with their own logged values. These problems can be detected by looking at the residuals of regression. The Durbin-Watson (DW) statistic is a test for first-order serial correlation. If there is no serial correlation, the DW statistic will be around 2. The DW statistic will fall below 2 if there is positive serial correlation (in worst case, it will be near 0). In Table 8.1, the DW is 1.463, which means that there are slight indications about a positive first-order serial correlation. In order to examine serial correlation more in detail, I use the Breusch-Godfrey Serial Correlation LM test and Q-statistics. These tests do not indicate any serial correlation. A White heteroskedasticity test does not give any indications about heteroskedasticity. Neither do there exist any structural breaks in the model, as tested by the Chow breakpoint

Table 8.1 OLS Regression Estimates of the Collaboration in R&D Process of Innovations, 1945–1984

Variable	Coefficient	Std. Error	t-Statistic	Prob.
C	0.622616	0.504247	1.234743	0.2256
LOG(INCRE)	0.758728	0.408109	1.859130	0.0719
LOG(PATENT)	0.756931	0.205800	3.678002	0.0008
LOG(LARGE)	0.872047	0.371702	2.346095	0.0251
R-squared	0.500746	Akaike info criterion		1.651986
Adjusted R-squared	0.455360	F-statistic		11.03289
Durbin-Watson stat	1.462644	Prob(F-statistic)		0.000036

test. Altogether, it can be concluded that the model works and the results are in line with expectations.

Cartels

After independence (1917), the first task for Finnish firms was to find new markets to replace Russian markets. At this time it was vital for the Finnish economy to gain a foothold in western Europe. Finnish firms in the export sector were mostly small, and even the international position of Finland was insecure. Thus, the problem with both the new independent state and its firms was a lack of confidence. In order to overcome this, the Finnish export sector chose cooperation as its strategy. By setting up extensive selling associations, that is, cartels, Finnish paper firms among others succeeded in getting access to western European and also overseas markets (Heikkinen and Kuusterä 2002, 5–8). As cartel data are combined with the innovation data, the results look as follows.

Beginning from the mid-1940s, the share of cartels in innovations increased more or less constantly, reaching a maximum value over 40 percent in the early 1960s. From late 1960s onwards, the share of cartels decreased, falling below 10 percent in the early 1980s. As the results indicate, the 'golden years' in cartel collaboration took place in the 1960s. As an average, one-third of all innovations commercialized during that decade included some type of cartel agreement.

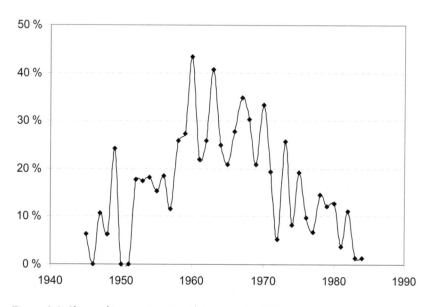

Figure 8.3 Share of innovations involving cartel collaboration.

The question now is in which types of innovations and innovative firms cartel collaboration was more likely to occur. Starting from the characteristics of innovations, the general assumption seems to be that radical type of innovations are more often involved in cartel arrangements. In Baumol's article on horizontal collusion and innovation he states that a clear danger of technology collusion is that it can be perverted into a monopolistic agreement to keep prices high and even to avoid the expense and turmoil of rapid innovation (Baumol 1992, 129–137). According to Jorde and Teece, the giant integrated enterprises are not most heavily at risk. Instead, most at risk are mid-sized enterprises that have developed and commercialized important innovations, because such firms are likely to have some market power and have the need to engage in complex forms of cooperation (1990, 77–80). Jorde and Teece's results can be interpreted in such a way that besides the radical nature of innovation, even the small size of the commercializing firm should affect positively the creation of cartel types of collaboration. Considering the protection of innovations as it involves cartel collaboration, I was not able to find any studies in which the relationship was analyzed well enough. The only examples for this came from the light-bulb market, which was highly cartelized at the beginning of the twentieth century. In that setting, the relationship between patenting and cartels was positive. Being not aware of any other studies, I use the question mark to illustrate my expectations. The model has the following form:

$$\log(CARTEL_t) = \alpha + \beta_1 \log(RAD_t) + \beta_2 \log(PATENT_t) + \beta_3 \log(SME_t) + \varepsilon_t$$

in which

$CARTEL$ = share of innovations, in which cartel type of collaboration is included;
RAD = share of radical innovations (+);[5]
$PATENT$ = share of patented innovations (-);
SME = share of small- and medium-sized-firm innovations (+).[6]

Expected outcomes of the estimation are presented in parentheses. The model is estimated for the period 1945–1984 by the method of OLS. All variables are in logarithms.

Table 8.2 displays the model estimates. There are statistically significant coefficients (at the 10-percent level of significance or less) for two of the included variables: share of radical innovations (RAD) and share of patented innovations ($PATENT$). Coefficient SME is statistically significant at the 1-percent level of significance. As expected, the share of radical innovations and share of small and medium-sized firms have a positive impact on the cartel type of collaboration in innovations, whereas patenting has a negative impact. This means that innovative SMEs seem to search for the

Table 8.2 OLS Regression Estimates of the Cartel Collaboration of Innovations, 1945–1984

Variable	Coefficient	Std. Error	t-Statistic	Prob.
C	-1.135982	0.696814	-1.630251	0.1129
LOG(RAD)	1.027340	0.544050	1.888319	0.0681
LOG(PATENT)	-0.495497	0.285632	-1.734739	0.0924
LOG(SME)	2.160104	0.713123	3.029075	0.0048
R-squared	0.391456	Akaike info criterion		2.090940
Adjusted R-squared	0.334405	F-statistic		6.861503
Durbin-Watson stat	1.161558	Prob(F-statistic)		0.001067

cartel type of collaboration in order to achieve success in the markets. In addition, increase in technical novelty promotes cartel collaboration. The more radical the innovation is to the firm and the markets, the more willingly firms rely on the market side of collaboration in the search for future profits from the new product.

Although the results strengthen some of my expectations, serial correlation and heteroskedasticity are always present as time-series data are concerned. In order to check these matters, similar tests were carried out as was done in the collaboration case. The results of these tests are presented in Appendix 8.2. These tests do not indicate any serial correlation, nor do they give any signs of heteroskedasticity. Nor do there exist any structural breaks in the model, as tested by the Chow breakpoint test. Despite the relatively low explanatory power of the model, it works well and gives reliable results.

Change in Collaboration Over Time

One of the impetuses for this study was that over the years, there has been a switch in networking activities of the firms. It was assumed that as networks on the markets (cartels) have decreased, R&D type of networking has become more popular. In order to illustrate that, I have concentrated only on innovations in which some type of collaboration has been included. Figure 8.4 displays the results.

In the beginning of the studied period, R&D collaboration was rather evenly distributed with cartel collaboration. Towards the late 1950s, cartel collaboration increased continuously, achieving its highest value of 80 percent around 1958. Since then, cartel collaboration has continuously decreased. From this it naturally follows that other types of collaborations have increased their importance—in this case it is R&D collaboration. To conclude, Figure 8.4 clearly illustrates the switch in

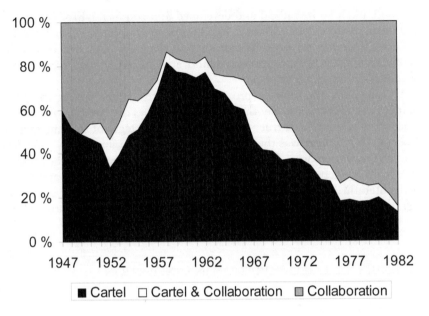

Figure 8.4 Change in collaboration over time (five years moving average).

networking activities of the firms during the studied period. This means that the arrow going to the left, presented in Figure 8.1, makes sense in this research environment.

CONCLUSIONS

This analysis has sought to highlight the changes in collaboration on new product development projects by Finnish innovative firms. Collaboration was divided into two different types depending on their appearance during the innovation process. It was assumed that as collaboration takes place during the product research and development process, cartels play a central role on the market side of the innovation process, after the commercialization of innovation. The chapter argued that over the years, there has been a switch in networking activities of the firms. As networks on the markets (cartels) have decreased, R&D types of networking have become more popular. The data consisted of Finnish innovation data and data on registered cartels in Finland during the years 1945–1984.

In the study, there were two econometric models tested for various types of collaboration. In R&D collaboration, innovations are incremental by their nature, they are usually patented and they are developed and commercialized by large firms. Considering cartel collaboration, innovations are more likely to be radical and developed and commercialized by small and medium-sized firms. When it comes to patenting, the relationship was negative. Together these results indicate that there are large differences in the characteristics of innovations and innovative firms in the different types of collaboration arrangements.

To conclude, the chapter provides new information concerning the changes in collaboration over the years. It also raises the question of importance of collaboration partners during the various stages of the innovation process. This chapter was the first attempt to combine cartel data with the Finnish innovation data. The results give some strong support to the switch in networking activities of the firms during the studied period. In addition, as the literature of innovation characteristics in the cartel context seems to be rather non-existent at the moment, this field will definitely be studied in the future as well.

APPENDIX 8.1: COLLABORATION IN INNOVATION

Correlation Matrix

	COLLA	INCRE	PATENT	LARGE
COLLA	1.000000	0.534846	0.536571	0.230487
INCRE	0.534846	1.000000	0.333944	-0.005819
PATENT	0.536571	0.333944	1.000000	-0.062282
LARGE	0.230487	-0.005819	-0.062282	1.000000

Descriptive Statistics

	COLLA	INCRE	PATENT	LARGE
Mean	0.165308	0.472467	0.249130	0.372894
Median	0.137626	0.464040	0.249529	0.369318
Maximum	0.400000	0.733333	0.454545	0.625000
Minimum	0.000000	0.258065	0.000000	0.178571
Std. Dev.	0.116807	0.112582	0.109009	0.089476
Skewness	0.478530	0.095534	-0.173325	0.355450
Kurtosis	2.075848	2.529077	2.238089	3.390642
Observations	40	40	40	40

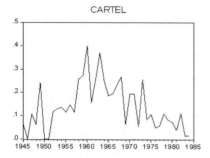

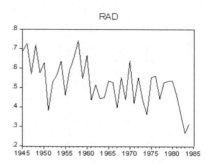

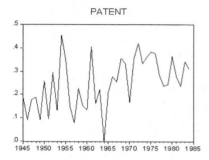

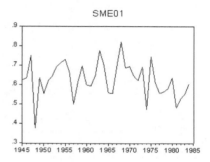

Estimation Output

Dependent Variable: LOG(COLLA)
Method: Least Squares
Sample (adjusted): 1945 1984
Included observations: 37 after adjustments

Variable	Coefficient	Std. Error	t-Statistic	Prob.
C	0.622616	0.504247	1.234743	0.2256
LOG(INCRE)	0.758728	0.408109	1.859130	0.0719
LOG(PATENT)	0.756931	0.205800	3.678002	0.0008
LOG(LARGE)	0.872047	0.371702	2.346095	0.0251

R-squared	0.500746	Mean dependent var		-1.941529
Adjusted R-squared	0.455360	S.D. dependent var		0.711746
S.E. of regression	0.525267	Akaike info criterion		1.651986
Sum squared resid	9.104877	Schwarz criterion		1.826139
Log likelihood	-26.56173	F-statistic		11.03289
Durbin-Watson stat	1.462644	Prob(F-statistic)		0.000036

APPENDIX 8.2: CARTELS IN INNOVATION

Correlogram of residuals

Autocorrelation	Partial Correlation		AC	PAC	Prob
. |**.	. |**.	1	0.210	0.210	0.184
. |* .	. |* .	2	0.129	0.089	0.294
. | .	. | .	3	0.055	0.012	0.462
. |**.	. |**.	4	0.228	0.215	0.303
. |**.	. |* .	5	0.260	0.191	0.162
. | .	. *| .	6	0.056	-0.069	0.234
. |* .	. |* .	7	0.162	0.138	0.231
. |* .	. |* .	8	0.169	0.100	0.217
. | .	. *| .	9	0.065	-0.104	0.279
. | .	. *| .	10	-0.044	-0.113	0.353
. *| .	.**| .	11	-0.161	-0.201	0.328
. |* .	. |* .	12	0.100	0.066	0.364

White Heteroskedasticity Test:			
F-statistic	0.686443	Prob. F(6,30)	0.661985
Obs*R-squared	4.466480	Prob. Chi-Square(6)	0.613815

Breusch-Godfrey Serial Correlation LM Test:			
F-statistic	1.145116	Prob. F(2,31)	0.331280
Obs*R-squared	2.545449	Prob. Chi-Square(2)	0.280067

Correlation Matrix

	CARTEL	RAD	PATENT	SME
CARTEL	1.000000	0.122491	-0.232439	0.424115
RAD	0.122491	1.000000	-0.312967	-0.007690
PATENT	-0.232439	-0.312967	1.000000	0.062282
SME	0.424115	-0.007690	0.062282	1.000000

Descriptive Statistics

	CARTEL	RAD	PATENT	SME
Mean	0.139436	0.523757	0.249130	0.627106
Median	0.115385	0.534565	0.249529	0.630682
Maximum	0.400000	0.741935	0.454545	0.821429
Minimum	0.000000	0.266667	0.000000	0.375000
Std. Dev.	0.100985	0.113658	0.109009	0.089476
Skewness	0.653850	-0.073187	-0.173325	-0.355450
Kurtosis	2.796981	2.547360	2.238089	3.390642
Observations	40	40	40	40

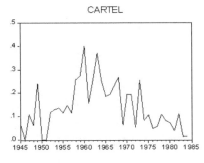

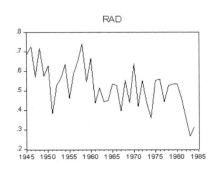

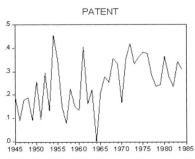

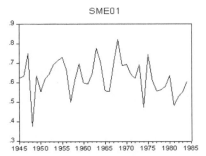

Estimation Output

Dependent Variable: LOG(CARTEL)
Method: Least Squares
Sample (adjusted): 1945 1984
Included observations: 36 after adjustments

Variable	Coefficient	Std. Error	t-Statistic	Prob.
C	-1.135982	0.696814	-1.630251	0.1129
LOG(RAD)	1.027340	0.544050	1.888319	0.0681
LOG(PATENT)	-0.495497	0.285632	-1.734739	0.0924
LOG(SME)	2.160104	0.713123	3.029075	0.0048

R-squared	0.391456	Mean dependent var		-2.163067
Adjusted R-squared	0.334405	S.D. dependent var		0.800794
S.E. of regression	0.653320	Akaike info criterion		2.090940
Sum squared resid	13.65846	Schwarz criterion		2.266886
Log likelihood	-33.63692	F-statistic		6.861503
Durbin-Watson stat	1.161558	Prob(F-statistic)		0.001067

Correlogram of Residuals

Autocorrelation	Partial Correlation		AC	PAC	Prob
. |***	. |***	1	0.336	0.336	0.036
. |* .	. | .	2	0.111	-0.001	0.086
. | .	. *| .	3	-0.042	-0.089	0.173
. *| .	. *| .	4	-0.155	-0.130	0.198
. *| .	. | .	5	-0.124	-0.027	0.245
. *| .	. *| .	6	-0.132	-0.077	0.278
. *| .	. *| .	7	-0.109	-0.059	0.328
. | .	. | .	8	-0.021	0.019	0.427
. *| .	. *| .	9	-0.095	-0.127	0.482
. |* .	. |**.	10	0.145	0.207	0.474
. |* .	. | .	11	0.083	-0.049	0.530
. | .	. *| .	12	-0.048	-0.131	0.604

White Heteroskedasticity Test:			
F-statistic	4.814771	Prob. F(6,29)	0.001607
Obs*R-squared	17.96537	Prob. Chi-Square(6)	0.006319

Breusch-Godfrey Serial Correlation LM Test:			
F-statistic	2.369447	Prob. F(2,30)	0.110810
Obs*R-squared	4.910927	Prob. Chi-Square(2)	0.085823

APPENDIX 8.3: INNOVATION DATA VARIABLES

1. Background data on the innovation
   The name of the innovation
   A brief description of the innovation
   TOL95 / NACE industrial field
   Complexity class

2. Year of commercialisation
   The commercialising firm:
   The name of the firm
   ID-number of the firm
   Firms previously involved in developing and commercialising the
   innovation

3. Characteristics of the innovation:
   Degree of novelty from the firm and market perspective

The nature of the required knowledge for the development of the innovation
Diffusion of the innovation

4. Patenting:
The name of patent assignees and patent authorities where patent granted
The origin of innovation and the time dimension:
Time taken from basic idea to prototype and commercialisation
Impulses for developing the innovation

5. Formal R&D
Yes / No

6. Public support:
The name of the public "supporter"

7. R&D collaboration:
The names of different partners during R&D collaboration

8. Other comments.

N

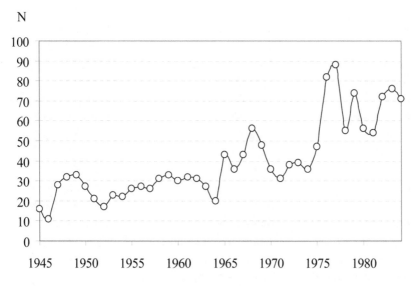

Appendix 8.3 Distribution of innovations 1945–84.

APPENDIX 8.4: LIST OF TECHNICAL AND TRADE JOURNALS

Name of journal	Years covered	Name of journal	Years covered
Tekniska Föreningens I Finland Förhandlingar	1945-58	Tielehti	1945-73
--> Tekniskt forum	1959-67	--> Tie ja Liikenne	1974-84
--> Forum för Ekonomi & Teknik	1968-84	Voima & Valo	1945-64
Suomen Kemistilehti	1945-73	Insinöörilehti	1952-70
Kemian Teollisuuden Tiedotuksia	1945-47	Teknillinen aikakauslehti	1945-70
--> Tekn. Kemian Aikakauslehti	1948-64	Teollisuuslehti	1945-70
--> Kemian Teollisuus	1965-73	--> Tekniikka	1970-82
--> Kemia	1974-84	Teollisuusteknikko	1945-66
Kuljetus	1959-84	--> Teollisuustekniikka	1967-84
Konepajamies	1951-84	Tehostaja	1945-68
Suomen Paperi- ja Puutavaralehti	1945-49	--> Yritystalous	1969-74
--> Paperi ja Puu	1950-84	--> Tehokas yritys	1975-80
Puumies	1956-79	Talouselämä	1945-84
--> Puu	1980-84	Työnjohto & Tekniikka	1955-74
Tekstiili	1945-84	Jäte & Ympäristö	1982-84
Keken uutiset	1977-80	Suomen Autolehti	1945-52
--> Keksintöuutiset	1981-84	Teollisuus & Tekniikka	1948-50
Teollisuus-sanomat	1946-77		
--> Teollisuus	1978-80		

APPENDIX 8.5: LIST OF COMPANY HISTORIES USED FOR THE INNOVATION DATA

Aga Oy Ab	Kaukas Oy	Rikkihappo- ja Super
Airam Oy	Kone Oy	Rosenlew Oy
Antti-Teollisuus Oy	Kymi – Kymmene Oy	Strömberg Oy
Aspo Oy	Kyro Oy	Sunila Oy
Atria Oy	Lemminkäinen Oy	Suomen Autoteollisu
Enso-Gutzeit Oy	Lokomo Oy	Suomen Kumitehdas
Fazer Oy	Lännen Tehtaat Oy	Suomivalimo Oy
Finlayson Oy	Medica Oy	Tampella Oy
Fiskars Oy	Nokia Oy	Typpi Oy
G.A. Serlachius Oy	Neste Oy	UPM-Kymmene Oy
Hackman Oy	Orion Oy	Vaasan Puuvilla Oy
Hartwall Oy	Outokumpu Oy	Vaisala Oy
Honkarakenne Oy	Paraisten Kalkkivuori Oy	Valmet Oy
Huhtamäki Oy	Raisio Yhtymä Oy	Wärtsilä Oy
Instrumentarium Oy	Rauma-Repola Oy	
Kaipio Oy	Rautaruukki Oy	

NOTES

1. On the basis of Chesnais' classification, OECD (1991) published a simplified version on different forms of collaboration. According to OECD, the most important forms of collaboration were (1) new research corporations, (2) equity-based agreements, (3) non-equity cooperative agreements and (4) agreements on completed technologies. In addition to these studies, the Maastricht Economic Research Institute on Innovation and Technology (MERIT) presented their own classification, which was based on the empirical data, collected from some ten thousand collaborative projects (Hagedoorn 1989, 1992; Hagedoorn and Schakenraad 1989). Despite of the identification of the different forms of R&D collaboration, and despite the large number of studies related to analyses means, effects, results and so on of collaboration, the time perspective and the historical evolution of collaboration has not been the subject of the studies.
2. In this context, 'innovative firms' mean firms which commercialized innovations during the studied period of time. Please note that innovative firms in my database are selected according to the object-approach criteria. This means that only firms whose innovations have been identified from the magazines are included.
3. 'Incremental innovation' is defined as an innovation which is (1) totally new to the firm and new to the domestic markets, (2) a major or incremental improvement to the firm and new to the world markets, or (3) a major or incremental improvement to the firm and new to the domestic markets.
4. 'Large firm' is defined as a firm with over one hundred employees.
5. 'Radical innovation' is defined as an innovation which is totally new to the firm and new to the world markets.
6. 'Small and medium-size firm' is defined as a firm with less than one hundred employees.

REFERENCES

Acs, Z., and D. Audretsch. 1990. *Innovation and small firms.* Cambridge, MA: MIT Press.
Allen, R. C. 1983. Collective invention. *Journal of Economic Behaviour and Organization* 4:1–24.
Baumol, W. J. 1992. Horizontal collusion and innovation. *Economic Journal* 102:129–137.
———. 1993. *Entrepreneurship, management and the structure of payoffs.* Cambridge, MA: MIT Press.
Becker, W., and J. Dietz. 2004. R&D cooperation and innovation activities of firms—evidence for the German manufacturing industry. *Research Policy* 33 (2): 209–223.
Brooks, H., and L. Randazzese. 1998. University-Industry Relations. In *Investing in Innovation: Creating a Research and Innovation Policy that Works,* ed. L. Branscomb and J. Keller, 361–399. Cambridge, MA: MIT Press.
Chesnais, F. 1988. Technical co-operation agreements between firms. *STI Review* 4:51–119.
Dachs, B., B. Ebersberger and A. Pyka. 2004. *Why do firms co-operate for innovation? A comparison of Austrian and Finnish CIS 3 results.* Volkswirtschaftliche Diskussionsreihe, Beitrag 255. Institut für Volkswirtschaftslehre.

162   Jani Saarinen

Edwards, K. L., and T. J. Gordon. 1984. *Characterization of innovations intro-duced on the U.S. market in 1982*. Report to the U.S. Small Business Adminis-tration. Glastonbury, CT: The Futures Group.

Fleissner, P., W. Hofkirchner and M. Poh. 1993. The Austrian experience with literature-based innovation output indicators. In *New concepts in innovation output measurement*, ed. A. Kleinknecht and D. Bain, 85–112. Houndsmill, U.K.: Macmillan Press.

Freeman, C. 1988. Japan: A new national system of innovation? In *Technical change and economic theory*, ed. Dosi et al. 330–348. London and New York: Pinter Publishers.

Fritsch, M., and R. Lukas. 2001. Who cooperates on R&D? *Research Policy* 30:297–312.

Gold, B. 1987. Approaches to accelerating new product development. *Journal of Product Development Management* 4:81–88.

Hagedoorn, J. 1989. *Economic theory and analyses of cooperation and alliances in R&D and innovation*. MERIT's Research Memoranda 89–006Maastricht: MERIT.

———. 1992. *Market structural hierarchies and networks of strategic technology partnering*. MERIT's Research Memoranda 92–026. Maastricht: MERIT.

Hagedoorn, J., and J. Schakenraad. 1989. *Some remarks on the cooperative agreements and technology indicators (CATI) information system*. MERIT's Research Memoranda 89–010. Maastricht: MERIT.

Halme, A., M. Pulkkinen and J. Tiilikka. 1999. *Tutkimuksen ja tuotekehityksen verkottumisen strategiat: Tutkimus yritysten avainhankkeista*. Teknologiakat-saus 78/99. Helsinki: TEKES.

Heikkinen, S., and A. Kuusterä. 2002. Institutions and crises: Finnish economy in the 20th century. Paper presented at the Thirteenth International Economic History Association Congress, Buenos Aires, 22–26 July 2002.

Jorde, T. M., and D. J. Teece. 1990. Innovation and cooperation: Implica-tions for competition and antitrust. *Journal of Economic Perspectives* 4 (3): 75–96.

Kamien, M. I., E. Muller and I. Zang. 1992. Research joint ventures and R&D cartels. *American Economic Review* 82 (5): 1293–1306.

Kankaala, K., E. Kaukonen, P. Kutinlahti, T. Lemola, M. Nieminen and J. Väli-maa. 2004. *Yliopistojen kolmas tehtävä*. Helsinki: Edita.

Katz, M. L., and J. A. Ordover. 1990. R&D cooperation and competition. *Brook-ing Papers on Economic Activity: Microeconomics*, 137–203.

Kleinkrecht, A. and Bria, D. (ed's) 1993. *New concepts in innovation output mea-surement*. Macmillan Press, Houndsmill.

Lemola, T. 1994. *Yritysten välisen teknologiayhteistyön tausta ja muutoksen suuntaviivat*. VTT Research Notes 1540. Espoo, Finland: VTT.

———. 2002. Tiede- ja teknologiapolitiikan muotoutuminen. In *Suomen Tieteen Historia*, ed. P. Tommila and A. Tiitta, 466–489. Helsinki: WSOY.

Lievonen, J. 1998. *Innovaatiot ja infrastruktuurit: Esimerkkinä internet-innovaa-tiot*. VTT Group for Technology Studies, Working Papers 36/98. Espoo, Fin-land: VTT.

Michelsen, K-E. 1993. *Valtio, teknologia, tutkimus: VTT ja kansallisen tutki-musjärjestelmän kehitys*. Painatuskeskus Oy. Espoo, Finland: VTT.

Negassi, S. 2004. R&D co-operation and innovation a microeconometric study on French firms. *Research Policy* 33:365–384.

OECD, 1991. TEP—the technology economy programme: Technology in a chang-ing world. Paris: OECD.

———. 1997. *Proposed guidelines for collecting and interpreting technological innovation data—'the Oslo Manual'*. Paris: OECD & Eurostat.

―――. 2003. Regulatory reform in Finland: The role of competition policy in regulatory reform. Paris: OECD.

Oksanen, J. 2003. *VTT:n alueellinen rooli ja vaikuttavuus* [*Regional role and impact of VTT*]. VTT Tiedotteita Research Notes 2205. Espoo, Finland: VTT.

Parkinson, S. 1982. Successful new product development: Having good customers helps. *The Business Graduate* 12 (1), Special Issue on Innovation:123–131.

Petit, M. L., and B. Tolwinski. 1996. Technology sharing cartels and industrial structure. *International Journal of Industrial Organisation* 15:77–101.

Purasjoki, M., and J. Jokinen. 2001. Kilpailupolitiikan odotukset, saavutukset ja haasteet. In *Asianajotoimisto Borenius & Kemppinen 90 vuotta*, ed. H. Arvanne-Potrykus et al., 99–123. Jyväskylä, Finland: Gummerus Kirjapaino Oy.

Rothwell, R. 1977. The characteristics of successful innovators and technically progressive firms (with some comments on innovation research). *R&D Management* 7 (3): 191–206.

―――. 1994. Issues in user-producer relations in the innovation process. *International Journal of Technology Management* 9 (5, 6, 7): 629–649.

Saarinen, J. 2005. *Innovations and industrial performance in Finland 1945–1998.* Lund Studies in Economic History 34. Stockholm: Almqvist & Wiksell International.

Unknown. 1951. Tutkimustyötä tekstiiliteollisuudessa. *Teollisuuslehti*, 410.

Virtanen, M. 1998. *Market dominance-related competition policy: An eclectic theory and analyses of policy evolution.* Turku, Finland: Turku School of Economics and Business Administration, Serie A.-1.

von Hippel, E. 1988. *The sources of innovation.* New York: Oxford University Press.

9 Networks of Opportunity and the Spanish Pharmaceutical Industry

Núria Puig

INTRODUCTION

Innovation is the ultimate source of economic progress. For innovation to occur there has to be an awareness and understanding of changes that take place in consumer demand, technological capabilities and the wider business and economic environments. This understanding depends on entrepreneurship. Entrepreneurs have played a fundamental role in the industrial and information eras by recognizing and responding to opportunities. How they seize and adapt them to their own environment is crucial for success. This chapter is concerned with the way entrepreneurs interplay with their institutional environment over time. By examining two intense periods of the history of the pharmaceutical industry—the antibiotics and the global eras—through six leading Spanish laboratories, the chapter seeks to understand how firms embedded in late industrializing countries and operating in technologically complex industries respond to major opportunities and try to catch up with the most advanced firms in the world.

As I write this, the world economic power is shifting from the historical leaders of industrialization to far less advanced yet fast-growing countries. If economic power continues to be linked with the ability to innovate, and there are signs that it does, this could change dramatically the rules and the geography of the pharmaceutical industry in the years to come. The stories chronicled here, however, were set in the previous scenario. Spain was a peripheral country with a poor historical record in innovation and entrepreneurship. Within this context, the firms, individuals and social groups under scrutiny were remarkable in terms of awareness and entrepreneurship, since they managed to (1) identify and seize business opportunities linked to the transnational diffusion of scientific and technical innovations, (2) create appropriate, if not privileged, conditions for their introduction in the Spanish market and (3) improve existing scientific-technical and managerial capabilities within their companies. But the outcomes were radically different. Whereas Antibióticos and CEPA failed to innovate and thus to reach the international market, Uriach, Esteve, Almirall and Ferrer have created their own specialized niches in the global market.

To explain why the former laboratories, unlike many comparable companies created at the same time in other parts of the world, did not succeed, I developed the concept of *opportunity networks* (Puig 2004). This was opposed to the concept of *innovation networks* brought about by Louis Galambos and Jane Sewell in their analysis of the American firm Merck, Sharp & Dohme (Galambos and Sewell 1995). I argued that formal and informal personal relations built and maintained over time, plus the remarkable ability of individuals and families to recognize business opportunities, lobby and design their own growth strategies, played a role of the utmost importance in the rise and consolidation of the Spanish pharmaceutical industry—a far more important role than the (rather mediocre) national system of innovation or the (frequently lacking) cohesiveness among the various professional bodies involved in the pharmaceutical business, two key elements in the innovative drive of American firms, according to Galambos and Sewell. As a result, short-term strategies have tended to prevail over the long-term strategies required by innovation in a science-based industry. The argument was sustained by the fact that the industrial and the scientific efforts displayed by the leading Spanish firms never became fully integrated into each other. In this chapter I re-examine, backed by new evidence, the development of the antibiotics manufacturers and approach the so far successful evolution of four leading and internationalized Spanish laboratories. Interestingly, all of them were built and sustained by networks of opportunity that, as the information and global ages develop further, are apparently becoming networks of innovation.

BETWEEN INDUSTRY AND ACADEMIA: THE CREATION OF THE SPANISH ANTIBIOTICS INDUSTRY

Antibiotics were an extremely important achievement of the American pharmaceutical industry. Built on scientific knowledge previously developed in British institutions, they turned into one of the most successful programmes of the so-called war effort (Parascandola 1980; Liebenau 1987). The new drugs were so effective against infections that their trade and manufacture spread fast throughout the world. Antibiotics did not only contribute to American industrial leadership: they gave rise to a wave of unlimited confidence in the power of scientific research. In late industrializing countries, the introduction of antibiotics brought with it the dissemination of American scientific and organization methods and the creation of the modern pharmaceutical industry (Redwood 1988; United Nations Industrial Development Organisation [UNIDO] 1992; Higby and Stroud 1990, 1997).

Conditions for the establishment of the antibiotics industry were apparently favourable in Spain. Local capital, industrial and scientific awareness, international contacts and the non-intrusive support of the Spanish government were all in place in the late 1940s. The pharmaceutical industry had developed considerably during the Second World War thanks to the pro-German neutrality maintained by Franco's dictatorial government. After the war, however, Spain adhered to the Bretton Woods agreement and German chemical and pharmaceutical assets were expropriated and sold to various Spanish groups (Puig 2001; Puig 2003a, 93–130; Puig and Álvaro 2007). Interestingly, most of the new owners were able to adapt to the extremely nationalistic policy of post-war Spain, while cooperating further with their former German home companies. This was indeed the case with Bayer and Schering, by far the most important investors from the German pharmaceutical industry in Spain and both of them remarkably sound businesses throughout the period that concerns us. It was on the basis of these two firms, along with the technical assistance of the American firm Merck, that the Compañía Española de Penicilina y Antibióticos (CEPA) was founded. Moreover, its scientific director managed to create a scientific institution, the Instituto de Farmacología Española (IFE), attached to his physiology chair at the University of Madrid and financed by the German subsidiaries (Santesmases 1999).

Another interesting feature of the institutional environment is that the Spanish government, which between 1939 and 1959 was embarked on a strongly nationalistic industrialization programme, based on self-sufficiency and the creation of a state-owned industrial holding, decided to leave the manufacture of penicillin and other antibiotics in private hands. Along the lines established by a law passed in 1948, two private companies 'of national interest' were founded: CEPA and Antibióticos. Both were granted fiscal and administrative privileges and the exclusive right to sell in the domestic market. A duopoly was thus born.

The development of the Spanish antibiotics industry was strongly influenced by its international and national environment, one which offered opportunities but at the same time created severe limitations on the development of a dynamic industry. Secondly, this promising sector was shaped by the cultural background of the business groups which supported it. These groups belonged to a liberal elite which, besides coming to terms with the new political rulers, regarded its own scientific and academic activities as being separate from its industrial and financial enterprises, which were often extremely successful. It is probably very telling that this elite's wealth and assets had their origins in partnerships with foreign, technologically advanced firms, which after the war made them suitable candidates for still further partnerships. The persistence and even strengthening of two separate cultures, a characteristic common to the industrial landscape in developing countries, underlies our story. The founders of CEPA and Antibióticos jumped at the chance to introduce antibiotics, recognizing the value of the new drugs and possessing the resources needed to make such an enterprise viable. In turn they reaped huge profits and were able to cultivate their own particular academic or cultural interests. As they demonstrated in thought and action, as did Spain's vindictive new authorities, industry and science were only apparently united. Establishing a clear and rewarding division of labour with the multinational firms assisting them, these Spanish partners actively contributed to the emergence of opportunity, rather than innovation, networks.

Antibióticos S.A.

Antibióticos was founded by five independent laboratories in 1949 (Antibióticos S.A. 1974). One of these, Instituto de Biología y Sueroterapia (IBYS), established by the more enterprising students of the prominent scientist Ramón y Cajal and linked to the University of Madrid, had played a leading role in the manufacture of sera and vaccines in the early twentieth century (IBYS 1944). IBYS was backed by the entrepreneurial and liberal-minded family Urgoiti (Cabrera 1994). In 1919, one of the Urgoiti brothers, Ricardo, professor of medicine at the University of Madrid, created IBYS on Cajal's advice with other prominent members of the Madrid medical profession, academic or otherwise, and with his own money (Ramón y Cajal 1923). Thanks to the proliferation of public health institutes in the early twentieth century and the position held by some of its partners in them, IBYS soon became a sound business and was able to support a prestigious in-house research institute with many prominent academics on its board and to publish a serious quarterly journal (Rodríguez-Ocaña 2000). Urgoiti's many international contacts, in addition to his own trips to the United States (where some of his colleagues had emigrated after 1939), gave him the opportunity of finding a partner for the import and manufacture of penicillin in Spain: Schenley. As we will see, Urgoiti and most of his colleagues belonged to the same social and intellectual milieu as CEPA's directors.

The focus of the American distilling firm on veterinary products was attractive for the first and most important founding member of Antibióticos, Abelló. Founded in the 1920s by a skilful Catalonian pharmacist and chemist, Juan Abelló, Fábrica de Productos Químicos y Farmacéuticos Abelló would become a very large and diversified business after the Spanish and world wars. Abelló's largest plant in León worked in association with a public veterinary station. It was there that Antibióticos built its first penicillin plant. In a way, Abelló was the industrial partner, promoting backward integration after 1960, while Urgoiti was regarded as the scientific (and academic) partner of Antibióticos. There is some evidence that Juan Abelló (who had excellent relations with the new regime) tended to be in charge of the bureaucratic affairs of the new firm, but it was Urgoiti who, in cooperation with CEPA's director, denounced and took action against a tolerated black market in penicillin that obviously damaged their interests and distorted the very nature of the existing duopoly. It was also Abelló who actively participated in the organization of the pharmaceutical lobby

Farmaindustria and the creation of the Spanish industry's legal framework in the late 1950s and 1960s.

The third founding firm was Leti-Uquifa, a Barcelona laboratory that distributed imported drugs, as did most Spanish companies, and produced some biological products and specialties. Interestingly, Uquifa (Unión Químico-Farmacéutica), founded in 1939, competed with Abelló in the new field of alkaloids. Its most prominent manager was Federico Mayor Domingo, the effective director of Antibióticos' main plant in León.[1]

Leti-Uquifa had strong links with the Barcelona medical and academic professions, among which the important collective action of the Spanish pharmaceutical industry emerged. The Madrid-based Instituto Llorente also specialized in sera and vaccines. During the wars, its owner, a renowned Madrid physician, established a partnership with Schering that allowed it to move into new fields, particularly that of hormones, but this was short-lived. Finally, Zeltia, a Galician firm, was founded in 1939 by an energetic self-made man and laid the foundations of various other successful firms.[2] At the core of Zeltia was a rather commercial joint-venture with the British company Imperial Chemical Industries.

According to Schenley's annual reports and Antibióticos' records, relations between the firms were determined by standard license agreements until 1980 (Schenley 1945–1955; Archivo General de la Administración [AGA], Industria 286). The introduction of the deep-fermentation process, unattainable by the Spanish partners, was fully assisted by the American firm, which built the León pilot plant and regularly trained Spanish technicians in Spain and in the United States. Most of the raw materials, such as steep corn, were imported, with royalties being paid. Serving a relatively small market, Antibióticos followed a very safe strategy: the first penicillin was manufactured in 1952, with streptomycin following in 1955, tetracycline in 1958 and vitamin B12 in 1960. The first semi-synthetic penicillin was patented in 1963 but for some reason abandoned. Semi-synthesis absorbed most of the research activities at Antibióticos, not that these were noteworthy. In 1963 the firm employed some one thousand people plus almost five hundred sales agents. Only fourteen were university graduates. The technically most complex tasks had to do with quality control. Tasks became more complex as did the firm's structure in the late 1960s, with the number of university graduates rising to forty, working in seven different departments, and around twenty-five university graduates and technicians occupied with scientific problems. All this led apparently to a better understanding of fermentation, on the one hand, and to an increasing number of vitamin patents (process variations of other patents), on the other. In 1976 several projects on quantitative methods, spectroscopy and chromatography were being carried out in cooperation with the optical department of the Consejo Superior de Investigaciones Científicas (CSIC). By then most of the original license agreements had expired.

The scientific background and technical expertise of Antibióticos was of little use in the area of antibiotics. Urgoiti and his colleagues came from the Madrid histology school, a field soon challenged by biochemistry and new scientific instruments, and had apparently no interest in antibiotics beyond a broad scientific understanding of established knowledge and ongoing research (Santesmases 2000, 2001). Their interests, reflected in *Revista IBYS* and other publications, took their own directions. Some, such as Urgoiti, kept their positions on the faculties of pharmacy and medicine at the University of Madrid while they worked at IBYS and sat on the board of Antibióticos.

CEPA

The creation of CEPA is a much more complicated story. It is closely linked to the construction of a pharma-chemical complex by the Urquijo Bank, the core of a business group formed around the aristocratic Urquijo family, whose wealth is associated with Rothschild's enterprises in Spain (Puig and Torres 2008). Although none of the family had a scientific background, the Urquijo Bank supported scientific and intellectual activities, particularly after the war, becoming in this way a sort of refuge for both established and excluded Spanish intellectuals. Moreover, the Urquijo group continued to be a natural partner in multinational firms, played a remarkable role in the economic and diplomatic relations between Spain and the United States and became the voice of the Ford Foundation beginning in the early 1960s (Puig 2003b).

The story of the Urquijo pharma-chemical complex also provides a fine example of the dynamics of Spain's post-war chemical industry. After a five-year-long process, in which Robert was instrumental, Proquisa and the Consorcio—two ad hoc firms backed by the Urquijo Bank and historically the Spanish partners of IG Farben and Nobel—acquired at a very low price the core of the German pharmaceutical business in Spain: Bayer and Schering. Bayer became the cornerstone of an ambitious coal-based chemical concern in La Felguera, in northern Spain, aimed at producing nitric, salicilic and acetilsalicilic acids, and methanol. The plant was built with the technical cooperation of the Italian and French multinationals Montecatini and Kuhlmann and the financial support of Bayer, a sound business working closely with Leverkusen and a captive customer for La Felguera's output. As for Schering, it became the basis of another ambitious pharma-chemical enterprise, CEPA, directed by Antonio Gallego, a brilliant scientist returning from the Rockefeller Foundation. He had been called by his brother José Luis, the scientific director of Bayer in Spain from 1936 to 1943 and from 1950 onwards. Before they acquired Productos Químicos, Schering's new Spanish owners made sure they could manufacture under licence from Berlin. As in the case of Bayer, the German firm's excellent sales network was used to commercialize the first antibiotics manufactured by CEPA under Merck license, and the rising profits of Schering itself kept CEPA going during its difficult start.

As mentioned previously, Bayer and Schering financed one of the few private scientific institutions of the time, IFE, founded in 1950 and located initially at CEPA's headquarters and moved later on to the University of Madrid, where Gallego became professor of physiology. Thus, IFE was originally an instrument for the transfer of technology, inspired and applauded by the new scientific authorities of the Consejo Superior de Investigaciones Científicas, as well as the only institution training industrial-minded scientists (Gallego 1958). There is evidence that the close relations between Gallego's academic circle and CEPA's people were driven by logistic and financial forces, not by an inner belief in academic-industry cooperation or by Gallego's desire to provide the growing pharmaceutical industry with his students. As academic career opportunities were scarce, many of IFE's university graduates ended up working at CEPA and other companies, particularly the many multinational subsidiaries established in the 1960s. As for IFE's research and publications, they became more and more aligned with the true academic interests of its director and with Spain's post-war physiology school.

An extremely interesting piece of the scientific-academic puzzle constructed by Gallego was the Natural Products Screening Programme, the origin of Merck's research centre in Madrid (Centro de Investigación Básica Española, CIBE) (Sturchio 1992; Mochales 1994; Strohl et al. 2001). Gallego persuaded CEPA's technological partner to establish in 1954 a branch of the newly launched screening programme, aimed at identifying natural active principles which were later synthesized in the United States. No doubt the pro-American atmosphere created by Spanish-American agreements favoured this move. The modest research unit focused on the continued work of the scientist Martínez Mata and his tiny team (fourteen people including laboratory technicians) and on the training and supervision of some of Merck's researchers at Rahway, particularly Oswald Stapley. This trans-Atlantic relationship was apparently an excellent one, meagre salaries (provided by CEPA) not spoiling the fundamental enthusiasm of its members. Joining the screening programme at such an early stage meant having a general overview of how this pioneering firm planned its research, an opportunity that no foreign firm has offered to Spanish researchers until very recently. It is truly astonishing that Merck, whose few foreign research units were located in highly developed countries, accepted Gallego's idea in those sombre years. For CEPA, the unit was a cheap luxury, expenses other than facility costs and salaries being paid by Merck, but the board of directors was increasingly reluctant to back its expansion. Given that progress was rather slow, and coinciding with the mounting difficulties of the Urquijo pharma-chemical complex and Gallego's personal disagreements with CEPA's management, the unit stagnated in terms of budget and staff. Its few university graduates were regular attendants of IFE's academic events, but there was no apparent interest within Spanish academia in what the Spanish branch of the screening programme was doing.

Effective as it was, the Urquijo pharma-chemical complex could not satisfy the expectations of its creators. Falling international prices of raw materials and some active ingredients, the prospect of liberalization, the inexorable advent of petrochemicals, a scandalous smuggling of penicillin and the approaching expiration of the licence contracts with Germany combined to bring down the entire structure in the late 1950s and early 1960s. As with most of the international chemical agreements in Spain, it was in the end a good deal for both parties. There is no doubt that it was extremely useful in creating entrepreneurial capabilities—and establishing further international contacts—within the liberal elite to which the Urquijo team belonged. In 1974 the Urquijo group sold off its chemical and pharmaceutical firms to Spain's largest chemical company, Explosivos Río Tinto, in which the Urquijo held a share. The new managers undertook an impressive expansion through backward integration and the acquisition of Spanish firms. The first scientific achievements of the screening programme (contributions to four new antibiotics—fosfomycin, cephamycin, cefoxitin and thienamycin—patented in the United States between 1972 and 1976) did not change Explosivos' initial lack of interest. At that time, Merck had established its own subsidiary and, in 1978, Martínez Mata and his team agreed to join it. A phase of expansion followed. Today CIBE has employees working with Spanish scientific institutions, a cooperation that began in the late 1980s. However, according to its long-time member and director, Sagrario Mochales, this was very hard to achieve. The early story of CIBE sheds light, in my view, on the roots of Spanish scientific and technical backwardness: the reluctance—if not unwillingness—of entrepreneurs to invest in research and development and the tendency to regard it as a purely intellectual activity, unrelated to business, even by those with a first-hand knowledge of both worlds. As for CEPA, after a rather turbulent period under Explosivos' management, it fell into the hands of Abelló's son, Juan, a doctor of pharmacy and a prominent figure in Spain's financial community. The firm was sold in 1999 to a German concern, becoming CEPA Schwarz Pharma. (Abelló 2000).[3]

To understand why the Natural Products Screening Programme, the result of a unique industrial-scientific constellation revolving around the unique personality of Antonio Gallego, did not give rise to a more innovative environment, first in the antibiotics field, then in further orientations, it seems reasonable to examine Merck's strategy. The question is not so much why the American firm did not expand CIBE's activities beyond its original, but why CEPA did not take full advantage of it, and how, serving as an intermediary between Merck and Spanish academia, it did not create the innovative capabilities that would guarantee its future.

In 1957, CEPA and Merck signed an agreement to distribute Merck's products through CEPA's (that is, Schering's) commercial networks. It was a common strategy among multinational firms seeking to avoid the many obstacles imposed by the Spanish administration on foreign investment before 1960. Taking advantage of the more liberal policy displayed by the Spanish government in the next decade and the impressive expansion of the domestic market, a subsidiary was established in 1968. It is interesting to note that the American firm did not refer to the screening programme in the documents sent to the Spanish Ministry of Industry (AGA, Industria 1.04 5112). Following OECD's guidelines, the administration sought to strengthen private research and logically looked to multinational firms for this. Wanting the required authorization, Merck argued that it had cooperated with CEPA in the development of new antibiotics since 1967. Indeed, that year Merck established a research department at CEPA that would become the subsidiary's platform. Influenced by the post-thalidomide framework, Merck looked for someone to direct a pioneering clinical testing unit in Madrid. The choice was Joaquín Mouriz, a medical researcher at CSIC who had spent some time in American universities and had no connection with CEPA or with Gallego's circles. It was with the University of Navarra, a private institution supported by the Catholic organization Opus Dei, that Merck cooperated regularly after 1970. In this way Merck helped to create the first clinical pharmacological department in Spain. Why Gallego did not seize this opportunity is not known. The clinical testing programme provided the University of Navarra (and, on a more modest scale, the new Autonomous University of Barcelona) with regular funding and launched a competitive biomedical programme for young graduate students and doctors.

The Rise of Four Spanish Global Laboratories[4]

This section deals with the development of four Barcelona-based laboratories, family owned and managed, middle sized, research committed, internationalized and increasingly involved in strategic alliances with national and foreign firms and research centres. The control of Uriach, Esteve, Almirall and Ferrer over a very dynamic domestic market alongside skilful lobbying have helped find or create their own niches in an extremely complex and competitive industry. Beyond this, one should note that (1) they have successfully managed their succession and professionalization processes; (2) their accumulated expertise is closely linked to their focus; (3) their turning points were responses to major economic challenges; (4) their most prominent members have been committed to collective action in association with Farmaindustria and the Instituto de la Empresa Familiar (IEF); (5) they hold many and varied connections with Spanish academia, which includes two private Catholic institutes, IQS and IESE; (6) international contacts and more recently strategic alliances have fuelled their internationalization; and (7) the relationship between industry and academia has apparently reached a new stage: the activity of their R&D departments is outstanding by Spanish standards, there are strong links with academic institutions and most of the philanthropic activity, channelled through foundations, is focused on pharmacology. Note, finally, that for the first time in the Spanish pharmaceutical industry short-term strategies are being replaced by long-term strategies, those that shape the innovative capabilities of any firm.

Uriach

Laboratorios Uriach was founded by Juan Uriach Feliu (Fundación Uriach 1988). Through hard work as a Barcelona chemist's employee, he was able to buy and rename the shop in 1860. He was joined by his three sons and succeeded by the eldest, Joaquín Uriach Uriach. Unlike his brothers, both of them pharmacists, Joaquín had no scientific education. In 1898 they added a laboratory to the traditional chemist and distribution business, in which they prepared cow-bone-marrow syrup and cough lozenges. They also manufactured a number of well-known foreign drugs, such as cough pills, cod-liver oil or laxatives, which they marketed and advertised with increasingly sophisticated and expensive methods borrowed from trend-setting German and Swiss laboratories.

On the eve of the Spanish civil war (1936–1939), the third generation, made up of three male cousins, took over. Again, only the younger members studied pharmacy. The eldest, Juan Uriach Tey, played the leading role. He agreed to keep his job as general manager throughout the war, when the firm was collectivized. The outbreak of the Second World War and Spain's particularly long and tough post-war period did not help to re-establish a business that was very dependent on foreign supplies and domestic demand. Like some of his fellow chemists and pharmacists, however, Uriach insisted on keeping the laboratory going and did actually start to do in-house research. It was a way to fight the general scarcity of raw materials and intermediate products and to take advantage of the nationalistic environment that followed the war. The result was the Instituto Farmacológico Experimental Biohorn. Founded in 1941, Biohorn did produce original products, such as *Nico-Hepatocyn, Bio-Digest, Biodramina, Lipograsil, Hipotensor, Hepatocyn, Conifit, Hiperbiol, Bio-Test* and *Taqui-Tyral*. Some of them remain best-selling over-the-counter (OTC) drugs. The increasing concurrence from equally national-minded laboratories and foreign multinational companies led Uriach to look for 'a niche of products with personality', to open commercial outlets all across Spain and to display new commercial techniques. Foreign markets, though, still made for a large share of Uriach's business.

In the mid-1950s, Uriach Tey's eldest son joined the firm. Dr. Juan Uriach Marsal (b. 1929) graduated with honours at the Faculty of Pharmacy of the University of Barcelona in 1955. In spite of his talent and fondness for academia, he joined the company immediately afterwards. Since his father also ran the firm in a quite patriarchal fashion, he directed his energy towards the research facilities, which he soon transformed into a true R&D department. The young Uriach's excellent links with the University of Barcelona (where he completed his Ph.D. a few years later) helped him to start and reinforce several research lines that would ultimately lead his company to integrate vertically. It was an example of synthesis and of many other innovations of the post-war world pharmaceutical industry.

The future of in-house research, however, depended not only on the efforts carried out by a specific department. The end of the autarchic politics that had exacerbated Spain's backwardness and isolation in the 1940s and 1950s was approaching when Uriach Marsal joined the firm. And a new generation of owners and managers of pharmaceutical companies had emerged—a generation that had been trained in science and management, knew how to deal with the Spanish administration, had foreign connections and was well aware of what was going on in the international pharmaceutical market. Furthermore, they felt that they belonged together, and on this basis they laid the foundations of Farmaindustria, used by the largest domestic firms to shape the legal framework of the Spanish pharmaceutical industry. It is important to note that Uriach was one of the first people to attend the post-graduate program PDG of the business school Instituto de Estudios Superiores de la Empresa (IESE) in the mid-1960s, as did Josep Esteve and one of the Gallardo brothers, along with many other members of Catalan family firms. IESE was instrumental in giving them the best business education available at the time in Spain, as well as an excellent platform for networking and lobbying. Indeed, the first chair of family business was created at IESE in 1987, and the lobby Instituto de la Empresa Familiar (IEF) was set up in 1992 in close association with the chair.

The transition from the fourth to the fifth generation has taken place gradually (Uriach 2002). It helped that in the 1980s Uriach Marsal became the sole owner of the laboratory after purchasing the shares of the other branches of the family. It was a key strategy for the survival of the firm. In the 1990s Uriach's five children have moved fully to the forefront of management of the company under the lead of one of them. Juan (b. 1958), Marta (b. 1960), Javier (b. 1961), Enrique (b. 1962) and Joaquín (b. 1966) have been trained respectively as pharmacist, designer, economist and lawyer. In addition, two of them have attended IESE.

Uriach's new strategy pursues collaborations or licences with pharmaceutical partners to develop its own product pipeline. The firm's research areas were defined between the 1960s and 1980s: cardiovascular, inflammatory and infectious diseases. It was here that the most successful drugs were developed: trifusal (Disgren), the most prescribed antithrombotic agent in Spain, marketed in over twenty-five countries; flutrimazole (Micetal), a topical antifungal agent with improved tolerability and a broad spectrum of activity, marketed in fifteen countries; and fosfosal (Disdolen), an anti-inflammatory agent with no gastric side effects. Collaborations with other firms or research institutions (and more recently also a Spanish venture capital firm) are expected to provide Uriach with an extra source of revenue and to enable the company to diversify scientific and financial risk and provide access to its collaborators' development, manufacturing and marketing resources. The current focus is in allergy, systemic fungal infection, inflammation and Alzheimers. Uriach, however, is a relatively small firm. Chemical synthesis and in vitro and in vivo screening are performed within Uriach's R&D centre, but pre-clinical toxicology and clinical trials are performed in collaboration with external contract research services. Bio-analytical and clinical support is retained in-house. Trial production is accomplished by the Uriach's chemical subsidiary Urquimia soon after a pre-clinical candidate has been identified. The group pursues rapid first-into-man clinical trials for both pharmacokinetic and dynamic testing, allowing early proof of concept. This strategy seeks to help the decision making process. All this work is organized through interdisciplinary therapeutic project teams that manage the drug development process, from discovery through marketing. The R&D portfolio is periodically reviewed by the Science and Commercial Executive Board. As of 2007, Grupo Uriach includes seven companies: J. Uriach y Cía (ethical), Biohorn (ethical), Pharmagenus (generics), Uriach OTC, Uriach Veterinaria, Urquimia (chemicals) and Dimportex (commercialization of chemicals), plus a scientific and cultural foundation, Fundación Uriach 1838, established in 1988.

Esteve

In 1929 Dr. Josep Esteve Subirana (1902–1979), a pharmacist who grew up in a family of pharmacists, founded Laboratorios Dr. Esteve in his home town, Manresa (Barcelona). Its first preparation was *Esterosol* (vitamin D), launched in 1931. In 1937, Esteve was able to synthesize *Neo-Spirol*, and *Amido-Sulfol* in 1941. The firm made further progress in the field of sulphonamides after the Spanish war, during which the family fled to France. The laboratory moved to Barcelona in 1942 and devoted more resources to research. Although Esteve also grew interested in penicillin (to the extent of being visited by Dr. Fleming in 1948), he abandoned this research line when the manufacture of penicillin was assigned to Antibióticos S.A. and CEPA.

The prestige of this laboratory was built on haemostatics. As a result of the war, Antoni Esteve grew obsessed with haemorrhages. Esteve began exporting *Antihemorrhagic 101* in 1954. It was the first time, according to internal sources, that a Spanish developed drug achieved international recognition. Ethamsylate, known outside Spain under the brandnames *Dicynone*, *Dicynene* and *Altodor*, was licensed and commercialized throughout Europe, Latin America and Japan after 1959. At the time, however, Esteve's eldest son, Dr. Josep Esteve Soler (b. 1930), had already joined the firm after completing his studies of pharmacy at the University of Barcelona (in

1953) and under the pressure of his father's weak health. His brother and sister, Joan and Montserrat (both vice-presidents of the group) also joined the firm, but Josep has been the one in charge ever since. While working for the laboratory, he graduated at IESE (1963) and got a Ph.D. at the University of Madrid (1970). Along with many of his Catalan colleagues, he helped to set the journal *Industria Farmacéutica*, mentioned previously, and the Spanish pharmaceutical lobby Farmaindustria. He held the chairmanship in 1975–1976 and 1987–1989.

There are many similarities between Josep Esteve and Juan Uriach: their background, their education, their commitment to research and growth and not least their drive for collective action. The just-completed processes of transition at Uriach and Esteve also bear striking resemblances. It was under the direction of Esteve Soler, actually, that the Esteve group was built. The veterinary division was established in 1963. Fine chemicals followed in 1966. The R&D department experienced an upsurge as a new product (Dobesilato Cálcico), the outcome of an in-house developed new chemical entity (NCE), reached the Spanish market in 1971. The drug has been licensed and is being marketed in eighty countries under the brand-names of *Doxium, Dexium, Doxiom, Dobesifar* and *Doxytrex*. In 1974 Esteve and Puig—a leading perfume and toiletry manufacturer—launched a joint venture, Isdin, focused on the development and marketing of dermatological products. A year later, Pensa Esteve was created after the acquisition of the former. During the 1980s Esteve became the leading Spanish pharmaceutical company, a new plant was inaugurated in Celrà (Girona) and two new divisions, OTC and Hospitals, were created.

The internationalization of the Esteve group was a relatively smooth process that took advantage of the company's accumulated capabilities in two areas: research and exports. Moreover, Josep Esteve played a relevant role in the design of the rules of the game that were to guide the modernization of the Spanish pharmaceutical industry from 1959 onwards. Not only from his position at Farmaindustria, but also as member of the Consejo Asesor para la Ciencia y la Tecnología from 1987 until 2001. This modernization encompassed a fundamental change in the patent system: the replacement of the patent of product by the patent of process and the subsequent eradication of a widespread practice: imitation. Needless to say, the new regime (coherent with Spain's membership of the European Union) led to further concentration in the pharmaceutical sector.

In the last fifteen years, Esteve has undergone two major changes. First, it has become a global knowledge-based firm by establishing strategic alliances with international partners, preferably American, and by creating a global commercial and manufacturing network that includes a joint venture with the Huadong Medicine Group (that has given rise in 2000 to the Zhejiang Huayi Pharmaceutical Company) and a new plant for fine chemicals in Mexico. The strategic alliances have linked Esteve with Discovery Laboratories Inc. (to develop and commercialize Surfanix, a new molecule against the respiratory distress syndrome), with Sugen (to develop NCEs against tumours) and with International Wex Technologies (to co-develop a new analgesic in the field of oncology and neurology). The second major change has been the generational transition, completed in 2005. Like Uriach, Esteve has relied on the professional advice of international family business consultants and the effective support of the IEF, which has helped create an excellent legal and fiscal framework for family firms in Spain. The two sons of Esteve Soler, Antoni (pharmacist) and Albert (economist), have come to the forefront of the management of the firm, the former as chairman and the two of them as joint CEOs.

Almirall

Almirall is the leading Spanish multinational in the pharmaceutical sector. The history of Almirall is closely linked to one family, the Gallardos, and its ability to research and market new active ingredients. The firm was founded by Antonio Gallardo Carrera (1908–1988) in 1944 (Almirall 1994). In contrast to most of the professionals working in the field, Gallardo had no scientific or technical background. After graduating at the Barcelona School of Commerce, he found work in what would later become Air France. He was the company's representative in Spain for twenty-five years. In the sad and isolated context of post-war Spain, a working knowledge of France and good contacts there were important advantages of which he was able to make good use. It was in France that he learned of the existence of new pharmaceutics and established contacts with the suppliers of the active ingredients. Not long afterwards in Barcelona he set himself up in the trade. He soon proved his talent and vision of the future. Almirall's first specialties were primarily balsams, which came from the international licence market which had developed following the Second World War. Almirall did make a qualitative leap when it obtained two licences from the Istituto De Agneli in Milan to manufacture and market one of the first antiulcer drugs to come into the Spanish market, Gefarnil (farnesilicerate of geranil), and a laxative popular around the world, known as Evacuol (sodium picosulphate).

It should be noted that in those days the creation of a social security system converted the state into the most important client of the pharmaceutical industry. This, together with the growth in quantity and quality of the Spanish market, aided Almirall and a whole generation of laboratories with an industrial vocation and local financing to grow and defend their common interests in dealing with the administration. It was then that Gallardo's two sons, Antonio (b. 1936) and Jorge (b. 1941) Gallardo Ballart, became fully involved the workings of the family business. They were responsible for the transformation of a national laboratory into a global enterprise. The eldest son had received a modern business education in Barcelona and the United Kingdom. At IESE he studied together with a good number of heirs to Catalan family enterprises. He furthered his training with periods spent working in different multinational pharmaceutical companies such as Rhône Poulenc. His brother Jorge had a more technical education at the Barcelona School of Engineering, from which he holds a Ph.D. To face the challenge of international competition, the Gallardo brothers created a R&D department. Research was centred in two main areas (gastrointestinal ailments and anti-inflammatories) and on certain molecules, defining the therapeutic areas which have brought the company most success at the beginning of the twenty-first century: allergies and respiratory pathologies, digestive alterations, central nervous system and cardiovascular illnesses. A new factory was built around the same time as the laboratory.

When Spain joined the European Economic Community, Almirall was better prepared to compete on the international market than the majority of its competitors. Despite the plans designed and financed by the Spanish government with the aim of promoting R&D, many laboratories retired from the race and the sector entered a dynamic period of spectacular concentration. By this time, Almirall had commercialized three products based on its own active ingredients: *Cleboril* (1979), *Almax* (1984) and *Calmatel* (1985). They opened the door to the international market and paved the way for the company's leadership in the Spanish market. The firm continued growing organically up to the mid-1990s. Half of its sales were products developed from its own investigation. Almirall embraced a new growth strategy based on mergers, absorptions and purchases. In 1997 it merged with Prodesfarma, a family firm that showed promise from a scientific and technical point of view and had a good international commercial network, but also problems in succession (Murray 2002). The operation helped Almirall develop products as successful as *Ebastel* and *Cidine* and annual growth figures of 10 percent. Further it helped the firm get *Almográn* approved in sixteen European countries and the United States.

Almirall's international expansion has recently accelerated through acquisitions in Europe and Mexico. Of particular relevance was the acquisition of the French laboratory Pharmafarm, with a complementary research program and an excellent commercial network in France. In order to promote ever more costly and risky research, Almirall has established several strategic alliances and developed a wide network of in and out licenses. So far the group markets seven principal active ingredients. It employs 3,200 people, 500 of those working in research in a recently inaugurated centre that has seen the largest investment of the Spanish pharmaceutical industry. Outside Spain, Almirall has one production centre and six affiliates.

Ferrer

Laboratorios Ferrer (later on Ferrer Internacional and Grupo Ferrer) was the personal creation of Carlos Ferrer Salat (1931–1998). A member of the Catalan bourgeoisie, Ferrer Salat graduated in chemical engineering, economics and liberal arts. In 1953, with the support of his family and the Instituto Químico de Sarrià, from which he had just graduated, he started his own business, a very modest facility from which he delivered a wide range of imported pharmaceutical products to hospitals and physicians. No doubt, his being both an international tennis player (he played between 1949 and 1954) and a pro-active modernizer of the Spanish economy (he was a founding member and first president of the Círculo de Economía in 1958) had a deep influence on his entrepreneurial activity: he was able to travel widely at a time when few Spaniards did so, he became proficient at networking at national and international scale and he committed himself to the construction of Europe and the liberalization of Spain. Among many other things, Ferrer Salat would be the founder and first president of the CEOE, Spain's first democratic employers' association (1977–1984), the vice-president and president of UNICE, the European association of employers (1988–1994) and president of the IOC, the organizing committee of the Olympic games (1987–). Besides this, Ferrer Salat founded a failed bank (Banco de Europa) and a successful company, Eyssa, in the rising electronic industry.

As with the other laboratories under examination, therefore, for Ferrer the representation of foreign firms was essential. This first commercial step was followed by a second step we are already familiar with: licensing, vertical integration and commercialization outside Spain. The third step, consisting of going international and developing and manufacturing its own products, was achieved as early as 1970 by acquiring the German pharmaceutical company (and this is a basic difference with the other laboratories under analysis) Trommsdorf. This was an audacious and farsighted move that helped Ferrer internationalize, on the one hand, and build commercial and scientific capabilities, on the other. The strategy followed after that reads like a textbook. Ferrer (since the mid-1970s under the management of the chemist Rafael Foguet) developed three management areas: (1) research (in Alsdorf and Barcelona, the R&D centre was created in 1977), (2) patents and authorizations and (3) backward integration (fine chemicals). A new factory in Sant Cugat del Vallès typified this new era. New acquisitions helped consolidate the strategy, particularly that of the chemical firm Zoster.

The fact that Ferrer Salat detached himself from the daily management of the pharmaceutical firm he had founded marks another difference. Ferrer underwent a precocious professionalization and did not play a visible role within the IEF (probably because it competed with the employer's body created by his founder, the CEOE). After the early and unexpected death of Carlos Ferrer Salat, his only son, Sergio, took over. Trained as an economist, he was still very young. Without introducing major personal or strategic changes, Sergio focused on the food sector (a relatively new activity for Ferrer) and continued the international expansion of the firm, particularly in Latin America and the Mediterranean, by means of alliances, joint-ventures and subsidiaries. Thus the current shape of the group has the mark of both Rafael Foguet and Sergio Ferrer-Salat. They are proud of being an all-round organization, able to cover the whole value chain from R&D&I (Research & Development & Innovation) to commercialization. Four departments (R&D&I, raw materials, specialties and commercialization) serve and oversee five divisions (domestic pharmaceuticals, international pharmaceuticals, hospital supplies, chemicals and food). Whereas the pharmaceutical divisions include thirty-one companies (eight in Spain, four in Germany, six in other European countries, twelve in Latin America and one in Hong-Kong), the chemical division is made up of Exquim (fine chemicals), Interquim (synthesis), Zoster (extraction and fermentation) and Medir Ferrer (intermediates); the food division includes the Morocco-based Beniquim (natural products), Exquim and Ferrer Alimentación (food ingredients). As for research, it is carried out in two centres. The main one is in Barcelona, where the all-round research of new drugs is carried out by a staff of some 150 people. Alsdorf specializes in new applications of pharmaceutical technology and the development of new galenic formulations. Besides these two centres, and several collaborations with various pharmaceutical companies and universities across Europe, the group has set up a strategic alliance with the French pharmaceutical company Bioproject. Ferrer's research is focused in four therapeutic areas: hypnotics, antibiotics, prokinetics and neuroprotectors.

CONCLUSIONS

There is rising awareness that the world economy is undergoing a historical shift from the countries that played the lead during the industrial age to the so-called emerging countries. This shift is about economic power and thus about innovation, an ability that until recently has seemed confined to the most advanced parts of the world. The main characters of the stories examined here lived in such a world. They worked hard to adapt foreign technologies to their specific national contexts while fostering industrial growth and scientific creativity at home. Their efforts and the outcome of such efforts were very different. However, they provide clues on the way a science-based industry arises and evolves in late-developing countries. I have argued that those firms were not so much part of the innovative networks described by Galambos and Sewell in an American setting as they were part of *opportunity networks*. Opportunity is understood here as a favourable combination of domestic and foreign circumstances that influences the development of a firm more than its own capabilities and favours the adoption of short-term strategies over long-term strategies.

The early history of the Spanish antibiotics industry shows that the individuals and social groups taking part in this fascinating process did recognize and actively seize the favourable circumstances created by industrial nationalism at home and the emergence of an international technological market abroad. It was the combination of an official duopoly, available foreign licences and managerial and financial capabilities that made both projects come true. In contrast to what happened in the early industrialized world after the Second World War, however, in Spain industry and academia remained two separate cultures even if they were supported by the same individuals. The inability—eventually lack of interest—to design and carry out long-term projects can be explained in terms of late industrialization and dominance of business groups (Guillén 2001). Antibióticos and CEPA proved to have remarkable capabilities to execute projects, but none of them developed or tried to develop the technological capabilities required to compete in the international markets.

This contrasts with the four family laboratories examined further on. Uriach, Esteve, Almirall and Ferrer were also creatures of the autarkic rule and shapers of the Spanish pharmaceutical policy and collective action. By taking advantage of a growing and highly protected domestic market and by seizing a new set of favourable circumstances, however, they have ended up integrating their industrial and scientific efforts to develop their own innovative capabilities. Their individual trajectories show that international experience, collective action, specialization, cooperative behaviour and a professional management of succession have helped them to grow and go international. The common preference for strategic alliances—a cooperative strategy where trust, culture and organizational learning matter a lot—is consistent with the proprietary structure of these firms. Strategic alliances are in fact a useful way to optimize research and development resources and to get access to highly competitive markets and to globalize. They are also a safe alternative to the more aggressive and risky policy of mergers and acquisitions for family firms seeking to remain independent.

NOTES

1. His son was Federico Mayor Zaragoza, a brilliant biochemist before becoming Spain's ministry of education and science and director of UNESCO; and his grandson, Federico Mayor Menéndez, is a professor of molecular biology at the Universidad Autónoma de Madrid.
2. The son of José Fernández, Dr. Fernández Sousa, would become professor of biochemistry at the University of Santiago de Compostela. He stands behind the successful research activities of Zeltia, particularly its subsidiary Pharmamar.
3. Productos Químicos y Farmacéuticos Abelló, soundly modernized by Abelló's son, Juan, in the 1960s and 1970s, was sold to Merck Sharp and Dohme in 1983. He had previously acquired the shares of the other founders of Antibióticos S.A. and sold the firm to the Italian concern Farmitalia in 1987. Under the umbrella of his own holding Torreal, Abelló manages today two very interesting pharmaceutical firms: Alcaliber (founded in 1973 on the basis of Abelló's alkaloids division and redesigned in 1984 after acquiring Uquifa) and Alergia (specialized in allergic products).

4. *Due to the extreme difficulty in getting access to the historical archives of the firms under analysis, this section is based on commemorative histories, journal and newspaper articles, corporate websites and personal interviews. I was also provided with biographical information on the main characters of this story that I used to write individual business biographies (Puig 2006a, 2006b, 2006c, 2006d, 2006e, 2008).*

REFERENCES

Abelló, J. 2002. *El opio, su aprovechamiento. La industria española de estupefacientes.* Madrid: Real Academia Nacional de Farmacia.
Almirall. 1994. *Almirall 1944–1994.* Barcelona: Laboratories Almirall.
Antibióticos, S.A. 1974. *XXV Aniversario.* Madrid: Antibióticos S.A.
Archivo General de la Administración (AGA), Industria. IDD 1.04, box 5112.
———. IDD 11, box 286.
Cabrera, M. 1994. *La industria, la prensa y la política. Nicolás María de Urgoiti (1869–1951).* Madrid: Alianza.
Fundación Uriach. 1988. *Uriach 1838–1988.* Barcelona: Fundación Usiach.
Galambos, L., and J. E. Sewell. 1995. *Networks of innovation: Vaccine development at Merck, Sharp & Dohme, and Mulford, 1895–1995.* Cambridge: Cambridge University Press.
Gallego, A. 1958. Entrevista al Dr. Antonio Gallego. *Industria Farmacéutica* 3:3–6.
Guillén, M. 2001. *The limits of convergence: Globalization and organizational change in Argentina, South Korea, and Spain.* Princeton, NJ: Princeton University Press.
Higby, G. J., and E. C. Stroud, eds. 1990. *Pill peddlers: Essays on the history of the pharmaceutical industry.* Madison, WI: American Institute of the History of Pharmacy.
———, eds. 1997. *The inside story of medicines: A symposium.* Madison, WI: American Institute of the History of Pharmacy.
Instituto de Biología y Sueroterapia (IBYS). 1944. *Memorias 1919–1944.* Madrid: IBYS.
Liebenau, L. 1987. The British success with penicillin. *Social Studies of Science* 17:69–86.
Mochales, S. 1994. Forty years of screening programmes for antibiotics. *Microbiología SEM* 10:331–342.
Murray, B. 2002. The secret of a successful merger. *Business in Family* 1(6): 31–33.
Parascandola, J., ed. 1980 *The history of antibiotics: A symposium.* Madison, WI: American Institute of the History of Pharmacy.
Puig, N. 2001. *La nacionalización de la industria farmacéutica en España: El caso de las empresas alemanas, 1914–1970.* WP 2001/2. Madrid: Fundación Empresa Pública.
———. 2003a. *Constructores de la química española: Bayer, Cepsa, Puig, Repsol, Schering y La Seda.* Madrid: Lid.
———. 2003b. La ayuda económica americana y los empresarios españoles. *Cuadernos de Historia Contemporánea: 50 años de relaciones entre España y Estados Unidos* 25:51–89.
———. 2004. Networks of innovation or networks of opportunity? The making of the Spanish antibiotics industry. *Ambix: The Journal of the Society for the History of Alchemy and Chemistry* 51 (2): 167–185.

———. 2006a. Almirall. In *El traç de l'excellència. Empreses, emprenedors, dirigents*, ed. F. Ribera Raichs, 41–51. Barcelona: Dobleerre Editorial.

———. 2006b. Antonio Gallardo Carrera. In *Cien empresarios catalanes*, ed. F. Cabana, 506–514. Madrid: Lid Editorial Empresarial.

———. 2006c. Carles Ferrer Salat. In *Cien empresarios catalanes*, ed. F. Cabana, 456–465. Madrid: Lid Editorial Empresarial.

———. 2006d. Joan Uriach Marsal. In *Cien empresarios catalanes*, ed. F. Cabana, 695–701. Madrid: Lid Editorial Empresarial.

———. 2006e. Josep Esteve Subirana. In *Cien empresarios catalanes*, ed. F. Cabana, 445–455. Madrid: Lid Editorial Empresarial.

———. 2009. Juan Abelló Pascual. In *Cien empresarios madrileños*, ed. E. Torres. Madrid.

Puig, N., and A. Álvaro. 2007. ¿Misión imposible? La expropiación de las empresas alemanas en España, 1945–1975. *Investigaciones de Historia Económica* 7:103–132.

Puig, N. and Torres, E. 2008. *Banco Urquijo: un banco con historia*. Madrid, Turmer.

Ramón y Cajal, S. 1923. *Reglas y consejos sobre investigación científica. Los tónicos de la voluntad*. Madrid: Espasa Calpe.

Redwood, H. 1988. *The pharmaceutical industry: Trends, problems and achievements*. Felixtown, Suffolk, U.K.: Oldwicks Press.

Rodríguez-Ocaña, E. 2000. Foreign expertise, political pragmatism and professional elite: The Rockefeller Foundation in Spain, 1919–1939. *Studies in History & Philosophy of Science Part C: Studies in History and Philosophy of Biological and Biomedical Sciences* 31 (3): 447–461.

Santesmases, M. J. 1999. *Antibióticos en la autarquía: Banca privada, industria farmacéutica, investigación científica y cultura liberal en España, 1940–1960*. WP 9906. Madrid: Fundación Empresa Pública.

———. 2000. Severo Ochoa and the biomedical sciences in Spain under Franco, 1959–1975. *Isis* 91:706–734.

———. 2001. *Entre Cajal y Ochoa. Ciencias Biomédicas en la España de Franco, 1939–1975*. Madrid: CSIC.

Schenley. 1949–1955. Annual reports.

Strohl, W. R., H. B. Woodruff, R. L. Monaghan, D. Hendlin, S. Mochales, A. L. Demain and J. Liesch. 2001. The history of natural products research at Merck & Co., Inc. *SIM News* 51 (1): 5–19.

Sturchio, J. 1992. *Values and visions: A Merck century*. Rahway, NJ: Merck.

United Nations Industrial Development Organisation (UNIDO). 1992. The world's pharmaceutical industries: An international perspective on innovation, competition and policy. Aldershot, U.K.: Edward Elgar.

Uriach, J. 2002. Our journey through transition. *Business in Family* 1(6): 35–38.

10 Knowledge Circulation in Innovation Networks in the Twentieth Century

Its Importance for Innovations in Small and Large Companies in the Netherlands

Mila Davids, Eric Berkers, Harry Lintsen, Arjan van Rooij, Sue-Yen Tjong Tjin Tai and Frank Veraart

INTRODUCTION

The innovative capacity of firms is considered as an essential element of the national competitiveness. Firms' ability to handle the challenges they face determines their innovative performance. It is a dance between what is needed from a market perspective and what is possible (Stefik and Stefik 2004). Moreover, innovation is path dependent. As formulated by Jorde and Teece,

> [I]nnovation is an incremental and cumulative activity that involves building on what went before, whether it is inside the organization or outside the organization, and whether the knowledge is proprietary or in the public domain. (1990, 75)

The ability to combine technological resources to generate new technological capabilities is considered essential for innovation processes. As Nonaka and Takeuchi concluded,

> [T]he potential to innovate of a business would depend on its capacity to create new knowledge, spread it through the organization, and incorporate it in new products, services and processes. (1993)[1]

We have to realize, however, that the expression 'create new knowledge' includes not only in-house research, but also all the knowledge-seeking and knowledge-acquiring activities. Innovative firms interact with other organizations in an institutional setting to gain, develop and exchange various kinds of knowledge and information and other resources. The importance of accumulation and exchange of knowledge for innovation processes supports the focus of this chapter, namely, the circulation of knowledge in innovation networks.

One of the most extended studies on the major success factors for innovations in the chemical and scientific instrument sectors, the project SAPPHO of the 1970s, pointed to the importance of internal networks of collaboration with users and external sources of technical knowledge (Rothwell et al. 1972). Since then these main results have also been confirmed by studies in other industries. Various studies focused on the importance of informal networks for innovations. Von Hippel's research on the U.S. steel mini-mill producers, one of the key studies on informal networks, showed that informal networks of engineers led to exchange of proprietary information (von Hippel 1988). More formal relationships exist between the companies in the supply chain or in a branch organization. Apart from these companies, knowledge institutes such as universities and research organizations can also play an important role in knowledge transfer.

The purpose of this chapter is to determine the companies' networks, the kinds of relationships and how they affected the transfer of knowledge. In this chapter we analyze four Dutch companies which were confronted with various challenges. Were these companies able to develop new products or processes, and how important was knowledge from external sources for the innovation processes? Although a lot of research pays attention to the role of universities and research institutes in the transfer of knowledge, we not only are interested in these sources but also pay attention to knowledge transfer between companies.

When we investigate knowledge we should be aware that innovation processes need various kinds of knowledge. Most attention is paid to the distinction between explicit and tacit knowledge (Nonaka and Takeuchi 1988; Polanyi 1958).[2] Less attention is paid to the various kinds of knowledge needed in the different phases of an innovation process. In line with the work of Gibbons, Faulkner and Senker show how important various kind of scientific and technological knowledge is for innovation (Faulkner and Senker 1995). While, for example, chemical knowledge can be sufficient to develop a new product, manufacturing it may need new mechanical knowledge. Moreover, innovations, especially when they are radical, can require changes in the organization, market innovations or a different commercial approach, for which other kinds of knowledge are acquired (Rothwell 1992). Innovative capacity needs also insight into consumer demand and business and economic developments. It requires understanding and aligning what is needed with what is possible (Stefik and Stefik 2004).

In the remainder of this chapter we pay attention to the importance of knowledge circulation in innovation networks for particular innovation processes at four Dutch companies. Two multinationals, the electronic company Philips and the chemical firm DSM, a medium-sized canning factory, Hero, and a small printing company, Budde, are studied.

A lot of studies have stressed the importance of innovation networks for small companies. Parsons and Rose, for example, illustrated how personal networks contributed to the innovative capacity of small entrepreneurs in the British outdoor trade (Parsons and Rose 2004; see also Chapter 3 of this volume). However, networks also play a role in large companies. Moreover, various studies have shown that external networks were just as important for firms which had their own R&D as for those which had none. We therefore focus on two companies with their own R&D (Philips and DSM), on Hero, whose parent company had a research laboratory, and on the small printing company Budde, which had no research facilities.

The innovations take place in a variety of sectors and in various periods. All four companies were confronted with major challenges. The economic depression in the 1930s necessitated that Hero come up with a new product at short notice, which led to the introduced of the apple drink 'Perl'. In the early 1950s the Philips company had to acquire the capacity to make transistors, which formed a threat for the existing tube market. In response to the run-down of the coal business, DSM diversified into lysine at the end of the 1960s and had to find a market for this amino acid. In the 1980s the printing industry was confronted with new developments in automation of composing equipment. Especially for a small company the large investments made the decision when to start with the new equipment even more difficult. In the early 1990s Budde integrated the Apple computer into its printing process.

HERO AND ITS CROSS-BORDER NETWORKS (1930s)

A broad network of actors was involved in the introduction of the apple drink Perl by the Dutch fruit and vegetable canning company N.V. Hero Conserven Breda (Hero Canning Breda Ltd.) (for this and the following, see Berkers 2008). Hero Breda was established in 1914 by Gustav Henckell and Karl Roth, the directors of a food-preserving company in Lenzburg, Switzerland. Although Hero could make its own decisions, it had strong ties with the Swiss 'parent factory'. The majority of the board of commissioners were Swiss, and during the 1920s and 1930s there was almost daily contact between the director, Reinier Jansen, and Gustav Henckell (Zwaal 1994). The factory, which due to World War I had a hesitant start, grew considerably in the 1920s, with around five hundred employees and six hundred seasonal workers at the end of that decade.

In the early 1930s the deteriorating economic situation was also noticeable in the Dutch canning industry. Confronted with decreasing exports and profits, Hero decided to introduce a radical new product. Via the branch magazines, Reinier Jansen knew that 'sweet must' (*zoete most*)—a non-alcoholic fruit and vegetable juice made of, for example, apples, grapes or tomatoes—was well on stream outside the Netherlands. The introduction of this new product was also motivated by requests from the horticultural sector, which was also affected by the economic crisis and searching for new markets (Bieleman 1992, 352–353).[3] When in 1931 profits from grapes decreased substantially New Honsel, one of the countries' biggest producers of grapes and (to a smaller extent) tomatoes, asked Hero to start producing 'sweet must' out of grapes (Berkers 2008). Hero considered it but finally chose another option. In March 1932 the board of directors of Hero decided to start producing a sparkling apple drink. In about one year's time Hero was able to build a production line, and in February 1933 the company launched Perl. To make it a marketable product at relative short notice various network contacts were important for Hero.

The information about producing 'sweet must' in the branch magazines was not sufficient to make the juice. Filtering and sterilization of the pulp and juice were crucial factors, which had to give the drink a good taste and make it not perishable. Hero did not rely on the Dutch agricultural research network, where Professor Sprenger from the horticulture laboratory in Wageningen did research into the making of 'sweet must'. On the other hand, Betuwe, another Dutch fruit-processing company that also wanted to expand into fruit juices, cooperated closely with Sprenger (Faber 2001).

For Hero its relationship with its Swiss parent company in Lenzburg proved to be essential to get access to the necessary knowledge in a relatively short time. Hero Lenzburg had its own chemical laboratory but also contacts with fruit-juice producers. The Swiss company Jules Schlör A.G., located near Hero Lenzburg, had developed a method for producing non-alcoholic apple juice in the 1920s and produced this on an industrial scale. Hero's Swiss director Henckell was enthusiastic about Schlör's apple drink and advised Jansen to use the Schlör process.

In the spring of 1932 Hero signed a licence agreement with the family firm Schlör. This official relationship implied that Schlör was obliged to share its knowledge about and experience with the production of non-alcoholic apple, grape and other fruit juices with Hero in exchange for compensation and part of the profit. The signing of an agreement was attractive for several reasons. While the research in Wageningen had just been started and was accompanied by financial problems, the Schlör process had already proved itself. This could give Hero a head start compared to Betuwe. Speed was also necessary because outside the Netherlands competition was well on stream. Moreover, signing a licence agreement had the advantage of exclusiveness, whereas the knowledge developed in Wageningen would be accessible by other competitors (Faber 2001, 109–110). Jansen also preferred the Schlör process to the more common Seitz process, on which the Wageningen laboratory elaborated. He found it tastier, less perishable and therefore commercially more interesting (Berkers 2008).

Well aware of the tacit elements in production knowledge, Hero insisted on recording the various ways of knowledge transfer, including exchange of personnel. Jansen received the right to visit the Schlör company and to gather information about the production process. The director Schlör himself had to instruct Jansen or one of his sons in the factory in Menzingen from 1 July 1932. Moreover, when Hero was about to start production Schlör personally, or one of his sons, had to be in the factory in Breda to '*persönlich mitzuarbeiten*'. By guaranteeing the involvement of experienced personnel, Jansen tried to minimize the risks of starting up this unknown production process (Berkers 2008). Visiting the factory and personnel assistance from the licensing party, however, was a common practice in licensing.

The fact that Lenzburg had a laboratory and contacts with other 'sweet must' producing companies proved to be important when the first samples in Breda were not optimal (the juice was cloudy) and Schlör was not very active in solving the problem. After investigating the possible causes of the problem, the chemist from the laboratory went to another 'sweet must' producer using the Schlör process, Mosterei Müller. Its director brought Meyer into contact with Dr. Widmer, director of the chemical department of the Swiss experimental station for fruit and wine in Wädenswill, who advised Müller when the latter had production problems. In sum, via its Swiss parent company and its network connections, Hero got access to other valuable sources of knowledge.

It was important for Hero's knowledge-acquiring activities that it realized that next to the process of making 'sweet must', other capabilities were also essential. Bottling, for instance. To get access to this new field Hero searched for contacts outside its usual ones and got in contact with the beverage industry. In April 1932 Jansen visited the neighbouring beer factory *De drie hoefijzers* (The three horseshoes) to investigate the production line. He judged the 'bottle-washing machine' suitable and ordered a comparable one from the company Holstein and Kappert. Because he found the bottling and labelling machines unsuitable, he decided to use the same machines as Schlör, which came from Süddeutsche Maschinen- & Metallwarenfabrik (Sümak) in Stuttgart. In fact Schlör acted as a mediator between Breda and the machinery supplier and received financial compensation for this role. The total costs of the new factory and inventory were more than 400,000 guilders, of which almost 250,000 were for machines and equipment (Davids et al. 2006; Berkers 2008).

For the production line, personnel had to be trained and new personnel were needed. Contacts in the beverage industry once again proved to be important. In February 1933 an expert from the brewery sector was appointed as technical manager to assist the manager of the Perl production plant.

The company realized very well that with Perl it would enter an unknown market. For market opportunities Jansen got access to market research via its Swiss parent company and also relied on its own market knowledge. He believed in the success of a non-alcoholic fruit juice made of grapes or apples, because he knew that the Dutch drank relatively a large amount of orange juice. Furthermore Jansen did some explorative research that convinced him that there was a demand for this product in the Netherlands. How he got the information on orange juice or what this explorative research implied is unknown, but it is a fact that Jansen was always very active in gathering market information. When in 1931 Jansen heard that the sales of Hero products decreased he wrote to Henckel, '*in den letzten 8 Tage viel im Lande herumgereist, um denselbe soviel wie möglich wieder zu beleben*' (travelled a lot in the country for the past 8 days, to experience things as much as possible) (Davids et al. 2006).

Convinced of the importance of marketing, Jansen started an intensive promotion campaign. Perl was brought to the attention of potential customers during events such as the 'nutrition and hygiene' fair held in Amsterdam in April 1933, and an advertisement campaign was started in various daily and sports papers '[to] introduce Hero Perl as the new national drink (Zwaal 1993, 71). Hero realized the importance of advertisements to reach its future customers, for which it used the skills and expertise of the Lenzburg factory, where a kind of company artist was employed who designed much of the promotion material.

Because the existing network of food retailers was not appropriate for the distribution of Perl, Hero got in contact with the beverage industry. Aware of the good prospects in the summer of 1932, the Heineken brewery approached Hero to explore the possibilities for cooperation. Hero, however, misjudged the eagerness of Heineken, which was in fact only interested in jointly producing Perl. When Heineken withdrew, Hero looked for other distribution channels. In February 1933 Hero signed an agreement with Bronnenbelang from Amsterdam for sales in the large cities and the west of the Netherlands.[4] The rest of the country was served by local salesmen. Some of them also represented Heineken, who were advised by Heineken's management to do this. Although not directly, the contacts with Heineken had been useful for the distribution of Perl. After a few years, the production, promotion and sales of Perl proved to be very successful. In 1933 4.2 million bottles were sold (around 1.7 million litres) (Zwaal 1993; Berkers 2008).

PHILIPS' R&D NETWORKS AND TRANSISTORS (1950s)

Despite Philips' Research and Development capabilities, relationships with American electronic companies proved to be essential for the production of transistors. Without these capabilities, however, establishing these contacts would have been impossible.

After the announcement in June 1948 that at the Bell laboratory the amplifying effect was produced by experimenting with a germanium crystal with two contacts close to each other, the so-called point-contact transistor, it became clear that transistors would supplant valves in electronics (Riordan and Hoddeson 1997, 177–182; Davids 2005; Choi 2007). As is illustrated by the economist Tilton (1971), the adoption of American knowledge in the field of semiconductors was essential for European electronic companies. This was also true for Philips, established in 1891 as a light-bulb factory and diversifying into electron tubes and radio sets in the 1920s. Philips was well aware that internal investments in R&D and production were not sufficient to become competitive in the transistor market. Because the Dutch universities were not active in solid-state physics at that time, the only knowledge source was other, especially American, companies. To acquire the latest knowledge, Philips focused on building a network with the American electronic industry. With success. It could make the switch to semiconductors and by the mid 1950s it was the main European transistor producer (for this and the following, see in more detail Davids 2005; Davids and Verbong 2007).

The existence of an industrial research laboratory at Philips proved to be important for its knowledge-acquiring and networking activity. The Philips Natuurkundig Laboratorium (Philips Physics Laboratory) (Natlab), established in 1914, had become an industrial laboratory with an excellent academic climate. Frequent seminars, regular visits to foreign research centres and good contacts with universities contributed to a lively exchange of knowledge, nationally as well as internationally. Natlab researchers frequently attended conferences and published in scientific journals. The good international reputation of the Natlab researchers also simplified visits to American firms and their research laboratories.

Next to informal contacts and exchange of knowledge, the existence of the research laboratory led to more formal relationships. Its prestige as a research institute had contributed to the exchange of technical-scientific knowledge with other electronic companies through cross-licensing (Blanken 2002, 125; Boersma 2002; De Vries 2005; Davids and Verbong 2006).

The research laboratory also provided Philips with the knowledge base necessary for absorbing the knowledge available in external sources. Although the research on semiconductor material in the 1930s and 1940s had bought only limited results, it had led to the building of research capabilities in the field of semiconductor materials. After Bell's announcement in the journal *Physical Review*, Philips also enlarged its research capacity in this field, with among others a special transistor group and more capacity for germanium research. This enabled Philips to produce transistors based on the codified knowledge published in the articles by Bell and RCA. At the beginning of 1952 Natlab could hand over the point-contact transistor to the development laboratory of the product division Electronic Tubes, which was also extended with a subdivision dedicated to the fabrication of semiconductors. In 1953 a factory dedicated to the fabrication of semiconductors was established in Nijmegen, where the point-contract transistors, the OC 50 and 51, were produced. The total number produced was limited to ten thousand a year (Davids 2005).

At the beginning of the 1950s, the Electronic Tubes product division and the development laboratory had some semiconductor expertise, and about ten academics were working at Natlab on various aspects of the transistor. The expertise in Philips' internal network, however, proved to be insufficient to produce layer transistors. The production of reliable point-contact transistors with equal qualities had caused substantial difficulties for Bell. In 1949 Shockley presented the idea of the layer transistor—a sandwich of emitter, base and collector integrated in one crystal, the so-called junction transistor. Production, however, proved to be difficult until the Bell researchers Sparks and Teal developed the grown-junction transistor by using the so-called 'double doping' technique, in which impurities were added in two stages to the semiconductor material. Due to its complexity this technique was not very useful for mass production (Riordan and Hoddeson 1997, 177–183).[5]

Despite Philips' access to the literature it soon became obvious that a gap in physical chemical knowledge prevented Philips from producing layer transistors on its own. It lacked tacit knowledge. Haaijman, from Natlab, said, 'We continued bravely and we had transistor action but it was of little importance, those guys at Bell were much better' (Davids and Verbong, 2009; for this and the following, see ibid). The possibility of getting access to Bell's knowledge by participating in the Bell Symposium was therefore more than welcome.

Scientists and engineers could get access to the knowledge of Bell labs not only through publications but also during visits to the Bell labs and at the transistor technology symposia held in 1951 and 1952. During the first conferences, transistor properties and possible applications were discussed, but no information on manufacturing processes was given. After several requests this item was put on the agenda of the 1952 symposium. After the issuing of Shockley's patent on the junction transistor in September 1951, the rights to manufacture transistors were licensed for a 25,000-dollar fee. The licensees—among which were also Philips—received an invitation to the Transistor Technology Symposium held in April 1952 (Davids and Verbong 2007).[6] Although Bell's position in semiconductor technology was beyond question, the development laboratory of Philips' product division, Electronic Tubes, doubted whether Bell had all the relevant knowledge. Nevertheless, everyone agreed that to make up arrears, acquiring as much knowledge as possible was necessary, and the contract was signed.[7] The Philips delegation to the Bell Symposium consisted of three Natlab researchers (Stieltjes, Haaijman and van Wieringen) and van Vessem, director of the development laboratory of the product division Electronic Tubes. This guaranteed that the knowledge was not only concentrated in the central research laboratory. The lectures and demonstrations during the symposium gave Philips insight into the manufacturing techniques and their theoretical background. Also the published description of the manufacturing process was given.

Everyone realized, however, that successful absorption of knowledge was a continuous interaction between internal knowledge building and external knowledge acquisition. 'The Natlab researchers realized that they had to push their R&D to build up sufficient knowledge necessary for the adoption of Bell information'. Most of 1952 was devoted to acquiring the necessary capabilities to develop the layer transistor using the double-doping technique and, at the end of 1952, Natlab provided about one hundred samples of layer transistors. Manufacturing these transistors proved to be a problem.

The strengthening of the capabilities of the product division Electronic Tubes was not sufficient. Philips had to expand its network to another player in the field and get access to its knowledge to be able to produce layer transistors. Important to this shift in focus was that van Vessem, the director of the development laboratory who had attended the Bell Symposium, preferred to give attention to other processes which were more suitable for producing transistors in large quantities. While Natlab focused on developing pnp-transistors using the double-doping technique from Bell, Van Vessem paid attention to the developments at RCA. Around the same period as General Electric, RCA developed the alloying technique, which was more appropriate than the grown-junction method for producing transistors in large quantities. The alloying technique used pellets of indium, which were heated and formed an alloy with the germanium (Choi 2007). Therefore it was no surprise that van Vessem hoped to get access to the developments at RCA.

But building a relationship failed, however, which hampered the access to RCA's knowledge. Due to the anti-trust policy, Philips had difficulties in continuing its pre-war exclusive licence agreement with RCA. Although negotiations were held to sign a new contract with RCA, the caution needed not to offend Bell hampered these. This proved that building relationships simultaneously with rivals was not that easy. The symposium held by RCA to offer its licensees 'all basic information to make germanium junction and point-contact transistors on a pilot production basis' could therefore not be attended by Philips representatives. The development lab had to wait until the information was officially published, and in 1954 the factory in Nijmegen started to produce junction transistors using the alloy process. Despite this delay, Philips was number one in the European transistor market around 1955.

The distribution of transistors was not a problem for Philips. It could build upon its existing network of customers, mostly radio-set manufacturers to which vacuum tubes and other devices had been delivered since the end of the 1920s. Moreover, Philips' own apparatus department purchased a substantial part.

DSM'S NETWORKING ACTIVITY IN
SEARCH OF A MARKET (1960s)

In contrast to Philips, the Dutch chemical company DSM could rely entirely on its internal R&D and production capabilities to develop lysine, while finding a market for its product was difficult, despite its networking activity in this field. DSM, established in 1902 by the Dutch state as a coal-mining firm, diversified into a chemical company from the 1920s onwards. Its diversification started with fertilizers and expanded further after World War II (WWII) into plastics, fibre intermediates and amino acids, among which was lysine.

Its internal knowledge network was considerable and solid. In the 1930s DSM had started to build internal research capabilities which resulted in the establishment of a formal R&D organization, the Central Laboratory. After WWII the engineering capabilities were institutionalized in Chemiebouw and the Central Laboratory grew in scale and scope, with, for instance, a semi-technical department to smoothen the conversion from laboratory to pilot-plant scale. Next to pilot-plant departments, the internal network also consisted of the research departments of the product development sector together with the pilot-plant work (for this and the following, see in more detail Lintsen, Veraart and Vincken 2000; van Rooij 2007).

Due to DSM's capabilities in organic chemistry, built up through experience with caprolactam (an intermediate for synthetic fibres), it was able to synthesize lysine, with which it started at the end of the 1950s. Lysine is one of the essential amino acids, which cannot be synthesized by the body but should be provided by food. Due to its various contacts with other chemical companies, DSM was well aware of the developments at foreign companies in this field. At the end of the 1950s, lysine was manufactured in various ways: extracting it from hydrolyzed soybeans, fish meal or other materials (Merck), or by fermentation (Kyowa, Anjinomoto and Pfizer) (Röthig 1968, 26; Wolf 1993, 247–250; Davids et al. 2006).

The Central Laboratory of DSM synthesized lysine from caprolactam, a process that had been explored by other companies. Starting with caprolactam was no more than logical. DSM produced this in house, and the caprolactam and lysine molecules had similarities. The project was feedstock driven and technology push. It began in 1957, and a year later the Organic Pilot Plants department and Chemiebouw started to design a pilot factory, which started in 1960. Trouble shooting was coordinated by the semi-technical department and the Organic Pilot Plants department, while the organic analysis group developed specific analytical procedures for the lysine project, and the lysine group in the organic chemistry department continued their research on the synthesis process. An extended internal network was involved in the development of lysine.

With lysine, DSM came in an unfamiliar field of technology, and its market possibilities were not clear. In the search for a possible market, DSM put a lot of effort in building a network of contacts with potentially interesting partners, customers, government agencies and research institutes. DSM, however, did not focus on one particular market, but put out feelers in various directions. Moreover, the idea that production would be large scale with low costs guided the searching for a market and thus DSM's networking activity.

One of the first ideas was the addition of lysine to bread. DSM approached TNO—a Dutch public research institute, established in the 1930s to improve the accessibility of research and development for smaller Dutch companies—to investigate the enlargement of the nutritional value of bread by adding lysine. In 1958 the TNO institute for dietary research, *Centraal Instituut voor Voedingsonderzoek* (CIVO), started tests to probe the feasibility of lysine-enriched bread. The results seemed promising; increasing nutritional value and no modifications in bread baking were needed to add lysine. In 1959 Berkhoff, the head of research who also coordinated external contacts, got in touch with Matthieu Dols, a crucial figure in the Dutch agricultural and food sector with many international contacts. Dols was an employee of the Ministry of Agriculture, a part-time professor and a member of the Food and Agricultural Organization (FAO) and the World Health Organization (WHO). It was important in this respect that he was a member of the governmental advisory council, which had to approve officially the marketing of lysine-enriched bread. Although Dols was interested in the lysine project, he did not see much priority in enriching human food in the Netherlands. Other experts in the council were even more sceptical, fearing an increase in the price of bread. Despite DSM network contacts, adding lysine to bread proved to be a non-starter (van Rooij 2007).

DSM had already got access to TNO and Dols via its existing contacts with the Agricultural Research Bureau. *Centraal Stikstof Verkoopkantoor (CSV)* (*Landbouwkundig Bureau CSV*), which was part of the Central Nitrogen Sales Office. The CSV sold all the nitrogen fertilizer produced in the Netherlands also for DSM. The agricultural research done by the Agricultural Research Bureau had stimulated the sale of fertilizer. The goal of networking activity with regard to lysine was comparable with that for fertilizer: building a relationship with a research institute for market stimulation. In this case, however, it did not work.

DSM used the same strategy to investigate the possibilities of adding lysine to animal feed as a substitute for animal protein sources such as bone and fish meal. Also in 1958 TNO got an order to test the increase of nutrition value of lysine-enriched feed for pigs and chickens. In the 1950s these were the largest feed markets in the Netherlands, with a production level in 1960 of 1.8 million tons each. As a result of the promising results from the TNO tests, Dols, acting as an adviser for DSM, saw the feed market as a possibility (De Boer 1974, 306, 311; van Rooij 2007).

Besides the research institutes, DSM also got in contact with prospective customers. The Dutch feed industry consisted of several large cooperative manufacturers, large and medium-sized private companies, and numerous small local mixers. Feed companies added bulk components such as cereals, peas and fish meal, for instance, but also other compounds such as vitamins, antibiotics and amino acids. Specialized companies produced and packaged these in so-called pre-mixes that feed companies added to their products. One of these manufacturers of pre-mixes, Handelsmaatschappij Trouw, approached DSM. They agreed that Trouw would target its own customers, and DSM a number of large feed companies, including the cooperatives (van Rooij 2007).

DSM's network also expanded internationally, in 1961, with the British branch of Unilever that had a large market share in the British feed market and was interested in using lysine. The contacts DSM had with cooperatives through its fertilizer production proved to be useful. Again the emphasis was on doing research to prove the effectiveness of adding lysine to feeds. In 1963, for example, Landbouwbelang, one of the large cooperatives, tested lysine-enriched feed for pigs. However, it never reached agreement with a feed manufacturer on market introduction (Davids et al. 2006; van Rooij 2007).

The focus on scientifically demonstrating the effectiveness of adding lysine to feeds is also illustrated by the establishment of a study committee with academics and representatives of agricultural research stations in 1960 to coordinate the various tests. DSM did not want to rely exclusively on the relationship with others and expanded its internal R&D network. In 1962 it started internal application research. A year later it also established a biological experimental station as an internal organizational unit to convince the feed industry that adding lysine to feed would be effective in increasing its nutritional value.

Other ideas—such as lysine-enriched baby food, adding lysine to the sweet potato, 'school milk' or peanut butter, or using it for pharmaceutical products—were considered (Röthig 1968, 20). Although, eventually, none of these materialized, they contributed to the idea that there existed a large market. This convinced the management of the Central Laboratory and the commercial-affairs department that there were sufficient market opportunities. They persuaded top management to build a lysine plant with a capacity of three thousand tons per year. In line with earlier DSM projects, lysine was considered as a bulk product, that is, involving large-scale and low-cost production. In 1964 the building of the plant started. Due to delays during construction the plant was operational in November 1968. There were, however, many mechanical problems, and the efficiency of the plant was low.

The feed market was still considered as most important. Despite the contacts with prospective customers no purchase agreements or joint projects had come into being. Cooperation with Unilever, for example, failed to materialize. DSM tried to overcome this weakness in its customer network by trying to acquire a pre-mix company in 1967. This only resulted in a cooperation with one feed manufacturer and in expected sales of no more than forty-five tons (van Rooij 2007).

Another problem was that the network relations had not even provided DSM with insight into the business economical aspects of adding lysine.

When in 1967 DSM's Biological Experimental Station evaluated the test with lysine-enriched pig feed, the conclusion was that it was not better than feeds with animal protein or with soy or fish meal and that adding soy and fish meal were much cheaper. The production costs of lysine proved to be higher than initially expected. Finally, the protein norms used by the feed companies hampered the addition of lysine to feed, which proved that DSM was insufficiently informed about the necessary requirements. In 1969 the production plant was closed. Producing a product for which there was no market was not economically justified.

Supplier and Branch Networks in the Graphic Industry (1980s–1990s)

The observation that transfer of knowledge in networks contributes substantially to the innovative performance of small firms is supported by the transition to new working processes in a small printing office called Budde. The introduction of computer-aided composing machinery in the printing process had far-reaching consequences for the graphic industry, especially for the many medium and small companies. The introduction of composing techniques at Budde illustrates how the existing networks facilitated this process innovation.

Budde was a small family firm, founded in 1947 in Utrecht by Sijbe Budde. A staff of around ten people in 1980 were responsible for the production of familial print, leaflets, brochures, books, theses of Utrecht University and multi-lingual brochures for the Open University (OU). In the 1980s general management was in the hands of Jan Koudijs, son-in-law of the founder (for this and the following, see in more detail Veraart 2008).

To keep abreast of new technological developments in printing, it was first of all important to get access to the publicly available sources of knowledge. Industry magazines such as *Compress*, *Grafisch Nederland* and others served as a platform for the wholesalers, trade organizations and other stakeholders and gave ample information for the graphic industry. In articles, general developments were discussed in terms of opportunities and dangers, and meetings of the different panels and the various trade fairs were covered. Announcements by dealers, coverage of the trade fairs and an occasional interview with a printer or typesetting shop showed new applications of technology.

Attending trade fairs was a more personal way to keep oneself informed. Producers showed their latest products and were approachable for getting background information. Sometimes experts gave lectures on the latest and future developments. Trade fairs functioned not only as a centre of knowledge exchange, but also as a platform for networking activities, as is also illustrated by Parsons and Rose (2004) in the case of the British outdoor industry. For Budde the generally accessible knowledge sources proved to be important when it came to changes in its printing process.

At the end of the 1970s Koudijs realized that the company should make the changeover from lead typesetting to photo typesetting. Linotype, one of the largest producers of photo-typesetting machines, launched a computer-aided photo-typesetting machine aimed at small firms, the Linotype CRTronic or 'Babytronic'. In 1980 Koudijs visited, together with some printer friends, the *Print* trade show in Chicago—with *Drupa* in Düsseldorf, the most important international fair—to see this Babytronic. Although impressed by the technical features, Koudijs decided not to purchase the Babytronic. He discovered that it could not produce foreign characters and accents (frequently used in, for instance, Spanish and Scandinavian languages) essential for the multilingual brochures for the Open University. Moreover, Koudijs found the investment costs too high. And even though it became clear at the trade fair that computer-aided photo typesetting and composing would be the future, he bought the latest conventional Compugraphic Editwriter, which he used until 1990. Koudijs also realized that closely monitoring the new developments in computer technology would be essential to keep in business.

Participating in a broad trade-oriented network was another way of acquiring the necessary business information and knowledge. Koudijs had always been very active outside the firm boundaries. He participated as a local representative in the trade organization Koninklijke Vereniging van Grafische Ondernemingen (KVGO) (the Royal Dutch Association for the Printing and Allied Industries) and also became a board member. His participation in the 'cost committee' of the KVGO, which executed time and motion studies and cost calculations on printing equipment for the associated firms, made him familiar with cost calculation and the latest technological developments in the printing industry and their cost-benefits. Due to his participation in the 'cost committee' Koudijs was, in 1984, invited to join 'Club Twelve', a collaboration of twelve small graphic firms with up to forty employees, mostly printers. These printers, who knew each other through Nederlandse Bond van Copieerders en Klein-offsetdrukkers (NBCK) (the Dutch Association of Copiers and Small Offset Printers), had founded Club Twelve in 1969. They met twice a month to discuss cost calculations, company results, new technologies, future developments and other firm-related issues. Also external experts were invited to give advice concerning new process innovations for printing firms. Club Twelve also operated as a user group to provide the printing-machine dealers and suppliers with relevant market information. In 1986, for example, the members were invited by Henk Gianotten, the market manager of Tetterode, to visit the Linotype plants in Frankfurt Germany. Tetterode was the largest wholesale business in graphic equipment. In the meeting, where a representative of the American Adobe company was also present, the possibilities of an integrated setup of Linotype-composing machinery with an Apple Macintosh computer was discussed with the Club Twelve members. This connection had become possible with the use of Adobe's development of the PostScript page-description language, a software interface that described the composition for output equipment. The PostScript file generated was fed into a Raster Image Processor, a single suite computer system that translated the PostScript instructions into a bitmap describing the whole page. This bitmap was processed by the phototypesetter that produced films. Overwhelmed by this new setup, the Club Twelve members subsequently cancelled all recent orders for other computer-aided typesetting and composing machinery. One of the members, the typesetting shop Reproka in Amersfoort, bought the new setup, including linotype-composing equipment, while its experiences were shared in the Club Twelve meetings (Veraart 2008).

The supplier network, in which, due to these new technological developments, new organizations were incorporated, was also important when the new methods were applied within the company. The wholesaler Tetterode functioned as an intermediary to get access not only to the new technical development, but also to those responsible for training and education. To get access to information about the Apple computer, Gianotten put Club Twelve in touch with MacVonk. MacVonk, a former printer and an Apple computer pioneer, had become an Apple and software dealer in the second half of the 1980s and also organized courses for printing firms. In 1989 he demonstrated the Macintosh-2 computers in combination with a 19-inch Sony Trinitron screen. On Reproka's advice Jan Koudijs took a course at MacVonk 'to check out what I am up to buy. First a course, than a purchase' (Versaart 2008, 284). After the course, Koudijs purchased an Apple Mackintosh-2 system, with an extra disk drive for five hundred sorts of type, a floppy cracker, a laser printer, and a 19-inch screen at a total cost of about 27,000 euros (22,000 dollars) (Davids et al. 2006). In 1990 the equipment was installed. Two female employees went to MacVonk for training on how to use DTP software. The first products at Budde for the new setup were black-and-white productions. In nine months' time, production went smoothly (Veraart 2008).

Remarkable is the 'division of labour' in Budde's essential branch network, Club Twelve. The cooperation in Club Twelve gave Budde the opportunity to invest solely in Apple computer equipment while it used the type-setting equipment of Reproka. Until Budde invested in 1993 in photo-typesetting equipment, Reproka transferred the computer file sent by Budde into a print on photo paper or film by a Raster Image Processor and Linotype photo-typesetting machinery. Its networking activity had made it possible for Budde to remain informed of the latest developments and in the meantime switch gradually to a new printing process.

CONCLUDING REMARKS

These four case studies underline the importance of networks for innovative capacity. Via network relations innovative firms get access to all kinds of information and knowledge for the innovation process. They draw on networks not only to become aware of market needs and possibilities but also to develop and improve their capabilities. As this chapter shows, the knowledge sources, kinds of relationships and their importance can vary considerably. They also give access to different kinds of knowledge.

For the early introduction of Perl on the Dutch market Hero's cross-border networks—crossing national as well as sectoral borders—were of prime importance. It was strongly stimulated by the supplier side: the horticultural sector. Well informed about the activities of foreign producers of sparkling fruit juices via its Swiss parent company Lenzburg, Hero was convinced of the market prospects in the Netherlands. It got access to the process of making 'sweet must' via a licence contract with the Swiss company Schlör. Also, for the necessary improvement of Perl's quality, Lenzburg—its laboratory and its knowledge network—proved to be important. To acquire knowledge of bottling and to get access to distribution networks, Hero got in contact with the Dutch beverage industry.

The development of the transistor at Philips shows how, even for large multinational companies with strong internal R&D and production capabilities, networks are of prime importance to get access to knowledge. Just like Budde, Philips built relationships with other companies in its sector, although the network was much more R&D oriented, mainly built by researchers and more international and formal of character. Philips' knowledge base proved to be important for its network building and knowledge-transfer capacity, because to produce transistors, physical-chemical and technical (production) knowledge was vital. Visits to other companies were important for information about the latest developments, while for information about specific consumer needs the existing internal and external consumer contacts were sufficient.

The chemical company DSM could rely entirely on its internal R&D and production capabilities provided by an extended internal network to develop and produce lysine. However, to find a market for lysine DSM built relationships with external actors: research institutes and customers, most of them Dutch in origin. The most promising idea was to add lysine to animal feed, and the research institutes had to prove its effectiveness. Also feed companies were asked to do tests. The relationships with possible customers, however, did not lead to purchase agreements or large amount of sales. It also had not provided DSM with insight into the business economical aspects of adding lysine to animal feed, nor in the protein norms used by the feed companies. DSM had concentrated too much on developing and producing lysine and believed in its market possibilities without proper knowledge of customer needs.

Budde's network contacts were essential for the introduction of computer-aided equipment in the typesetting and composing process. Dealers of equipment offered important information and knowledge by supplying the latest equipment and offering access to courses and training. Even more important were the relationships with other printing companies in Club Twelve. Although this cooperation can be labelled as a formal network (the goal of this closed cooperative—you had to be invited—was to exchange information), most exchange of knowledge and information was done in a more informal setting. Via these semi-formal relationships Budde not only kept informed about the latest technological developments and management information but was also able to learn from the experiences from another company, which already worked with new computer-aided photo-composing equipment. The network even gave Budde the opportunity to gradually make the switch to the new equipment as a result of a division of labour.

Our cases confirm other studies which conclude that when existing information and knowledge is not available in the innovating company, it seeks for it outside its company's boundaries. Such companies use information and knowledge available by other organizations in the network to keep informed and also to solve their problems. The external relations of DSM and Philips were less numerous and were needed only to get access to specific knowledge. For the smaller companies Hero and Budde external contacts were needed to gain information about the market situation and to enable innovation (Mowery, Oxley and Silverman 1996; Lorenzoni and Lipparini 1999; Stefik and Stefik 2004).[8]

Another important conclusion drawn from these four case studies is that the networking activity of the firm is very important for the effectiveness of its innovation networks (see also Mason, Beltramo and Paul 2004).[9] It determines if and how easily knowledge is transferred, along with the quality of the knowledge transferred.

The networking activity is determined by a firm's external orientation. While Philips and especially Budde were considerably focused on developments outside its boundaries, DSM was not. Although Hero was mainly concentrated on its Swiss parent company, it followed the developments at its competitors and their partners, while Hero Lenzburg was very externally oriented. Because the more in- or outward-looking attitude is part of the firms' culture—or, to phrase it in Nelson and Winter's concept, 'organizational routines'—it is not always easy to establish new network relations when confronted with technological or market developments (Nelson and Winter 1982).

The purposes of networking varied. Not all of the four companies built relationships to get access to and acquire as much knowledge as possible for *all* the stages of the innovation process (research, development, production, marketing). For Budde and Hero, and to a lesser extent also for Philips, getting access to knowledge was an integral aspect of their innovation strategies from the outset. At DSM efforts to get access to knowledge about the market through network building was less well related to the developmental stages of lysine. A complicating aspect for the R&D-oriented actors within DSM was that it was less familiar with market knowledge than, for example, Philips, where the knowledge was related to development and production aspects. The search for knowledge by Hero and Budde was less limited to specific areas. They used their contacts to gain a broad range of information and knowledge.

The cases also illustrate how perception influenced the networking activity. DSM, which believed in the superiority of the 'technologically pushed' product lysine and in its substantial market opportunities, had less access to networks when market demand failed to materialize. The relationship building of Hero was largely determined by the wish to get a new product into the market as soon as possible. This urge for speed led to Hero's focus on the Swiss innovation network. The driving idea behind the network building of Budde was the importance of cooperation in this self-regulating sector, to keep informed about the latest technological developments, but also to keep risks as small as possible. As a consequence Budde was able to choose the most appropriate time to start with new computer-aided equipment. At Philips the opposing ideas of the Natlab researchers and the production department influenced their relationship building. While for Natlab, knowledge to develop a layer transistor was sufficient, the production department attached great importance to the mass-production process and preferred a license agreement with RCA.

Past experiences also play a role in the nature of the network activity. Which, or which kind, of organizations are approached, what kind of relationship is established and what kind of knowledge is acquired is often rooted in earlier network activity. The tendency of DSM to get in touch with research institutes to prove the applicability of lysine was a well-known strategy, which DSM had successfully used in the case of fertilizer production and was established via its 'fertilizer contacts'. For lysine, however, this networking strategy was less efficient. The Philips' transistor case illustrates that the earlier license agreement with Bell hindered a contract with RCA. Building a strong network in a completely new field is even more difficult, but not impossible. Hero was aware that making contacts in the beverage industry would offer access to their distribution network. Although much is written about the importance of networks and exchange of knowledge, these aspects of the networking activity itself have received only slight attention.

ACKNOWLEDGEMENTS

This chapter is part of the research programme *The Co-evolution of the Dutch Knowledge Infrastructure and Innovations in Dutch Business,* which in turn is embedded in the research programme *Business in the Netherlands in the Twentieth Century* (BINT) (see http://www.bintproject.nl/ innovatie). An earlier version was presented at the International Economic History Conference (Helsinki, August 2006). We thank the commentators, the participants at that conference and the editors of this volume for their comments. The research is funded by the Netherlands Organisation for Scientific Research.

NOTES

1. Under the influence of scholars from history and evolutionary economics, the notion that technological advance and innovation proceeds through an

evolutionary process, the dynamic nature of the innovation process and especially the importance of accumulation of technological know-how over time
is widely accepted.

2. While explicit knowledge is highly codified, tacit knowledge is, as pointed out
   by Polanyi in the 1950s, the knowledge which exceeds what can be expressed
   verbally. Most studies illustrate that the transferability of tacit knowledge is
   much more difficult than that of codified knowledge and demands considerable effort.

3. The Federation Westland, representing the market-gardeners in its region
   tried to promote the producing and drinking of fruit juices. It used its
   influence with the Dutch government for example to lower wine excise,
   because it hindered the production of grape juice by the fruit processing
   industry.

4. Bronnenbelang was obliged to purchase a substantial amount of bottles at
   once (40,000) for 9 cents a piece, which were sold for 12.5 cents to hotels,
   restaurants and shops, and for 11 to middlemen.

5. The double-doping technique, as described by Riordan and Hoddeson, was
   as follows: 'Starting with a melt of N-type germanium, they first doped it
   with a gallium pill to grow a P-type layer on a N-type crystal. About ten sec-
   onds later, they added a second pill containing 100 micrograms of antimony,
   a fifth-column element located under arsenic in the periodic table. A donor
   element supplying excess electrons to the crystal lattice, the antimony more
   than compensated for the electron deficit caused by gallium, converting the
   melt back to N-type' (1997, 182).

6. Participants came from twenty-six U.S. companies and fourteen foreign
   companies.

7. This meant that Philips had to pay 5 percent royalty for the transistors (1)
   sold or produced in countries with Western patents, being part of appli-
   ances not falling under the scope of the main agreement; (2) sold as single
   devices in the United States; and (3) sold separately in other countries for
   other purposes than transmitters, receivers for sound, facsimile and televi-
   sion. The license agreement opened the way to the Transistor Technology
   Symposium.

8. The large number of studies on strategic alliances often pays attention to
   these kinds of knowledge transfers. The innovative efforts can also be spread
   over various organizations in a network in which specialized roles are highly
   complementary, which is, for example, seen in the Italian packaging-machin-
   ery industry.

9. An important aspect of network building is that the establishment of a
   relationship and the forming of a network are largely dependent on the
   willingness to do so. Are management as well as employees willing and
   able to engage in 'networking' activity, that is, in building and maintaining relationships (informal or formal) with (individuals) in other firms and
   organizations to acquire knowledge? (See also Mason, Beltramo and Paul
   2004.)

REFERENCES

Berkers, E. 2008. Tastes differ. Comparing company strategies: Innovation trajectories and knowledge sources in Dutch soft drink production in the 1930s.
Business History 50 (3): 351–367.

Bieleman, J. 1992. *Geschiedenis van de landbouw in Nederland 1500–1950: Veranderingen en verscheidenheid.* Meppel: Boom.

Blanken, I. J. 2002. *Een Industriele Wereldfederatie (1950-1979).* Vol. 5 *Geschiedenis van Koninklijke Philips Electronics N.V. Een Industriële Wereldfederatie. V: 1950–1970.* Zaltbommel: Europese Bibliotheek.

Boersma, K. 2002. *Inventing structures for industrial research: A history of the Philips Nat.Lab. 1914–1946.* Amsterdam: Aksant.

Choi, H. 2007. The boundaries of industrial research: Making transistors at RCA, 1948–1960. *Technology and Culture* 48 (4): 758–782.

Davids, M. 2005. Solid-state technology and international knowledge transfer: The case of Philips. Paper presented at the Society for the History of Technology (SHOT), Minneapolis, MN, 3–5 November.

Davids, M., E. Berkers, A. Van Rooij and F. Veraart. 2006. Knowledge circulation in innovation networks in the 20th century: Its importance for innovations in small and large companies in the Netherlands. Paper presented at the XIVth International Economic History Congress, Helsinki, Finland, 21–25 August.

Davids, M., and G. Verbong. 2006. Intraorganizational alignment and innovation processes: Philips and the transistor technology. *Business History Review* 80 (Winter): 657–688.

———. 2007. Absorptive capacity in solid-state technology and international knowledge transfer: The case of Philips. *Comparative Technology Transfer and Society* 5 (1): 1–27.

De Boer, I., ed. 1974. *Boer en markt. Ontwikkeling van de Nederlandse land- en tuinbouw en de Cebeco-Handelsraad organisatie in de periode 1949–1974. Een uitgave van Cebeco-Handelsraad ter gelegenheid van zijn 75-jarig bestaan.* Rotterdam: Cebeco-Handelsraad.

De Vries, M. J. 2005. *80 years of research at the Philips Natuurkundig Laboratorium (1914–1994): The role of the Natlab at Philips.* Amsterdam: Pallas Publications.

Faber, J. 2001. *Kennisverwerving in de Nederlandse industrie 1870–1970.* Amsterdam: Aksant, 130–133.

Faulkner, W., and J. Senker. 1995. *Knowledge frontiers: Public sector research and industrial innovation in biotechnology, engineering ceramics, and parallel computing.* With L. Velho. Oxford: Clarendon Press.

Jorde, T. M., and D. J. Teece. 1990. Innovation and cooperation: implication for competition and antitrust. *Journal of Economic Perspective* 4 (3): 75–96.

Lintsen, H., F. Veraart and P. Vincken. 2000. De onvervulde belofte: Lysine. In *Research tussen vetkool en zoetstof: zestig jaar DSM Research 1940–2000,* ed. H. Lintsen, 70–81. Zutphen: Walburg Pers.

Lorenzoni, G., and A. Lipparini. 1999. The leverage of interfirm relationships as a distinctive organizational capability. *Strategic Management Journal* 20:317–338.

Mason, G., J. P. Beltramo and J. J. Paul. 2004. External knowledge sourcing in different national settings: a comparison of electronic establishments in Britain and France. *Research Policy* 33 (1): 53–72.

Mowery, D. C., J. E. Oxley and B. S. Silverman. 1996. Strategic alliances and interfirm knowledge transfer. *Strategic Management Journal* 17:77–91.

Nelson, R. R., and S. G. Winter. 1982. *An evolutionary theory of economic change.* Cambridge, MA: Harvard University Press.

Nonaka, I., and H. Takeuchi. 1995. *The knowledge-creating company: How Japanese companies create the dynamics of innovation.* Oxford: Oxford University Press.

Parsons, M. C., and M. B. Rose. 2004. Communities of knowledge: Entreprenuership, innovation and networks in the British outdoor trade, 1960–1990. *Business History* 46 (4): 609–639.

Polanyi, M. 1958. *Personal knowledge—towards a post-critical philosophy.* Chicago: Chicago University Press.

Riordan, M., and L. Hoddeson. 1997. *Crystal fire: The birth of the information age.* New York: W. Norton.

Röthig, F. W. R. 1968. *Toepassing lysine voor menselijke voeding en als therapeuticum. Contacten CL/DSM met derden.* Heerlen: Staatsmijnen, Centraal Laboratorium.

Rothwell, R. 1992. Successful industrial innovation: critical factors for the 1990s. *R&D Management* 22 (3): 221–239.

Rothwell, R., et al. 1972. SAPPHO updated. *Research Policy* 3 (3): 259–291.

Stefik, M., and B. Stefik. 2004. *Breakthrough stories and strategies of radical innovation.* Cambridge: Cambridge University Press.

Tilton, J. E. 1971. *International diffusion of technology: The case of semiconductors.* Washington: The Brookings Institution.

van Rooij, J. W. 2007. *The company that changed itself: R&D and the transformations of DSM.* Amsterdam: Amsterdam University Press.

Veraart, F. C. A. 2008. *Vormgevers van Persoonlijk Computergebruik, De ontwikkeling van computers voor kleingebruikers in Nederland, 1970–1990.* Eindhoven: Stichting Historie der Techniek.

von Hippel, E. 1988. *The sources of innovation.* New York: Oxford University Press.

Wolf, M. 1993. *Im Zeichen von Sonne und Mond: Von der Frankfurter Muenzscheiderei zum Weltunternehmen Degussa AG.* Frankfurt am Main: Degussa.

Zwaal, P. 1993. *Frisdranken in Nederland. Een twintigste eeuwse produktgeschiedenis.* Rotterdam: Stichting BBM.

———. 1994. Hero Nederland in beeld. Een bedrijfshistorisch profiel 1914–1994. Unpublished manuscript.

Contributors

EDITORS

Paloma Fernández Pérez is Professor of Economic and Business History at the University of Barcelona and ICREA Academic researcher. Her research interests are family business, innovation, entrepreneurial networks, and lobbies. She has published *El rostro familiar de la metrópolis* (Madrid, 1997) and *Un siglo y medio de trefilería en España* (Barcelona, 2004), has edited with P. Pascual *Del metal al motor* (Bilbao, 2007), and has published articles in *Business History, Enterprise & Society, Business History Review, Revista de Historia Industrial, Revista de Historia Económica,* and *Investigaciones de Historia Económica.* She is principal researcher of a project on entrepreneurial networks in Spain and member of the *Centre d´Estudis Antoni de Capmany.*

Mary B. Rose is Professor of Entrepreneurship in the Institute of Entrepreneurship and Enterprise Development in the Management School at Lancaster University, UK. She specialises in evolutionary approaches to innovation and the relationships between innovation, entrepreneurship and communities of practice. She has published widely on the evolution of business values, networking behaviour by family firms and the problem of leadership succession. Publications have included numerous articles in refereed journals and she has authored and co-authored three books and edited nine. With Mike Parsons she co-authored *Invisible on Everest: Innovation and the Gear Makers* (Old City Publishing, 2003), which was winner of the 2005 Design History Society Prize and runner up for the 2004 Wadsworth Prize.

CONTRIBUTORS

Eric Berkers is Assistant Professor of History of Technology at the sub-Department of Innovation Sciences of the Eindhoven University of Technology. He participated in research projects about the History of

Technology in the Netherlands in the 19th and 20th century and the History of Dutch Business in the 20th century. Within the latter his focus was on innovations in small and medium sized firms. He has published on topics such as water management, land registry, energy supply and research, and now studies transitions in health care.

Mark Casson is Professor of Economics at the University of Reading and is Director of the Centre for Institutional Performance He has published over 30 books on entrepreneurship, business culture and the economics of the multinational enterprise and these include *The Economics of Business Culture* (1991),. *Enterprise and Leadership* (2000), and *Economics of International Business: A New Research Agenda* (2000). His research interests also include business history and transport studies.

Andrea Colli is associate professor of Economic History at Bocconi University, Milan. He specializes in Business History, his fields of interest comprising the structure and evolution of small and medium sized enterprises, the role of family firms in modern economic growth, entrepreneurship and entrepreneurial history, Corporate Governance in a comparative and historical perspective and foreign direct investments and economic growth in the long period. He is member of the board of the European Business History Association, and Vice Director of the Research Centre on Entrepreneurship and Entrepreneurs (EntER) at Bocconi University.

Mila Davids is Assistant Professor of History of Technology at the sub-Department of Innovation Sciences of the Eindhoven University of Technology. As one of the editors of the History of Technology in the Netherlands in the 20th century (TIN-20) project she was responsible for the volume on Industrial Production. Within the project on Dutch Business in the 20th century (BINT project) she is responsible for the book on Innovation and the knowledge infrastructure. Her publications focus on innovations, circulation of knowledge and innovation networks of Dutch firms.

Matthias Kipping is Professor of Strategic Management and Chair in Business History at the Schulich School of Business in Toronto, Canada. His main research interest has been the international transfer of management knowledge, with a particular focus on the role of management consultants and management education. He has published widely on these topics in business history as well as management journals and edited volumes. He is currently finalizing a manuscript on the history of the management consultancy business, tentatively entitled "From Racket to Riches". He has recently commenced work on a new research project examining the long-term economic and social effects of cross-border mergers and acquisitions.

Dr. Juha-Antti Lamberg is Professor in Strategic Management at the Helsinki University of Technology. He publishes research in Strategic Management Journal, Industrial and Corporate Change, Organization Studies, Business & Society, Human Relations, European Management Journal, the Scandinavian Economic History Review and other journals. His research interests focus on continuity and change in strategy; especially in the contexts of retail industry and paper industry. He has he won the Sloan Foundation's Industry Studies Best Paper Prize in 2008 and been several times a nominee or finalist for the Carolyn Dexter Award at the same conference.

Harry Lintsen is professor of History of Technology at the sub-Department of Innovation Sciences of the Eindhoven University of Technology. The most important scholarly work of Lintsen has consisted of putting together two monograph series about the history of technology in the Netherlands during the 19th and 20th centuries (up to approx 1970) TIN-19 and TIN-20. At this moment his research is focused on a historical analysis of the period after 1970. He also intends to relate the historical analyses to major socio-technological issues, especially sustainability.

Anders Melander is an Associate Professor in Business Administration at Jönköping International Business School (JIBS). In 1997 he defended his Phd thesis; Industrial wisdom and Strategic Change in the Swedish Pulp and Paper Industry 1945-1990. After this he has written several articles and book chapters further researching strategic issues in the Swedish Pulp and Paper Industry. In the period 2000-2006 Melander was the Program Director of the krAft program - a national development programme including more than 600 SMEs and 19 universities. Today he is continuously engaged in research on evolutionary issues such as strategic networks, dynamic capabilities and strategic choice.

Jari Ojala, PhD, is professor of history in the department of history and ethnology at the University of Jyväskylä, Finland. He specializes in business history and is leading a research group entitled 'organizational evolution and dynamics'. He has written articles for journals such as European Review of Economic History, Business History, International Journal of Maritime History, and Scandinavian Economic History Review. Recently he has co-edited volumes 'Information Flows: New Approaches in the Historical Study of Business Information' (SKS 2007), 'The Road to Prosperity: An Economic History of Finland' (SKS 2006) and 'The Evolution of Competitive Strategies in Global Forestry Industries: Comparative Perspectives' (Springer 2006).

Mike Parsons was the CEO responsible for the development of Karrimor from a micro-business making cycle bags in 1960 to the UK's largest rucksack manufacturer. The designer of many path breaking outdoor products, Mike is currently innovation director of outdoor equipment manufacturer OMM Ltd. He is an honorary fellow at the Institute for Entrepreneurship and Enterprise Development at Lancaster University, where he has co-designed and co-delivers courses in innovation with Mary B. Rose. Their undergraduate innovation course won a university prize for innovative teaching in 2005.

Nuria Puig is associate professor of Economic and Business History at the Universidad Complutense de Madrid. Her research interests include transnational business influences and the role of business groups and family firms in 20th century Spain. She has published a book and a number of articles on the historical development of the chemical and pharmaceutical industries in Spain, focusing on the interplay between foreign multinationals and domestic family firms. The co-authored book *Banco Urquijo. Historia de un grupo empresarial* (Madrid 2008) is her most recent publication.

Dr. Jani Saarinen works as innovation and technology policy manager at PricewaterhouseCoopers. He holds a PhD in economic history from School of Economics and Management, Lund University, Sweden. Trained in both research policy and economic history, Saarinen has extensive knowledge about innovation at the intersection of science, technology, and industry, including the impact of innovation and technology policies in various contexts.

Sue-Yen Tjong Tjin Tai is a sociologist and mechanical engineer. She studies knowledge circulation during the development of plant equipment in the coal mining industry and the starch industry. In addition, she is one of the team leaders of the maintenance turnaround department of an oil refinery.

Arjan van Rooij works as a researcher at the sub-Department of Innovation Sciences of the Eindhoven University of Technology. His interests include technology, research and business. Arjan has worked extensively on the history of the chemical industry, chemical technology, R&D and innovation, and laboratories. His recent publications include an R&D history of the Dutch chemical firm DSM.

Frank Veraart is Assistant Professor at the Eindhoven University of Technology School of Innovation Sciences. In 2008 he published his thesis *Vormgevers van Persoonlijk Computergebruik* (Designers of Personal Computing), a historical analysis of the introduction and appropriation of computers by Dutch small-scale users at home, in schools and printing industries. He contributed to the series on the History of Technology in the Netherlands in the twentieth century (TIN-20). Moreover he has published on the histories of bicycle use, plastics in building engineering, knowledge exchange in mechanical engineering and Dutch computing history.

Index

Page numbers in *italics* denotes a figure/table

For Product Safety Concerns and Information please contact our
EU representative GPSR@taylorandfrancis.com Taylor & Francis
Verlag GmbH, Kaufingerstraße 24, 80331 München, Germany